GREAT MUSLIMS OF UNDIVIDED INDIA

GREAT MUSLIMS OF UNDIVIDED INDIA

Nikhat Ekbal

KALPAZ

Great Muslims of Undivided India

Rs. 675

ISBN: 978-81-7835-756-0

Published in 2009 in India by
Kalpaz Publications
C - 30, Satyawati Nagar,
Delhi - 110052
E-mail: kalpaz@hotmail.com
Phone: 9212729499

Printed at: Singhal Print Media, Delhi

Contents

Section: II

FREEDOM FIGHTERS

Section: III

LEADERS

Section: IV
PHILOSOPHERS

Section: V
SCIENTISTS

Section: VI
SCHOLARS

Section: VII
SOCIAL REFORMERS

Section: VIII
SPORTS PERSON

Section: IX
WRITERS

Preface

History tells us that India had remained under the domination of Muslim warriors and the kings for about six hundred years. After the death of Aurangzeb in 1707 AD., the Muslim rule over India crumbled. The British wrested sovereignty from the Muslims and established the British Rule over India, and they ruled for two hundred years.

The contribution of Muslim revolutionaries, poets and writers is very finely documented in India's struggle against the British. Maulana Abul Kalam Azad, Hakeem Ajmal Khan and Rafi Ahmed Kidwai are some of the examples who engaged in this purpose. Muhammad Ashfaq Ullah Khan of Shahjehanpur conspired to loot the British treasury at Kakori (Lucknow). Khan Abdul Gaffar Khan, was a great nationalist who spent 45 of his 95 years of life in jail. In the fields of sports, literature and politics,l the Muslims have played a significant role. However, after the partition of India, a great number of Muslims settled in Pakistan, but their significance and contributions in their respective fields of expertise is not less significant. They are all duly respected and recognized among the people of both the lands. This book brings out about their life, career, achievements and the art they propounded. By Undivided India, we mean the geographical area of India before independence.

Undersigned is hopeful that her work will be valuable to the readers. Comments and suggestions of the readers are always welcome.

Introduction

As far as the history goes, many today wrongly think that Islam first entered Indian subcontinent through the violent invasions of Muslim invaders in the North India. While it is true that invasions of Timur, Babur, Ghazni and Ghori caused a lot of destruction in North India. On the contrary, the first entry of Islam in India was as early as 8th century AD in a peaceful manner. The Muslim Mappilas of South East India in the Malabar Coast are the earliest known Indian Muslim community, since the 8th century AD, when Arab merchants who had been trading with the Chera kingdom converted them to Islam, based on the preachings of Prophet Muhammad.

On the contrary Christianity entered India by the violent invasion and occupation of Portuguese and the forced conversions by them on the native people of the same Malabar Coast in the 16th century. The Muslim Mappilas were known for active armed attacks against the British, including the 1921 Moplah rebellion. Mappilas fought hand in hand with Hindus to stop European invaders and protected coast of Kerala from cultural and religious conversions.

More Muslims live in the region of undivided India (India, Pakistan and Bangladesh) than in any other place on this planet. This area has produced many illustrious Leaders, Philosophers, Scientists, Scholars, Social Reformers, Sports Person and Writers.

Great lyricists like Javed Akhtar who has written many beautiful songs, singer Mohammed Rafi, Naushad is still unmatched. Everyone enjoy the wonderful tabla of Zakir Hussain, the shahanayi of Ustad Bismillah Khan. One of the most patriotic songs "Saare Jahan Se Achchha" was written by Muhammed Iqbal, a Muslim. This song is called Tarana-e-Hindi i.e Anthem of the people of Hindustan.

Mansoor Ali Khan Pataudi was captain of Indian cricket team. So was Azharuddin, one of the most successful cricket captains of India. Syed Kirmani who kept wickets for India for years, and now is a selector of the Indian cricket team. At present, they have Mohammed Kaif, Zaheer Khan, and Irfan Pathan in their Test squad.

From Dilip Kumar to Naseeruddin Shah, the Muslims have dominated the silver screen in India. From Naushad to Talat Aziz, they are loved, admired and respected in the film industry. The late Nusrat Fateh Ali Khan is revered to this day as master musician among his peers. Remember M. F Husain, who can deny his contribution to the field of arts?

When India launched on its struggle for freedom from British rule, its two major communities, the Hindus and the Muslims, joined in it with equal enthusiasm, like they had done so during the First Indian War of Independence in 1857. The Indian National Congress was formed in 1885. Nationalist leaders from all communities participated in its activities in the first four decades of its existence. Indeed, its second President was a Muslim, Badruddin Tyabji.

Under Gandhi's inspired leadership, the social base of the Congress was widened and it acquired the character of a mass national organization. Meanwhile, in pursuit of their worldwide imperial interests the British decided to dissolve the Islamic Caliphate in Turkey. The repression let loose in Muslim countries in the wake of this decision caused a stir in the Indian Muslim community which launched its own separate movement against the British, referred to as the Khilafat. Mahatma Gandhi, who perceived that the common impulse behind both movements was nationalism, called for a united effort. The Indian National Congress made common cause with the Khilafat, and leaders of the two organizations conducted a common struggle against British imperialism.

Among the most steadfast freedom fighters were the Pathans of undivided India's North-West Frontier Province (NWFP), now a part of Pakistan. Led by their austere leader, Khan Abdul Ghafar Khan, who was popularly known as Frontier Gandhi, the Pathans were throughout uncompromising in their opposition to British rule. Since NWFP was a sensitive border area, the British had to employ even more repression here than elsewhere in the country. They resorted to strong-arm methods to suppress the Khudai Khidmatgars, the soldiers of the disciplined and non-violent militia raised by the Khan. Thousands of these volunteers were victims of this repression. They not only spent years in British prisons but fell victims to their batons and bullets.

Muslim intellectuals like Sir Sayyad Ahmad Khan, founder of Aligarh Muslim University, Shibli Numani, Mohammad Iqbal, Mohammad Ali Jinnah, Abul Kalam Azad and other Muslim intellectuals of this sub-continent carried the noble tradition of fighting for independence.

Sir Sayyad Ahmad Khan was known to be the principal founder of 'modernist Islamic thought'. A known advocate for scientific and modern education to Muslims he renounced the Islamic orthodoxy. Mohammad Ali Jinnah, a westernised Muslim intellectual began his political career with the Indian National Congress. H joined the Muslim League in 1913. He succeeded in making Muslim League as the representative organisation of Indian Muslims. With mass support of his community, he emerged as a third political force in Indian politics during the freedom struggle between Congress and the Britishers.

Mohammad Iqbal, a renowned Muslim scholar and poet, left a deep imprint on Indian Muslim psyche. In his early years he was an advocate of a common nationality, but after his return from England, he advocated for a separate homeland for Muslims. He is credited and admired as the conceptual founder of Pakistan.

In science also many Muslims have contributed greatly to the field. Salimuzzaman Siddiqui was a leading Pakistani scientist in natural products chemistry. He is the pioneer in extracting chemical compunds from the Neem and Rauwolfia, and is also known for isolating novel chemical compunds from various other flora in the Indian subcontinent. As the director of H.E.J. Research Institute of Chemistry, he carried out extensive research with a team of scientists on pharmacology of various plants to extract a number of chemical substances of medicinal importance.

Bangladeshi engineer Fazlur Khan, regarded as the "Einstein of structural engineering" and "the greatest architectural engineer of the second half of the 20th century" for his designs of structural systems that remain fundamental to all high-rise skyscrapers, designs and constructs the John Hancock Center.

Bangladeshi economist Muhammad Yunus, founder of Grameen Bank, successfully applies the concept of microcredit to the first microfinance banking system.

Pakistani theoretical physicist, Abdus Salam, received the Nobel Prize in Physics for his pioneering work on the electroweak interaction theory, which is the mathematical and conceptual synthesis of the electromagnetic and weak interactions.

India's former President and one of the eminent technological figures in India, the master mind behind missiles like Prithvi and Agni and one of the big hands behind the India's nuclear programme, A. P. J. Abdul Kalam is a miracle man. Look at the success of sports persons like Sania Mirza, Azharuddin, Mohd Kaif, Irfan Pathan, Pataudi, etc.

This area has produced numerous Muslim social reformers who have played a significant role in the society. These social reformers have fought against several social evils. These social reformers got themselves engaged in long-drawn social movements in several regions of our sub-continent. Fearless in the condemnation of what they considered culturally decadent, morally unconscionable and socially backward in religious practice, they not merely championed the spirit of rationalism and social reform, but also raised political demands designed to facilitate reforms. These include personalities such as Syed Waheed Akhtar, Muhammad Zakariya Al-Kandahlawi, Muhammad Shahidullah, Muhammad Hussain Najafi, Maulana Tariq Jamil, Maulana Muhammad Ilyas, Azizul Haque and Abul Kashem.

Section: I

ARTISTS

1. AKBAR PADAMSEE

Akbar Padamsee was born in year 1928, in Mumbai (Bombay), state of Maharashtra, India. Akbar Padamsee is a confirmed modern artist. He went to Paris in 1951 and dwelt and worked there until his come back in 1967. Though he is best acknowledged as a painter, Akbar Padamsee has tried out with film-making, sculpting, and writing as an art columnist. Akbar Padamsee is an individual of wide- ranging interests- an artist, a philosopher and a Sanskritist. His thoughtful individuality finds itself reflected on his landscapes where he brings out the original accord in the landscape instead of making a grid. He considers the totality of things with all its opposing factors. To him painting is a deed of question into one's self, a deep challenging action.

His images are lucid, made with traditional formal accord which is an efficient instrument in Padamsee's words. Dialectically contradicted aspects meet in his paintings, like the sense of closeness and withdrawal that his landscapes radiate. Having started his early life in art in J.J.School, he shortly went to Paris becoming one amongst the few Indian artists in the sixties functioning successfully in the global field.

He was granted Diploma in Fine Arts from J.J. School of Art, Mumbai (Bombay) in 1949. He acquired JRD third Foundation Fellowship, NY; and was granted Jawahar Lal Nehru Fellowship.

Akbar Padamsee, since the starting of his artistic career, never hesitated from his strength of line and sharp vision. His idea, even as a very young painter, didn't yield to persisting patterns. Even as Padamsee broke free from the established European schooled thought, which was prevailing then, he maintained a traditional equilibrium in all his work. Padamsee's forms bounded by the line and produced from an assemblage of strokes on the surface are both real and surpassing. In current years he had painted pictures which are relative variations of the same landscape. He held a lot of expositions and his works exhibited were acknowledged well all over the world.

List of his exhibitions held all over world is given below:

- 1952: (Solo exhibition) Galerie Saint Placide, Paris. 1953, 55 Venice Biennale, Italy.

- 1957: (Solo exhibition) Galerie Ventadour, France.
- 1958: Seven Indian Painters, Gallery One, London.
- 1959: Sao Paulo Biennale, Brazil.
- 1959: Tokyo Biennale, Japan.
- 1960: (Solo exhibition) Painting in Grey, Gallery '59, Mumbai (Bombay).
- 1967: (Solo exhibition) Museum of Contemporary Art, Montreal.
- 1980: Retrospective, organized by Art Heritage, Mumbai (Bombay) and New Delhi.
- 1981: Myth and Reality- Aspects of Modern Indian Art, Museum of Modern Art, Oxford.
- 1982: Contemporary Indian Art, Royal Academy of Arts, London.
- 1985-86: Artistes Indiens en France, Foundation Nationale des Arts Graphiques et Plastiques, Paris.
- 1987: Festival of India, Moscow, USSR.
- 1991: National Exposition of Contemporary Art, National Gallery of Modern Art, New Delhi.
- 1992: Sanskriti Art Gallery, Calcutta.
- 1993: Sakshi Gallery, Bangalore & Madras.

Padmasee received following awards in his career:

- 1965: Granted JDR 3rd Foundation Fellowship, New York.
- 1965: Rockerfeller III. Fund Fellowship, United States.
- 1967: Artist - in - Residence, Stout State University, Wisconsin.
- 1969-70: Granted Jawaharlal Nehru Fellowship.
- 2004: Lalit Kala Ratna, Lalit Kala Akademi, New Delhi.

Padmasee now live in the city of Mumbai, India

2. ALTAF RAJA

Altaf Raja is an Indian musician born in October 1967 in the district of Nagpur, state of Maharashtra, India. He has made many pop albums in Hindi along with his rise to fame music album "Tum to thehre pardesi".

His songs are admired for both their lyrics and for his exceptional tone. He is also a playback singer. Born to obscure qawwals Rani Roop Lata and Ibrahim Iqbal, Raja went together with his parents for appearances all over the country. He studied concert skills, stage craft and the skill of extempore entertainment. Raja also spent time at Vazir, an eating place in south Mumbai's Bhendi Bazar where musicians and qawwals talked about sur and taal over chai. Nevertheless, his parents were highly aware of the requirement for a good education. So he was sent to school, first in Pune and then in Mumbai (Bombay). They also asserted that he get schooled in a profession which would get him in any case his daily earning.

So Raja learned dress designing. But making clothes didn't measure up to his dreams. He was eighteen when he came to conclusion that music was his true vocation. His parents gave in and sent him to learn under Pandit Govind Prasad Jaipurwale.

By the time he was twenty, Raja was singing Islamic devotional songs in true Sufi custom at Urs and public functions. With the assistance of Muhammad Shafi Niazi of Venus company, Raja made his first music disc in 1993. It may have been a cover variation — devotional songs in qawwali custom named Sajda rab ko karle — but it also marked the starting of Raja's excellent future. Raja was signed by Venus company for a qawwali album Jungi Qawwali Muqabla with Yasmin Akhtar in 1995 and a solo Mujko Baghdadwale Ka Dar Chahiye. More music albums were followed by invitations for appearances from various parts of the country.

But Raja was not contented. To him, singing only devotional songs was life on-the-periphery. To get nationwide attention, he knew he would have to give a major hit. This meant a mix of music, along with those for films, which eluded him, unflustered, he played on. "I studied books, went across the words of over 2,000 songs, listened to Ghulam Ali and Jagjit Singh who are my favourites." And kept going to Venus company for a break. In the meantime, Raja recollects, "I went on singing in chorus, singing the cue for major singers and, naturally, my solo appearances of devotional songs and other qawwalis. I was certain my break would come soon."

In 1996, Raja recorded his first commercial music album. Venus company released it as Panga Le Liya, based on a admired number on Side A. Amazingly, it was a number on the opposite side, "Tum to thehre pardesi", — that made waves. Venus company was quick to benefit from the hit. It renamed the music album as Tum To Thehre Pardesi.

Inside a couple of weeks, TTTP had taken the market by storm. At first nevertheless, the music album swept only the small towns. In the wake of TTTP's success, Venus company had spun out two more music discs a devotional one named Maiya Meri Jholi Bharde brought out during Navratras and another on Sai Baba. And, naturally, a sequel to TTTP named Aaj Ki Raat Na Ja Pardesi which was on countdown appearance and Liberty Top Ten, a non-film music program.

His blockbuster music albums are:

- 1997: Shapath
- 1998: Yamraaj
- 1998: Tirchi Topiwale
- 1998: Keemat
- 2001: Dil Ke Tukde Hazaar Hue
- 2003: Dil Ka Haal Sune Dilwala
- 2004: Taaza Hawa Lete Hain
- 2007: Harjaiie

He gave his voice for following movies as play back singer:

- 1998: Pardesi Babu
- 1998: Keemat: They Are Back
- 1998: Tirchhi Topiwale
- 1998: Chandaal
- 1999: Benaam
- 1999: Mother
- 2002: Company
- 2003: Market
- 2006: Main hun na
- 2007: Haarjai

3. BARI SIDDIQUI

Bari Siddiqui was born on November 15, 1954 in Netrokona district of Bangladesh. He is a classical flautist, who created his own genre folk fusion by fusing North Indian Classical Music with Baul music.

Abdul Bari Siddiqui, more familiar as Bari Siddiqui, comes from the Pt. Pannalal Ghosh gharana of North Indian Classical Music and a direct disciple of Ustad Aminur Rahman and Pt. V.G. Kannad. Bari Siddiqui is the only musician in the Indian subcontinent who plays North Indian Classical Music in flute as well as sings Baul Songs.

To add to his versatile quality, he composes and directs music, writes lyric and sings as well. Bari Siddiqui started to sing since 2000, with the award winning album of 'Shrabon Megher Din'. His unique contribution in the music of folk fusion is originated from the sub-continental classical music. With authentic background in music and originality of his voice quality, he created his own genre.

He comes from a family of musicians. His formal vocal training began at the age of 12 under Gopal Dutta of Netrokona. His career takes flight in 1981, when he was taken under the wings of Ustad Aminur Rahman, direct disciple of Pt. Pannalal Ghosh (1911- 1960) and Dabir Khan (Beenkar). Ustad Aminur Rahman spotted Bari Siddiqui during a concert, and offered to tutor him. For the next six years he trained under Ustad Aminur Rahman.

Ustad Aminur Rahman's house was frequented by the contemporary legends like Devendra Muddereshshor, Director All India Radio (also the son-in-law of Pt. Pannalal Ghosh), VG Karnad, Daagar Brothers, Ustad Zia Mohiuddin (Veenakar), Ustad Asad Ali Khan Veenakar, Pandit Sriram Tewari. After Ustad Aminur Rahman, he continued to take special training on Alap from Tawfique Nawaz (second son of Ustad Aminur Rahman).

At one stage, Bari Siddiqui went to Pune and got professional tutelage under Pandit VG Karnad. For many years to come, being in an environment surrounded by musical maestros, he kept his search for his own true self and to achieve newer heights of infinite journey of music.

Bari Siddiqiui performed in countries like India, Pakistan, Singapore, Indonesia, Thailand, Burma, USA, England, Switzerland, France and many other European countries. In 1999 at the World Flute Conference in Geneva, where representatives from seventy countries took part, Bari Siddiqui was the only representative from the Indian subcontinent. He received many awards for his performances at Fajar Music Festival award in Iran, World Flute Conference Award in Geneva, International Film Movement Association Award, and Bachshash Award.

Bari Siddiqui started to sing since 2000, with the award winning album of 'Srabon Megher Din'. Success of 'Srabon Megher Din' was followed by popular albums like 'Lokkho Tara', 'Lilua Batash', 'Dukkho Roilo Mone', 'Valobashar Boshotbari', 'Aporadhi Hoileo Ami Tor', etc giving the local music industry a new dimension in terms of authenticity and originality.

Bari Siddiqui lives and works from Dhaka, Bangladesh.

4. DILIP KUMAR

Dilip Kumar, was born on December 11, 1922 as Muhammad Yusuf Khan, in Qissa Khawani Bazaar in Peshawar, Pakistan, in a Pashtun household of twelve children. He is a renowned Bollywood film artist and a past Member of Parliament (Rajya Sabha). His father, Ghulam Sarwar was a fruit vendor and possessed large plantations in Peshawar and Devlali in Maharashtra close to Mumbai (Bombay). The household shifted to Mumbai (Bombay) in thirties and in the early forties Yusuf Khan shifted to Pune and started his canteen business and supply of dry fruits. There he was found by a major performer of those years, Devika Rani, who was also the wife of the founder of Bombay Talkies, Himanshu Rai, and assisted his admission into the Bollywood film industry. She also gave him the screen name "Dilip Kumar".

A small tiff with his father made young Yusuf run away to Pune. There he started to work in a British Army canteen and later having saved some amount, set up his own fruit stall. As far as his interest in art goes, even from a young age Yusuf was fond of gazals and was himself a good singer and sitar player never knowing that later, he was to render his voice in a Hrishida film.

In the 40's Yusuf was initiated to the world of films by the leading actress of those days Devika Rani, who was also the proprietor of the famous studio Bombay Talkies. Yusuf who was re-christened Dilip Kumar by a famed Hindi novelist made his debut in their film 'Jwar Bhatta' in 1944. He became successful as a hero opposite singing actress Noorjehan in the film 'Jugnu', next came 'Mela' in which he played the doomed lover and then Mahboob Khan's 'Andaz', a love triangle, opposite superstars, Nargis and Raj Kapoor, which became a big hit and elevated him to a superstar level.

His first film Jwar Bhata, was brought out in 1944 which was a flop. In 1947 he shot to fame with the film Jugnu which was his first main hit. In 1949, he acted with Raj Kapoor in the romantic melodrama film Andaz, which became a big success and made him a star. During the fifties he was amongst the greatest stars of Bollywood together with Raj Kapoor and Dev Anand. He became famous for acting tragic roles in admired films such as Deedar, Amar, Devdas and Madhumati, which earned him the name of "tragedy king".

He was also successful in playing light roles such as playing a swaggering peasant in Aan and a comical role in Azaad. In 1960 he acted in the historical film Mughal-e-Azam which is as of 2008, the second highest earning film in Hindi film history, in which he played the character of the Mughal crown-prince Jehangir, the son of Akbar.

In 1961 he made and acted in the hit Ganga Jamuna in which he and his real-life brother Nasir Khan played the title roles. In spite of the film's success he didn't make any film after this. Dilip had a narrow encounter with global fame in 1962, when British director David Lean offered him the role of Sherif Ali in his 1962 megahit, Lawrence of Arabia. Nevertheless, he refused the part. The role finally went to Omar Sharif, the Egyptian artist. After a short period of box office failures in the mid sixties, he bounced back when he played a double role of twins separated at birth in the film Ram Aur Shyam which was amongst the greatest box office successes of the year. The hit of Ram Aur Shyam started a number of remakes and imitators.

In the seventies he starred in lesser films as younger actors such as Rajesh Khanna and Amitabh Bachchan had started to take the attention. A lot of his films failed at the box office throughout this period of time and after the release of his 1976 film Bairaag in which he played triple roles, he took a five year pause from acting.

He made a reappearance in 1981 with the multi-starrer Kranti which was the greatest hit of the year. He went onto play character roles as an aged household family head or a policeman in a succession of box office successes along with Shakti (in which he acted together with the ruling superstar of the time Amitabh Bachchan), Vidhaata, Mashaal and Karma. In his last main successful film, Saudagar, he appeared together with another renowned artist Raj Kumar after three decades since they last acted together in Paigham. In 1992 he won the Filmfare Lifetime Achievement Award.

In 1996 he was attached to make his directorial entry with a film named Kalinga but the film was postponed. In 1998 he made his last film appearance to date in the box office failure Qila where in an uncommon form he played a villainous role. He has since retired from the film industry though he has continued to get film proposals in current years but the films have either been postponed due to his indifferent health or because he declined them.

He is believed to be amongst the biggest actors of Indian cinema. Beginning his profession in 1944, Dilip Kumar has acted in some of the greatest commercially successful films from the late forties, fifties, sixties and eighties. His acting have been looked upon as the height of acting in Indian Cinema. He was the first actor to get a Filmfare Best Actor Award and holds the record for most number of Filmfare Awards won for that class. Although he has done all kinds of films - he balanced different kinds of roles such as the vivid Andaz with the swaggering Aan, the dramatic Devdas with the comical Azaad and the historical romance Mughal E Azam with the social Ganga Jamuna. He has now retired from the film industry.

Given below is list of some of his famous films in chronological order:

1944: Jwar Bhata
1945: Pratima
1947: Milan
1947: Jugnu
1948: Shaheed
1948: Nadiya Ke Paar
1948: Mela
1948: Ghar Ki Izzat
1948: Anokha Pyar
1949: Shabnam
1949: Andaz
1950: Jogan
1950: Babul
1950: Arzoo
1951: Tarana
1951: Hulchul
1951: Deedar
1952: Sangdil
1952: Daag
1952: Aan
1953: Shikast
1953: Footpath
1954: Amar
1955: Udan Khatola
1955: Insaniyat
1955: Devdas
1955: Azaad
1957: Naya Daur
1957: Musafir
1958: Yahudi
1958: Madhumati
1959: Paigham
1960: Kohinoor
1960: Mughal-E-Azam
1961: Gunga Jumna
1964: Leader

1966: Dil Diya Dard Liya
1967: Ram Aur Shyam
1968: Sunghursh
1968: Sadhu Aur Shaitan
1968: Aadmi
1970: Sagina Mahato
1970: Gopi
1972: Daastan
1972: Anokha Milan
1974: Sagina
1974: Phir Kab Milogi
1976: Bairaag
1981: Kranti
1982: Vidhaata
1982: Shakti
1983: Mazdoor
1984: Duniya
1984: Mashaal
1986: Dharam Adhikari
1986: Karma
1989: Kanoon Apna Apna
1990: Izzatdaar
1990: Aag Ka Dariya
1991: Saudagar
1998: Qila

5. ISMAIL GULGEE

Ismail Gulgee was born on October 25, 1926 in Peshawar city, Pakistan. He was an prizewinning, world renowned Pakistani artist. He was a certified engineer in the United States and self-taught abstractionist and portrait painter. Before 1959, as portraitist, he painted the whole Afghan Royal Household. From about 1960 on, he was noted as an abstractionist shaped by the custom of Muslim calligraphy and by the American "action painting" idiom.

He attended Aligarh University to learn civil engineering before moving to USA for carrying on his higher education. Gulgee began to paint while gaining his education as an engineer in the United States at Columbia University and then Harvard.

His first exhibition was in 1950. Gulgee was a talented and gifted expert naturalistic portrait painter who had enjoyed generous state backup and lots of best commissions in this ability. However, he was possibly best known all over for his abstract work, which was motivated by Muslim calligraphy and was also inspired by the "action painting" trend of the fifties and sixties. This is possibly a natural enough rhetorical combination, as in both Muslim calligraphy and action painting a great value is placed on the unity and energy of gestural flow. As with the works of other action painters or abstract expressionists, Gulgee's canvases were often quite large. He was also famous for employing materials such as mirror glass and gold or silver leaf in his oil paintings, so that they were in reality mixed media pieces.

Gulgee's calligraphy paintings are abstract and gestural interpretings of Arabic and Urdu letters. His swinging layers of paint explore the formal qualities of oil paint while they addresses the Muslim design elements. Starting in the 1960s, Gulgee also produced sculptings, along with bronze pieces that were (like several of his paintings) calligraphic in form and motivation, and occasionally explicitly founded on verses from the Quran.

His paintings were brilliant and awash with colour, but the paint was put on with great feeling, and paintings pulsate with strong feeling. Areas sing with lucent, thin colour; thick blobs of paint quiver with fibreglass tears, the brush twirls strong and free. The total impression used to be very free, however considered and thoughtful. They work tremendously well, because it was all organized with great care and concentration.

Guljee, as he was notably known, received a lot of requests for his paintings globally, from the Saudi royal house to the Islamabad presidency. A lot of his works are placed in the "Faisal Mosque" in Islamabad. Guljee received a lot of awards, along within Pakistan, Saudi Arabia, Japan and France. Guljee's expositions have mainly been accessible to a small number of individuals.

Holding that in mind and great demand from public and fans of his works, an art gallery for Guljee has been made in Clifton, Karachi close to South City Hospital and Sea View Karachi. Guljee mainly painted for his own motivations and dream, though certain paintings are available for sale in Guljee art gallery. Guljee was last based in Boat Basin in Karachi.

Gulgee, his wife Zarrin Gulgee and a maidservant were found dead in their house in Karachi on the evening of December 19, 2007 by his servants. Police believe that all three had been murdered. Although the bodies were found on the nineteenth, officers report that they had evidently been dead for three days, leading to a tentative death date of December 16, 2007. Their bodies were found bound and strangled in different rooms of the house. The original cause of death for all three has been assigned to asphyxiation. Gulgee was buried on the evening of December 20, 2007, in Karachi.

6. LUBNA AGHA

Lubna Agha was born in 1949 in Pakistan. She is a leading South Asian artist belonging to Pakistan. Lubna Agha, one of Pakistan's leading artists, is famous for her free, novel, and significant body of work. Officially recognized as an influential and crucial figure in the growing Pakistani female art movement, Agha has proven herself to be a constantly developing and stylistically smooth artist during her respected thirty-year career.

Nearly twenty years ago, Agha left her native Pakistan and relocated to the United States. During her stay in the United States, Agha has continued to incorporate and reflect the principles, challenges and mannerisms of her adopted land. The developing scenery of the American Experience is explored in her most recent works-in-progress series, named, InfoSeries. Agha feels that staying cued to the beat of American life and its influences furnishes a lively source of motivation and guidance in her work that improves her creative growth.

Never wandering too far from her native Persian origins, such as customary miniature painting and Sufi theology, Agha has also been evenly inspired by Western creative movements initiating from the Colonial Era and beyond. Agha feels that her work bridges the soul of the East with that of the West, ensuing in a blending of the literary influences and acutely stylized miniature painting of the East, with the distinctive and emotive aesthetic concerns of the West.

Her art is a type of "lyrical artistic movement," and favours a flourishing, aesthetical, and bold use of colour. Her changeover to acrylics has granted her a bigger amount of liberty and suppleness to use colour as a thematic element that enlivens and improves her canvases. Her use of vibrant colour deepens the sensation of robustness and fertile possibilities built-in in her works.

Agha's thematic interests often focus on notions of personal individuality and individual limitations. These limitations are either self-enforced or traditionally enforced, and can be emotional, scholarly, sexual, theoretical or individual in origin. Oftentimes these limitations and identities constrict and burden the person, inhibiting their spiritual growth and development. These limitations can even cloud and deform our percepts of truth. At times, enforced limitations separate and remove us-from others, from ourselves, from truth, from that which supplies nourishment.

Agha's aesthetic dissertation is that the conflict with and examination of these limitations and restraints allows us a pathway into spectral and individual transcendence. This transcendence allows us to confirm our connections with others and with ourselves, thereby restoring us to the sensation of whole we starve for spectral realization. This journey of disclosure and revelation leads us to an understanding of a higher, cosmopolitan truth.

Agha offers an option to her barren environment of deconstruction, doubt, and abolition. She responds with a realized vision of realization, which is based in the commonalties of recurring happenings. These recurring happenings can be deduced from universe or from human knowledge. Frequently their portrayal is a representative microcosm of the entire that ties us together. The cycles of birth, life, death and disintegration are an inescapable reality for each human being. By identifying with and analysing our commonalties, we can transcend enforced limitations.

In no work is this better exemplified than in Roots. The elements portrayed all sustain life-from the umbilical cord in the womb, to the roots of a tree. The enlacing of the two symbolize how we, as human beings, are tied into a bigger reality and reincarnation and life. It becomes impossible to split one from the other.

She has displayed in art museums and galleries all over the world - in her motherland, Pakistan, and also in Britain, Japan, Jordan, Switzerland, and the United States. Agha's most recent paintings draw motivation from Asian and Muslim design and from customary Islamic crafts such as woodcarving, metalworking, and textile fabrication.

Her work is part of the permanent collections at the Asian Collection at Bradford Museum, UK, National Council of the Arts, Pakistan, and the Jordan National Gallery of Fine Arts, Jordan.

A volume about the artist by Marcella Sirhandi named Lubna Agha: Points of Reference was printed by The Foundation of Museum of Modern Art, Pakistan in 2007.

Lubna Agha resides and works in Brookline, Massachusetts, United States.

Given below is the list of her famous Exhibitions:

- 1969: Pakistan American Cultural Centre, Karachi, Pakistan
- 1971: Arts Council of Pakistan, Karachi, Pakistan

- 1972: Contemporary Art Gallery, Rawalpindi, Pakistan
- 1973: Indus Gallery, Karachi, Pakistan
- 1975: Pakistan Art Gallery, Lahore, Pakistan
- 1976: Contemporary Art Gallery, Rawalpindi, Pakistan
- 1980: Indus Gallery, Karachi, Pakistan
- 1981: Alta Galleries, Sacramento, California
- 1981: Stuart/Scott Gallery, Fair Oaks, California
- 1983: Rara Avis, Sacramento, California
- 1985: Djurovich Gallery, Sacramento, California
- 1987: Indus Gallery, Karachi, Pakistan
- 1991: Himovitz Solomon Gallery, Sacramento, California
- 1996: Chawkandi Gallery, Karachi, Pakistan
- 2001: Chawkandi Gallery, Karachi, Pakistan
- 2007: International Visions Gallery, Washington DC

7. M. F. HUSAIN

Maqbool Fida Husain was born on September 17, 1915, in city of Pandharpur in the state of Maharashtra, India. He is commonly known as M F Husain and is one of India's better known artists. As per Forbes magazine, he has been named the "Picasso of India". Husain comes from an Islamic Indian household. His mother expired when he was one and a half years old. His father remarried and shifted to Indore, where Husain attended school. In 1935, he shifted to Mumbai (Bombay) and was accepted to the Sir J. J. School of Art. He began by painting cinema billboards.

Husain first became famous as an artist in the late forties. In 1947, he became member of the Progressive Artists' Group, established by Francis Newton Souza. This was a camp of young artists who wished to break with the nationalist customs founded by the Bengal school of art and to promote an Indian avant-garde, engaged at a global level. He has also worked (produced & directed) on a small number of movies, along with Gaja Gamini (with Madhuri Dixit who was the subject of a series of his paintings which he signed Fida). The film was meant as a compliment to Ms. Dixit herself. In this film she can be seen impersonating various forms and manifestations of womanhood along with the muse of Kalidasa, the Mona Lisa, a rebel, and musical ecstasy. He went on to make Meenaxi: A Tale of Three Cities (with Tabu). His autobiography is being made into a movie tentatively named "The Making of the Painter." starring Shreyas Talpade as the young Husain.

In 1952, his first solo exhibition was held at Zürich and over the next few years, his work was broadly seen in Europe and United States. In 1955, he was granted the esteemed Padma Shree award by the Government of India. In 1967, he made his first film, Through the Eyes of a Painter. It was shown at the Berlin Film Festival and won a Golden Bear. M. F. Husain was a distinctive invitee together with Pablo Picasso at the Sao Paulo Biennial in 1971. He has been granted the Padma Bhushan in 1973 and was nominated to the Rajya Sabha in 1986. He was granted the Padma Vibhushan in 1991.

Husain moved on to become the biggest paid painter in India. His single canvases have fetched up to two million dollars at a recent Christie's auction. The Peabody Essex Museum (USA, Massachusetts) showed a solo exhibition from November 4, 2006 to June 3, 2007. It displayed Husain's paintings motivated by the Hindu epic, Mahabharata.

In early 2008, Husain's Battle of Ganga and Jamuna: Mahabharata twelve, a large art, from the Hindu epic, fetched $1.6 million, setting a world record at Christie's South Asian Modern and Contemporary Art sale. This talented artist rose to international fame from a humble beginning and now has become the highest paid painter in India. His single canvases have fetched up to 2 million dollars. The immensely popular artist now lives and works in Bombay and remains a central figure in the contemporary Indian art scene.

8. MADHUBALA

Madhubala was born on February 14, 1933 in Delhi, India. She was born Mumtaz Begum Jehan Dehlavi and was a well liked Hindi film actress who acted in many successful films in the fifties and early sixties, a lot of which have attained classic and cult status today. With her contemporaries, Nargis and Meena Kumari, she is broadly looked upon as amongst the most gifted and important actresses to have appeared on the screens of Hindi Cinema.

Mumtaz Begum Jehan Dehlavi is famously known as Madhubala, She was Muslim and an ethnic Pathan, the fifth child of a traditional household of eleven children. After Madhubala's father, Ataullah Khan lost his work at the Imperial Tobacco Company, the household suffered a lot of hardships along with the deaths of four of Madhubala's sisters and her two brothers. Madhubala and four other sisters remained. In search of a better life for his poor household, her father shifted them to Mumbai (Bombay). There they struggled for over a year and often frequented the Mumbai (Bombay) film studios in search of job. Young Mumtaz came into films at the age of nine.

Her first film was the box-office hit, Basant, in which she acted the daughter of the well liked actress, Mumtaz Shanti. She then moved on to act in many films as a child artist. It was the famous actress, Devika Rani, struck by her performances and potentiality, who suggested to her to alter her name to Madhubala. Her gift was explicitly apparent and she soon garnered a status as a dependable and professional performer. By the time she was a teenager, her remarkable good looks and tall, lissome figure, meant she was already being prepared for lead roles.

Her first break came when filmmaker, Kidar Sharma paired her opposite Raj Kapoor in Neel Kamal (1947). Till that point, she had always been called as Mumtaz but after this film she was accredited as Madhubala. She was only fourteen years old, but Madhubala had finally arrived on the Indian screen in a lead role. Although the film was not a commercial hit, she was noticed and her performance well received.

In the next two years she bloomed into a attractive beauty (film media and fans referred to her as the Venus of the Screen). Nevertheless it was not till she acted in the sought after lead role of Bombay Talkies production, Mahal in 1949, that Madhubala became a full-fledged star and a household name. Audiences enthused over Madhubala's enigmatic screen charisma and beauty. Although she was only sixteen at the time, critics widely admitted that her pernicious and proficient performance upstaged her experienced co-star, Ashok Kumar. The film became a well liked hit and the song Aayega Aanewala heralded the arrival of two new superstars both Madhubala and playback singer Lata Mangeshkar.

Madhubala's heart problem was discovered in 1950 after she frequently coughed up blood on the sets. She was born with a cardiac flaw commonly acknowledged as a "hole in the heart". At the time, heart surgery was not broadly accessible.

Her sickness was kept a secret from the industry for a lot of years, although one event was broadly reported by the film media in 1954. Madhubala was filming in Madras for S.S. Vassan's film Bahut Din Huwe. She got very sick and vomited blood on the set. Vassan and his wife were very friendly and cared for her till she was well again. Madhubala was tremendously thankful and as a result broke her own rule of never attending film premieres, even her own, by making an exception for Bahut Din Huwe and the following year, another Vassan production, Insaniyat. The event in Madras was down-played and shortly forgotten, enabling Madhubala to continue functioning and to make herself as an A-grade star.

As a consequence, Madhubala's household was tremendously protective. When filming at the studios, she would only eat home prepared food and drink water that came from a specific well in an attempt to minimize risks of sickness or infection. Finally her condition would take its price and cut her life and profession, but for most of the fifties, Madhubala performed successfully in spite of her sickness and physical limitations.

Her famous films are:

1942: Basant	1944: Mumtaz Mahal
1945: Dhanna Bhagat	1946: Rajputani
1946: Pujari	1946: Phoolwari
1947: Saat Samundaron Ki Mallika	1947: Mere Bhagwan
1947: Khubsoorat Duniya	1947: Dil-Ki-Rani Sweet-Heart
1947: Chittor Vijay	1947: Neel Kamal
1948: Parai Aag	1948: Lal Dupatta
1948: Desh Sewa	1948: Amar Prem
1949: Sipahiya	1949: Singaar
1949: Paras	1949: Neki Aur Badi
1949: Mahal	1949: Imtihaan
1949: Dulari	1949: Daulat
1949: Apradhi	1950: Pardes
1950: Nishana	1950: Nirala
1950: Madhubala	1950: Hanste Aansoo
1950: Beqasoor	1951: Tarana

1951: Saiyan
1951: Nazneen
1951: Nadaan
1951: Khazana
1951: Badal
1951: Aaram
1952: Saqi
1952: Sangdil
1953: Rail Ka Dibba
1953: Armaan
1954: Bahut Din Huye
1954: Amar
1955: Teerandaz
1955: Naqab
1955: Naata
1955: Mr. & Mrs. '55
1956: Shirin Farhad
1956: Raj Hath
1956: Dhake Ki Malmal
1957: Yahudi Ki Ladki
1957: Gateway of India
1957: Ek Saal
1958: Police
1958: Phagun
1958: Kalapani
1958: Howrah Bridge
1958: Chalti Ka Naam Gaadi
1958: Baghi Sipahi
1959: Kal Hamara Hai
1959: Insaan Jaag Utha
1959: Do Ustad
1960: Mehlon Ke Khwab
1960: Jaali Note
1960: Barsaat Ki Raat
1960: Mughal-E-Azam
1961: Passport
1961: Jhumroo
1961: Boy Friend
1962: Half Ticket
1964: Sharabi
1971: Jwala

Madhubala in her final years was very ill and died on February 23, 1969, in Mumbai (Bombay), India.

9. MEHMOOD

Mehmood was born on September 29, 1932, as Mehmood Ali, in the city of Mumbai (Bombay), Maharashtra, India. Commonly known simply as Mehmood, he was an Indian actor, director and producer. He was famous and appreciated for acting comic roles in Hindi films. He worked in over three hundred Hindi films in a career crossing three decades.

Mehmood was one of eight children born to actor and dancer Mumtaz Ali in Mumbai (Bombay). Mehmood had an elder sister and the rest of the six siblings were younger to him. Mehmood began acting as an unwilling child actor in Bombay Talkies films like Kismet. Some of his early jobs before he began acting were driving, doing odd jobs, selling poultry. He worked as director P. L. Santoshi's driver (Later Santoshi's son Rajkumar Santoshi cast Mehmood in his venture Andaz Apna Apna). He was employed to teach table tennis to Meena Kumari in those days. He afterward married her sister Madhu.

It was after marriage and becoming a father that he decided to act to earn a better living. He got a small break as a murder victim in CID. He began by doing small overlooked roles in films like "Do Bigha Zameen" and "Pyaasa". He afterward moved on to act in lead roles but he was appreciated for his comedy.

Mehmood was Bollywood's best-known comedian. There were many other comedians in Bombay Talkies before he came to the screen, but they merely functioned as excuses to take the audience's mind off the melodramatic plot for a few minutes of the film's running time. Then, along came Mehmood and he made the comedian's role an integral part of the story line. Often the comedian's plight proved more interesting than even the hero's romance. And, for a brief period in the 60s, thanks to him, comedy was king. And Mehmood was the uncrowned King of Comedy.

Some of his famous films are:

- 1961: Chotte Nawab
- 1961: Sasuraal
- 1962: Dil Tera Diwana
- 1964: Zindagi
- 1965: Gumnaam
- 1965: Johar Mehmood in Goa
- 1966: Pyar Kiye Ja
- 1966: Love in Tokyo
- 1967: Patthar ke Sanam
- 1968: Padosan
- 1968: Aankhen
- 1968: Do Phool

- 1968: Sadhu aur Shaitan
- 1970: Humjoli
- 1971: Main Sundar Hoon
- 1971: Johar Mehood in Hong Kong
- 1972: Bombay to Goa
- 1974: Kunwaara Baap
- 1974: Vardaan
- 1976: Ginny Aur Johnny
- 1976: Sabse Bada Rupaiya
- 1995: Guddu

He won many awards, the most notable being:

- 1962: Filmfare Best Supporting Actor Award - Dil Tera Diwana
- 1966: Filmfare Best Comedian Award - Pyar Kiye Jaa
- 1974: Filmfare Best Comedian Award - Vardaan

He expired on July 23, 2004 in Pennsylvania, United States where he had gone for cure of lung disease after suffering poor health for many years.

10. MEENA KUMARI

Meena Kumari or Mahjabeen Bano was born on August 1, 1932 in the city of Mumbai (Bombay), Maharashtra, India. She was an outstanding Indian movie actress. Mahjabeen Bano was the third daughter of Ali Baksh and Iqbal Begum; Khursheed and Madhu were her two elder sisters. At the time of her birth, her parents were unable to pay the fees of Dr. Gadre, who had delivered her, so her father left her at an Islamic orphanage, nevertheless, he picked her up after a couple of hours.

Her father, a Sunni Islamic, was a expert of Parsi theatre, played harmonium, taught music, and wrote Urdu poetry. He played minor roles in films like Id Ka Chand and compiled music for films like Shahi Lutere.

Her mother, Prabhwati Devi, was the second wife of Ali Baksh. Before encountering and then marrying Ali Baksh, she was a stage actress and dancer, under the stage name, Kamini. After marriage, she converted from Hinduism to Islam, and altered her name to Iqbal Begum.

When Mahjabeen was born, Ali Bakhsh aimed to get roles as an actor in Rooptara Studios. At the pressing of his wife, he got Mahjabeen too into movies in spite of her protests of wanting to go to school. Young Mahjabeen is said to have said, "I do not want to work in movies; I want to go to school, and study like other children."

As Mahjabeen embarked on her acting profession at the age of seven, she was renamed Baby Meena. Farzand-e-Watan or Leatherface was her first movie, which was directed for Prakash Studios by Vijay Bhatt. She became nearly the only breadwinner of her household during the forties. Her early adult acting, under the name Meena Kumari, was mostly in mythological movies like Veer Ghatotkach, Shri Ganesh Mahima, and fantasy movies like Alladin and The Wonderful Lamp.

Meena Kumari earned recognition with her role as a heroine in Vijay Bhatt's Baiju Bawra. This heroine always negated herself for the material and spiritual advancement of the man she loved and was even eager to annihilate herself to supply him the experience of pain so that his music would be enriched. She became the first actress to win the Filmfare Best Actress Award in 1953 for this performance.

Meena Kumari extremely successfully played the roles of a suffering woman in Parineeta, Daera, Ek Hi Raasta, Sharda, and Dil Apna Aur Preet Parayi. Although she cultivated the image of a tragedienne, she also acted commendably in a couple of light-hearted movies like Azaad, Miss Mary, Shararat, and Kohinoor.

One of her better known performance was of an alcoholic wife in Sahib Bibi Aur Ghulam, which was made by Guru Dutt. In one unforgettable scene, the heroine, Choti Bahu, dresses for her husband, providing a poignant presentation of a woman's expectations and sexual desire.

In 1962, she made history by being nominated for three Filmfare Best Actress Awards for her roles in Aarti, Main Chup Rahungi, and Sahib Bibi Aur Ghulam. She won the award for her role in Aarti.

There are some eerie commonalties between the lives of Choti Bahu and Meena Kumari: The estranged marital relationship, the taking to drinking, the searching of younger male company, and the starving to be understood and loved by all.

For four more years, Meena Kumari acted admirably in Dil Ek Mandir, Kaajal, and Phool Aur Patthar. Nevertheless, she relied more and more on close relations with younger men like Dharmendra, and often dulled her senses with liquor. She spent the last years of her life acting the doomed woman. Because of serious drinking, she progressively lost her good looks, and began playing character roles in B grade movies like Jawab and Dushmun.

She developed an affection to writer-lyricist Gulzar and starred in his directorial entry, Mere Apne Meena Kumari presented a strong portrayal of an aged woman who got caught between two street gangs of disturbed, unemployed youth and got killed, her demise making the youth realize the uselessness of aggression. In 1972, she acknowledged that she had a limited time left on this earth, and so she went out of her way to complete at the earliest the cult classic, Pakeezah. At first, after its release in February 1972, Pakeezah opened to a half-hearted reaction from the public; nevertheless, after Meena Kumari's demise less than two months afterward, individuals flocked to see it. During her life, Meena Kumari had a love-hate relationship with movies.

Some of her famous films are:

1939: Leatherface
1940: Ek Hi Bhool
1940: Pooja
1941: Nai Roshni
1942: Garib
1943: Pratiggya
1947: Piya Ghar Aaja
1948: Bichchade Balam
1950: Magroor
1950: Shri Ganesh Mahima
1951: Hanumaan Pataal Vijay
1951: Lakshmi Narayan
1952: Baiju Bawra
1953: Dana Paani
1953: Do Bigha Zamin
1953: Baiju Bawra
1954: Parineeta
1954: Chandni Chowk
1955: Azaad
1955: Bandish
1956: Bandhan
1956: Ek-Hi-Rasta
1956: Halaku
1956: Mem Sahib
1956: Naya Andaz
1956: Shatranj
1957: Miss Mary
1958: Yahudi
1959: Ardhangini
1959: Shararat
1960: Dil Apna Aur Preet Parai
1962: Aarti
1962: Sahib Bibi Aur Ghulam
1964: Maain Bhi Ladki Hun
1965: Kaajal
1965: Jadui Angoothi
1967: Bahu Begum
1967: Noorjehan

1968: Baharon Ki Manzil 1971: Dushmun

1972: Pakeezah

She won many awards, the most notable being:

- 1953: Filmfare Best Actress Award - Baiju Bawra
- 1954: Filmfare Best Actress Award - Parineeta
- 1962: Filmfare Best Actress Award - Aarti
- 1965: Filmfare Best Actress Award - Kaajal

11. MUHAMMAD RAFI

Muhammad Rafi was born on December 24, 1924 in Kotla Sultanpur, a town close to Amritsar in the state of Punjab, India. He was a well known Indian playback singer. A versatile singer, Rafi sang in a lot of Indian languages along with Hindi, Urdu, Punjabi, Bengali, Marathi, Kannada and Telugu. He is mainly remembered, nevertheless, for his Hindi songs, which still remain very well liked in the Indian subcontinent as well as amongst the Indian diaspora. Together with Mukesh and Kishore Kumar, he was amongst the major male Bollywood playback singers from the 1950s to the 1970s. He was granted the Padma Shri in 1965.

Muhammad Rafi was born the youngest of six sons of Haji Ali Muhammad. Rafi, whose nickname was Pheeko, began singing by imitating chants of a fakir in his village. In 1935-36, Rafi's father moved to Lahore, and the rest of the household followed later. Rafi's household managed a men's salon in Lahore's Noor Mohalla. It was his brother-in-law Muhammad Hameed who found the gift in Rafi and encouraged him. Rafi studied Hindustani traditional music from masters Ustad Bade Ghulam Ali Khan, Ustad Abdul Wahid Khan, Pandit Jiwanlal Matto and Firoze Nizami.

Rafi's first public performance came at the age of thirteen, when he was permitted to sing at a concert featuring the renowned K. L. Saigal. Rafi, under Shyam Sunder, made his entry in playback singing with the duet Soniye nee, Heeriye nee with Zeenat Begum in a Punjabi film Gul Baloch in 1942. Shortly after, Rafi was invited by the Lahore radio station to sing for them. In 1944, Rafi moved to Mumbai (Bombay). He was introduced to some of the major film producers of the time such as

Abdul Rashid Kardar, Mehboob Khan and actor-director Nazeer by Tanvir Naqvi. Rafi contacted the renowned music director Naushad, who at first employed him as part of the singing group. Rafi's first song with Naushad was Hindustan ke hum hain with Shyam Kumar, Alauddin and others, from A. R. Kardar's Pehle Aap (1944). Around the same time, Rafi recorded another song for the film Gaon ki Gori (1944) for Shyam Sunder, Aji dil ho kaaboo mein with G. M. Durrani and chorus. He considered this song as his first Hindi language song. In 1945, Rafi got married to his cousin Bashira, nicknamed "Majhi", in his village.

In 1945, Rafi appeared on the screen for the famous song "Tera Jalwa Jis Ne Dekha" in the film Laila Majnu. He sang a number of songs for Naushad as part of the chorus, along with "Mere sapnon ki rani, Roohi Roohi" with K. L. Saigal from the film Shahjahan (1946). Rafi was first noted for the song Tera Khilona Toota Balak from Mehboob Khan's Anmol Ghadi (1946). His duet with Noor Jehan in the film Jugnu 1947, Yahan Badla Wafa Ka became a success. After division, Rafi decided to stay back in India and had his household flown to Mumbai (Bombay). In 1948, Rafi sang "Suno Suno Aye Duniya Walon Bapuji Ki Amar Kahani, scripted by Rajendra Krishan, which became a big success. In 1949, Rafi was given solo songs by music directors such as Naushad (Chandni Raat, Dillagi and Dulari), Shyam Sunder (Bazaar) and Husnalal Bhagatram (Meena Bazaar).

Rafi, in his life time was awarded many times. Some of his famous awards are:

- 1948: Rafi received a silver medal from the Indian Prime Minister Jawaharlal Nehru, on the first anniversary of the Indian Independence Day.
- 1960: Filmfare Best Male Playback Award for Chaudhvin Ka Chand Ho song in the film Chaudhvin Ka Chand
- 1961: Filmfare Best Male Playback Award for Teri Pyaari Pyaari Surat Ko song in the film Sasural
- 1964: Filmfare Best Male Playback Award for Chahunga Mein Tujhe song in the film Dosti
- 1965: He was honoured with the Padmashri by the Government of India
- 1966: Filmfare Best Male Playback Award for Baharon Phool Barsao song in the film Suraj
- 1968: Filmfare Best Male Playback Award for Dil Ke Jharoke Mein song in the film Brahmachari

- 1968: National Award for Best Male Playback Singer for Neel Kamal compiled by Ravi
- 1977: Filmfare Best Male Playback Award for Kya Hua Tera Vaada song in the film Hum Kisi Se Kum Nahin
- 1977: National Film Award for Best Male Playback Singer for Kya Hua Tera Wada song in the film Hum Kisi Se Kum Nahin), compiled by RD Burman, words by Majrooh Sultanpuri
- 2001: Rafi was honoured with the "best singer of the millennium" by Hero Honda and Stardust magazine in Mumbai on January 7, 2001

Rafi died on Thursday, July 31, 1980, in Mumbai, India after a massive heart attack.

12. NASEERUDDIN SHAH

Naseeruddin Shah was born on July 20, 1950 in the city of Barabanki, Uttar Pradesh, India. He is a famous Indian film actor widely acclaimed. He has seen triumph in both conventional Bollywood cinema and also in Parallel Cinema. He also appeared in a lot of global films most notably playing Skipper Nemo in the Hollywood comic book adaptation "The League of Extraordinary Gentlemen."

He became active in normal movies, commonly acknowledged as Bollywood with the 1980 film Hum Paanch. His next main success in conventional films was the 1986 multi-starrer film Karma where he starred together with expert Dilip Kumar. Sole hero films such as Ijaazat, Jalwa and Hero Hiralal followed. In 1988 he played opposite his wife Ratna Pathak as Inspector Ghote, the fictional detective of H. R. F. Keating's novels in the Merchant-Ivory English language film The Perfect Murder.

He starred in many multi-starrer Bollywood films as well such as Ghulami, Tridev and Vishwatma. In 1994, he acted as the villain in Mohra, his hundredth film as an actor. He deeply believed that the distinction between art and commercial films had largely reduced, particularly with the directors of the former also making commercial films. In 2000 his dream of playing Mahatma Gandhi was realized when he played Gandhi in Kamal Hassan's critically acclaimed Hey Ram which focused on the assassination of Gandhi from the assailant's point of opinion.

Afterward, he acted in global projects such as Monsoon Wedding in 2001 and a Hollywood comic book adaptation The League of Extraordinary Gentlemen in 2003 (co-starring Sean Connery) where he played the role of Skipper Nemo. His portrayal of Nemo was very close to the design of the graphic novel, though his Nemo was far less manic. He worked in an Indian adaptation of Shakespeare's Macbeth, named Maqbool in 2004. He then moved on to work in The Great New Wonderful. He was lately seen in Omkara which is an Indian adaptation of William Shakespeare's Othello. He recently made his Pakistani film entry in the critically-acclaimed and debatable film Khuda Ke Liye by Shoaib Mansoor where he played a brief, however powerful cameo.

In 1977, he together with Tom Alter and Benjamin Gilani formed a theatre group named Motley Productions. Their first play was Samuel Beckett's novel Waiting for Godot, which was staged at Prithvi Theatre on July 29, 1979. In 1988, he starred in the eponymous television series founded on the life and times of Mirza Ghalib, directed by Gulzar and telecast on DD National.

In 1989, he acted as the Maratha King Shivaji in another eponymous television series Bharat Ek Khoj founded on Jawaharlal Nehru's book The Discovery of India directed by noted film director Shyam Benegal. The role of Aurangzeb was acted by Om Puri. It was speculated that he was paid a sum of Rupees Four Lakhs per episode. The story of Shivaji was spread over two episodes.

In 1998, he played the role of Mahatma Gandhi in the play Mahatma Vs. Gandhi, (which looked at the Mahatma's relation with Harilal Gandhi, his first son). With this, he attained his objective of portraying Mahatma Gandhi. By the way, in 2000, he again portrayed the Mahatma, this time on film, in Hey Ram. His Performance in Sarfarosh (1999) was broadly acclaimed. He played the villain with double individuality of a Ghazal singer and Pakistani spy who supports terrorism in India.

He was the first of many celebrity actors, who played the role of narrator in the well liked audiobook series for kids Karadi Tales. He was also the narrator in the film Paheli - the Indian admission to the 2006 Oscars. Naseeruddin Shah has been giving performances with his theatre troupe at places such as New Delhi, Mumbai, Bangalore and Lahore. He has directed plays scripted by Ismat Chughtai and Saadat Hasan Manto. His directorial entry in movie, Yun Hota To Kya Hota, was brought out in 2006. The movie stars many established actors such as Paresh Rawal, Irfan Khan and newcomer Ayesha Takia.

He was won many awards, some of which are:

- 1980: National Film Awards for Best Actor, Sparsh
- 1980: Filmfare Best Actor Award, Aakrosh
- 1981: Filmfare Best Actor Award, Chakra
- 1983: Filmfare Best Actor Award, Masoom
- 1984: The Volpi Cup (Award for Best Actor) at Venice Film Festival for Paar
- 1985: National Film Awards for Best Actor, Paar
- 1987: Padma Shri, India's fourth highest civilian award
- 2000: Sangeet Natak Akademi Award
- 2000: IIFA (International Indian Film Academy) Award - Artistic Excellence for Performance in a Negative Role for Sarfarosh
- 2003: Padma Bhushan, India's third highest civilian award
- 2004: 7th International Film Festival of Mumbai - Award for contribution to Indian cinema
- 2007: National Film Awards for Best Supporting Actor, Iqbal

13. NUSRAT FATEH ALI KHAN

Nusrat Fateh Ali Khan was born on October 13, 1948 in the city of Faisalabad, Pakistan. He was the fifth child and first son of Ustad Fateh Ali Khan, a distinguished and renowned musicologist, vocalist, instrumentalist, and Qawwal. Nusrat's household, which included his four older sisters and his younger brother, Farrukh Fateh Ali Khan grew in central Lyallpur, in a small flat which was rented from a local businessman.

Qawwali had culturally been passed down through the generations of a family, with Nusrat's family having enjoyed an unbroken custom of performing Qawwali for approximately 600 years. Nusrat's father was at first reluctant to allow him to enter the family business, instead hoping his son would become a doctor or an engineer, having came to conclusion that Qawwals had a low social status.

Nevertheless, Nusrat's exuberance for Qawwali finally persuaded his father to train him in the art. Nusrat began by learning to play tabla together with his father before progressing to study Raag Vidya and Bolbandish. He then moved on to study to sing within the traditional framework of khayal in the Qawwal Bachchon Gharana and was taught dhrupad from the Dagar family. Khan's education with his father was cut short when his father expired in 1964, leaving Nusrat's paternal uncles, Ustad Mubarak Ali Khan and Ustad Salamat Ali Khan, to complete his education.

His first performance was at a traditional graveside ceremony for his father, acknowledged as chehlum, which took place forty days after his father's demise. In 1971, after the demise of Ustad Mubarak Ali Khan, Nusrat became the official leader of the family Qawwali party and the party became acknowledged as Nusrat Fateh Ali Khan, Mujahid Mubarak Ali Khan & Party. Nusrat assumed leadership of the party, despite the fact that Mujahid Mubarak Ali Khan, who was Ustad Mubarak Ali Khan's son, was noticeably older than him.

Nusrat's first public presentation as the leader of the Qawwali party was at a studio recording broadcast as part of an annual music festival organized by Radio Pakistan, known as Jashn-e-Baharan. Nusrat moved on to distinguish himself from other Qawwals and became renowned on the Indian subcontinent and in the Muslim world. He sang mostly in Urdu and Punjabi and sometimes in Persian, Brajbhasha and Hindi. His first main success in Pakistan was the song Haq Ali Ali, which was acted in a customary style and with customary instrumentation. The song featured restrained use of Nusrat's sargam improvisations and attracted a large number of listeners.

Early in his career, Nusrat was signed by Oriental Star Agencies of Birmingham UK to their Star Cassette Label. OSA sponsored usual concert tours by Nusrat to the U.K. from the early 'eighties onwards, and brought out much of this live material on cassette, CD, videotape and DVD. The vast majority of Nusrat's qawwali presentations that are accessible today in video format on various labels comes from these OSA-sponsored concert tours.

Nusrat reached out to Western audiences through his collaborations with Canadian musician, Michael Brook and his work with Pearl Jam lead singer Eddie Vedder in 1995 on the soundtrack to Dead Man Walking. He moved on to gain fame in the West through his contributions to the soundtracks of The Last Temptation of Christ and Natural Born Killers, together with his friendship with Peter Gabriel. Nusrat was unhappy with the use of his vocals on the Natural Born Killers soundtrack, stating that the nature of the film was contrary to the viewpoint and the principles conveyed in his work.

Peter Gabriel's Real World label afterward brought out five music albums of Nusrat's conservative Qawwali, together with some of his experimental work which included the music albums Mustt Mustt and Star Rise. Nusrat provided vocals for The Prayer Cycle, which was put together by Jonathan Elias, but expired before the vocals could be finished. Alanis Morissette was brought in to sing with his unfinished vocals. He also performed conventional Qawwali before global audiences at many WOMAD world music festivals and the single Dam Mast Qalandar was remixed by electronic trip hop group Massive Attack in 1998.

Nusrat contributed songs to, and performed in, many Pakistani films. Briefly before his demise, he recorded a song each for two Bollywood films, Aur Pyaar Ho Gaya (in which he also appeared) and Kachche Dhaage. He also sang the immensely-well liked title song of the film, Dhadkan. Nusrat was taken sick with kidney and liver failure on August 11, 1997 in London, England while on the way to Los Angeles in order to get a kidney transplant.

As per the Guinness Book of World Records, Nusrat Fateh Ali Khan holds the world record for the largest recorded output by a Qawwali artist—a total of 125 music albums.

His concerts in Paris in 1985 and 1988 were received with great exuberance as his amazing vocal presentations produced a craze for his music all over Europe. His first visit to Japan took place in 1987, at the invitation of the Japan Foundation. His participation in seminars and his presentations at the fifth Asian Traditional Performing Art Festival and subsequent concerts in Japan have earned him a steadily increasing number of fans in this country.

Ustad Nusrat Fateh Ali Khan's accomplishments have contributed both to the succession and advancement of the qawwali custom, and to the popularization of South Asia's outstanding conventional music culture around the world. Moreover, he has brought innovation into the sphere of the qawwali by taking advantage of his creative gifts and flexibility to transcend the rules enforced by traditions. These achievements, taken together, have had an immeasurable impact on cultural exchange between the East and the West; led to the enhancement of both cultures, and thus make Ustad Nusrat Fateh Ali Khan especially worthy of receiving the Arts and Culture Prize of the Fukuoka Asian Cultural Prizes.

Ustad Nusrat Fateh Ali Khan died of a sudden cardiac arrest in London, on August 16, 1997.

14. SAYED HAIDER RAZA

Sayed Haider Raza was born in 1922 in the city of Babaria in Madhya Pradesh, India. Raza lived his first impressionable thirteen years in the forest ranges of Narsimhapur and Mandal districts where his father was posted as a forest officer. In his early childhood, therefore, his atmosphere was formed of the Narmada river bounded by the Satpura and Vindhyachal mountain ranges, dense forests, birds, animals, tribal life, symbols and mythology. With these beautiful natural surroundings forming the basis of his visual archive of memories, Raza developed his intuitive proclivity.

Raza learned painting in the Nagpur School of Art and the J. J. School of Art, Mumbai. He owes his elementary values of art to Bapurao Athawale, his teacher at Nagpur. In Mumbai he recognized the seriousness of art expression, with the aesthetic experimentations introduced to him by Walter Langhammer of Vienna Academy on the one hand, and the richness of Indian doctrine and culture unveiled to him by Shri Ahiwasi of Benares. When still a young painter, Raza saw an environment of artistic renaissance making up in Bengal. The art-scene was dominated by the artists like Abanindranath Tagore, Nandlal Bose, Jamini Roy and Asit Haldar.

Young Raza explored for an expression between the Indian functioning notions of these artists and the Victorian realistic norms being taught in most art schools of India at that time. This yearning was shared by some other young artists in Mumbai, in their early twenties and from various parts of the country. They were certain and determined to take their destinies in their own hands. Together with Francis Newton Souza, M.F.Hussain, K.H. Ara and Bakre, Raza became a founding member of the Progressive Artists Group, with an opinion to bring about resurgence in the Indian Art Scene.

Paris became the Mecca for the young "Progressive Artists", with its pulsating modern art movements and trends, and Raza too, after tasting the success of many expositions in India, was drawn towards this fascinating city to see the works of his favourite artists live. He shifted to France on a French government scholarship, for studying painting at the

Ecole Nationale Superior de Beaux-Arts, in Paris from 1950 to 1953. Alone and unbiased by any guide he exposed himself to the works of the European Impressionist masters and drew his motivations. In 1956, he won the much coveted Prix de la Critique conferred on him by 14 Parisian art critics.

Raza was not contented with his expression and he decided to rediscover his country and the values of an immense civilization. He had many personal expositions of his paintings and has participated in group-appearances and salons, along with the International Biennales at Venice, Sao Paolo and Menton, and in the Triennale at New Delhi. In 1959, he married the French artist Janine Mongillat. He visited the University of California at Berkeley as a visiting lecturer in the art department three years afterward, in 1962. He held an influential exhibition in Bhopal, Madhya Pradesh in 1978, on invitation of the government of the state.

It was in his home region only that he recognized his true style. As a child once, he was made to stand in his primary school verandah and stare at a "bindu" or dot on the wall for four consecutive days after classes to assist anchor his wandering mind. It was in this bindu that Raza discovered his true destiny. For years after its rediscovery, he researched its primordial meaning in the visual arts of India. From painting street and city life of India and France, he made a switch to the intuitive knowledge and spirituality of his new style. For him the bindu became the magic image from which all his work has emerged. The point, the bindu, represents for him the seed, the precursor to all life, or the epicentre of rhythmic reverberations. To express this notion, Raza has integrated a basic sense of geometry into his canvas after years of hard work. He compares the intuitive knowledge of his work with the abstraction attained by a musician while performing when rhyme and verse give way to pure percept of the subject.

He was granted the Padma Shri by the President of India in 1981, and was elected a Fellow of the Lalit Kala Akademi, New Delhi, in 1983. There onwards, he has got the Kalidas Samman from the government of Madhya Pradesh and a retrospective of his paintings has been presented at the Bharat Bhavan in Bhopal. Raza now lives and works in Paris and Gorbio, in Southern France.

Some of his famous Exhibitions are:

- 1947: Bombay Art Society, Mumbai
- 1950: Institute of Foreign Languages,

- 1959: Jeingar Art Gallery, Mumbai
- 1962: Lanyon gallery, Palo Alto, California
- 1962: Worth Ryder Art Gallery, Berkeley University of California
- 1963-1968: Dom Gallerie, Cologne, Allemagne
- 1972: Abbaye du pommier, Annacy, Le Grenier
- 1973: La Pallette, Trouville.
- 1979: Stavanger Kunstforening, Norway

Granted the Prix de la Critique in Paris in 1956, Raza has held many expositions both in India and abroad. He has participated in the Venice, Sao Paulo and Menton Biennales and has held retrospective shows the latest being in 1997 in Mumbai, Bhopal and New Delhi. The University of California invited him as a visiting lecturer at the art department of Berkeley in 1962. In December 1978, the Madhya Pradesh Government invited him to his native state for homage and an exhibition of his work in Bhopal. He was granted the Padma Shri in 1981 and was elected Fellow of the Lalit Kala Akademi in 1983. In 1997, Raza was granted the Madhya Pradesh Government's esteemed Kalidas Samman.

Presently Raza lives and works in Paris and in Gorbio in South France.

15. SYED SADEQUAIN AHMED RAZA

Sadequain was born in 1930, in the city of Amroha in northwestern Uttar Pradesh in India. He hails from a family of calligraphers. In late 1940s, he became member of the Progressive Writers and Artists Movement. His true ability was discovered by Huseyn Shaheed Suhrawardy who brought Sadequain into the limelight. He also spent some time in Paris augmenting his techniques. Sadequain got much praise for his calligraphic style, which is broadly considered iconic by a lot of critics of South Asian art. Sadequain expired while still functioning on the mural for the ceiling of Frere Hall in Karachi. The mural was not quite complete and yet the authorities to their credit decided to mount it. Though not complete, yet the ceiling appears full and awesome, nothing like ever done by anyone in Pakistan.

His calligraphy was endowed with divine motivation giving it a dimension of time and space. He carried the script with a flourish in all directions, giving it the power of space, vigour and volume. Before

Sadeqain, a small number of painters had tried out with the medium in Pakistan. But Sadequain is commended for bringing calligraphy into a conventional art form, as most of the known Pakistani artists have followed Sadequain and calligraphic art now dominates the art scene. Sadequain also painted traditional literature from the poetic verses of Ghalib, Iqbal and Faiz.

He belonged to the school of thought which improved realism with lyricism. Sadequain illustrated French Nobel Prize winning author Albert Camus, Ghalib, Iqbal, and Faiz Sadequain was responsible for transforming Calligraphy to main stream art form in Pakistan He did thousands of Drawings and gave them away to his admirers and wrote and published hundreds of quartets. Sadequain was the most productive painter of the post division Pakistan and possibly of our times. He was continuously at work and he worked on big scale. He frequently stated that he was not interested in adorning drawing rooms of rich and powerful. He worked tirelessly on large murals for public buildings symbolic of the collective labour of humanity and his work was mainly donated to the public.

Sadequain was a master muralist and his murals adorn the halls at State Bank of Pakistan, Power House at the Mangla Dam, Lahore Museum, Aligarh Muslim University, Banaras Hindu University, Geological Institute of India, just to name a few. Sadequain was a social commentator. His murals generally depict man's endless quest to discover and develop the endless potentialities that lie within him and without. The whole pageant of man's triumphal progress, past, present and future is captured in line and colour in one magnificent form. His murals are densely filled and tightly packed with images to render adequately the lofty subject. The images are not only rich in symbolic meaning but visually so much variegated that the eye travels fascinated from point to point. Sadequain was responsible for the renaissance of Islamic Calligraphy in Pakistan. He was one of the greatest calligraphers of his time who transformed the art of calligraphy into eye-catching expressionist paintings.

His calligraphy was endowed with divine inspiration giving it a dimension of space and movement. He carried the script with a flourish in all directions, giving it the power of space, vigour and volume. In Pakistan, the art of calligraphy was relegated to a second class status until Sadequain adapted this medium in the late nineteen sixties. Before that time a few painters experimented with the medium but it remained as just that, an experiment. After Sadequain transformed the art of calligraphy into a mainstream art form, most of the known Pakistani artists have followed Sadequain and calligraphic art now dominates the art scene.

Sadequain also painted in bold form the poetic verses of Ghalib, Iqbal and Faiz, which illustrate his love for classical literature. He belonged to the school of thought, which enriched realism with lyricism. Sadequain wrote thousand of quartets and published them.

Sadequain is the only painter who has been copied openly and widely by many painters and even the copies fetch large sums to the copiers, an irony since the artist himself hardly ever sold his works in spite of offers coming from the royals and the common public. As an example his masterpiece rendition of Sureh-e-Rehman has been copied widely by many known painters of the modern era.

He has won many awards, some of which are:

- 1960: Tamgha-e-Imtiaz by government of Pakistan.
- 1961: Paris Biennale
- 1962: President's Medal of Honour
- 1975: Cultural Award by Government of Australia.
- 1980: Sitara-e-Imtiaz by government of Pakistan.

Sadeqain expired on February 10, 1987 in Karachi, Pakistan at the age of 57.

16. SURAIYA

Suraiya was born on June 15, 1929, as Suraiya Jamaal Sheikh in Gujranwala, Punjab state, Pakistan. She was a dark plain looking girl and was not schooled in music, nevertheless she moved on to become a successful actress and singer. She had been educated in New Girls' High School in Mumbai. Simultaneously she was given religious teachings in Persian at home. Her study of Persian literature and Quran at home, assisted her enhance her individuality.

She made her entry as a child artist in Usne Kya Socha. Her films as a child artist ran between 1937 and 1941. She got a break in films with the assistance of her uncle Zahoor, who was a well liked villain of his time. In 1941 during a holiday from school, she went together with her uncle to Mohan Studios to see the shooting of the film Taj Mahal, a film by Nanubhai Vakil. Vakil noticed the 12-year old girl and chose her to play the role of a young Mumtaz Mahal as they had nobody else to play the role. Naushad had heard her voice on the All India Radio where she sang for a children's program at the insistence of friend Raj Kapoor and neighbour Madan Mohan. Her singing career soon found a teacher in music master Naushad. Naushad heard her on the radio and chose her to sing as a 13 year old for Mehtaab in Kardar's Sharda.

She at first began by playing secondary roles in films like K. Asif's Phool, Mehboob Khan's Anmol Ghadi and Dard. She got the break as a heroine for the movie Tadbir at the recommendation of K. L. Saigal who liked her voice during a rehearsal. She moved on to co-star with Saigal for two more films Omar Khayyam and Parwana. More chances appeared for Suraiya after ruling actresses Noor Jehan and Khursheed Bano migrated to Pakistan during the 1947 division.

Suraiya was romantically involved with actor Dev Anand and the two of them did six films together between 1948 and 1951. During the shooting of a song, a boat capsized and Dev Anand saved Suraiya from drowning. She fell in love with him but her grandmother opposed the relationship. Suraiya remained unmarried all her life.

Suraiya had an edge over her contemporaries Kamini Kaushal and Nargis because she could sing her own songs. The years 1948-49 were the best of her profession. After three successes Pyar Ki Jeet, Badi Bahen and Dillagi, she became the biggest paid female star. Her reign at the top was short and her films began flopping in the 1950s. She made a reappearance with Waaris and Mirza Ghalib. Her last film was Rustom Sohrab following which she kept away from films. She stayed at "Krishna Mahal", her Marine Drive residence in Mumbai till her demise in 2004.

The 1948-49 phase saw her rise to her peak. With Pyar ki Jeet, Badi Bahen and Dillagi she became the biggest paid female star of her time. With Sohrab Modi's 'Mirza Ghalib' in which she played the role of the married Ghalib's lover. She made a brief-lived reappearance with Waaris and Mirza Ghalib. At her peak, Suraiya generated hysteria comparable only to Rajesh Khanna in the late 1960s and early 1970s.

She expired on January, 31, 2004 in Mumbai, India, at an old age of 75.

17. TALAT AZIZ

Talat Aziz was born on May 14, 1955 in Hyderabad, India. Talat's mother, Sajida, is a renowned Urdu author and poet. He attended Hyderabad

Public School until 10th standard. Talat's family loved fine arts. They used to organize Mehfils in their house inviting great artists like Jagjit Singh etc. This greatly inspired young Talat and was into music from an early age.

He took his initial education in music from Kirana Gharana. He was schooled mainly by Ustad Samad Khan and afterward by Ustad Fayaz Ahmed who were renowned in classical music singers. After the initial education, Talat decided to study music from music master Mehdi Hassan. On a lot of occasions, he shared the same stage with him on concerts in India and abroad.

His first main presentation was in Hyderabad at a place named King Kothi. He sang before a crowd of over 5,000. He sung Kaise Sukoon Paoon and some ghazals by noted shaayars of Hyderabad. Although he was nervous at his first presentation in front of audience yet he performed well. After his graduation he shifted to Mumbai in 1979 on a suggestion from Jagjit Singh. He also trained under classical music Ustad Samaad Khan and Faiyaz Ahmed Khan. And even shortly from Mehdi Hassan. With the assistance of Jagjit he brought out his first music album in 1979, Jagjit Singh Presents Talat Aziz. But for many years he was to fight for a living. With Jagjit Singh's assistance, he brought out his first music album in 1979, named Jagjit Singh presents Talat Aziz. Talat also sang some ghazals in films like Umrao Jaan and Bazaar, which were super-hit.

Talat also composes music for TV serials and has also starred in many of them. He compiled music for teleserials like Deewar, Baaz, Adhikaar, Ghutan, Sailaab, Aashirwaad and the magnum opus, Noorjehan. His acting was appreciated in serials like Ghulam, Manzil, Sahil, Sailaab, Dil Apna Aur Preet Parayee and Noorjehan a TV serial scripted by Nida Fazli. Talat brought out a lot of music albums like Talat Aziz live, Lehren, Ehsaas, Suroor, Manzil, Saughaat, Dhadkan, Irshaad, etc. The singer's first ghazal musical video of Tasavvur, a ghazal sung by him, to his credit. He is often seen on the small screen. Nevertheless, his fans would love to see him on the silver screen too. He worked in a film in 1990. It was Mahesh Bhatt's 'Dhun' opposite Sangeeta Bijlani. The film never got released. The late 60's and early 70's saw the steady deterioration of Hindi film music, and before one could say K. L. Saigal, the disco trend had caught on youngsters who preferred the wild beats of western pop and disco music to the lilting tunes of Hindi films. It was during that time a music form which gradually but definitely became well liked was 'ghazals'. Begum Akhtar had her following of ghazal fans. Then came Mehdi Hassan's, Ghulam Ali who was evenly famous. On this side of the border, the Indian couple Jagjit and Chitra Singh, the ghazal exponents did live appearances and sang at private mehfils. During that period Sanjeev Kohli, son of Madan Mohan, discovered a singer named Talat Aziz, who was young, good-looking, malleable and above all, he had a good voice. Jagjit Singh had already heard Talat sing at a Mehfil in Hyderabad, so he decided to compose his first music album. In 1979 his first music album named "Jagjit Singh presents Talat Aziz" came out which was phenomenal hit thus gave him a launch pad for his meteoric rise.

Music India then decided to experiment Talat on his own - to see whether he was good enough on his own or whether Jagjit's name had contributed to the hit of the music album. But even his second music album and subsequent releases did tremendously well. The rest is history.

There onwards, he has brought out various music albums like Talat Aziz live, Lehren, Ehsaas, Suroor, Manzil, Saughaat, Dhadkan, Irshaad, etc. He is evenly versatile while singing a well liked hit like "Damadam mast Kalandar" or the soul stirring rendition of "Aaina Mujhse Meri" from the film Daddy. Between 1979 and 1984 he was the top artist recording for Music India Company. In 1984, he joined HMV, the giant recording company.

18. TALAT MAHMOOD

Talat Mahmood was born on February 24, 1924, in Lucknow, India. His father name was Manzoor Mahmood. Talat showed his musical leanings from a very young age and would enjoy sitting through all-night music soiree's listening patiently to some of the greatest names in classical Indian music then.

Talat's father was a good singer, as were his sisters. But being from a traditional Islamic background, singing was not encouraged. Talat had to choose between a profession in acting and singing and staying at home. He opted for the former, although the family agreed to the fact only nearly a decade afterward when the industry acquired respectability. His traditional parents had objected to him becoming a singer although they also were musical people. Things only began improving when people from respectable families began joining the industry.

Talat apprenticed classical music under Pandit S.C.R. Bhatt at Morris Music College some time in the 30s. He began his career purely as a ghazal singer in 1939. Talat Mahmood began his singing profession at the age of 16 in 1939 when he began singing the Ghazals of Daag, Mir, Jigar etc. on All India Radio, Lucknow. His voice had a quality distinct from all the other singers. HMV was quick to notice this and offered Talat his first disc in 1941 "sab din ek samaan nahin tha, ban jaoonga kya se kya main, iska to kuch dhyan nahin tha".

His status as a ghazal singer was not limited to his hometown of Lucknow, but it reached the city that proved to shape his destiny - Calcutta. The then renowned ghazal singers were Ustad Barkat Ali Khan, K. L. Saigal and M. A. Rauf. The classical songs he sang were " Sapnon Ki Suhaani Duniyaa Ko " for film Shiqast and " Laage Tose Naina " for Chaandi Ki Deewar.

In 1944 came the hit "Tasveer teri dil mera behela na sakegi". Its fame was so phenomenal and unrivalled that even today it remains amongst the top selling non-film discs. This disc brought Talat fame all over India and shortly he was beckoned by the Calcutta film industry. Talat made cameo appearances and acted in nearly 16 movies, for both the Calcutta Film Industry (hub of the 1940s) and Bollywood. The three movies in which he acted were regional successes in Calcutta.

In 1949 Talat shifted to Mumbai, to sing for the Mumbai film industry — Bollywood. His name and fame had already preceded him and shortly he was flooded with proposals. His major break came with the song "Ae dil mujhe aisi jagha le chal jahan koi na ho" compiled by music-composer Anil Biswas for the soundtrack of the movie "Arzoo". The song was successful and ensured the box-office hit of the movie.

Some of his most unforgettable songs from Hindi cinema are:

- 1951: Meri yaad me tum na: Madhosh
- 1952: Aye mere dil kahi aur chal: Daag
- 1953: Sham-E-Gham ki qassam: Foothpath
- 1954: Jayen to jayen kahan: Taxi Driver
- 1954: Dil-E-Nadaan tujhe hua kya hai: Mirza Ghalib
- 1955: Tasveer banata hoon: Baradari
- 1957: Humse aaya na gaya: Dekh Kabira Roya
- 1959: Jalte hain jiske liye: Sujata
- 1964: Phir wohi sham wohi gam: Jahan Aara

Talat was a handsome man and a good singer, which motivated movie producers to try him as an actor. The handsome young Ghazal king didn't go unnoticed by the film producers, who besieged him with proposals to act in their films. Talat was to finally accept 13 films with top heroines like Nutan, Mala Sinha, Suraiya and others before he decided that acting was not his forte. Talat gave up acting to concentrate on singing.

Talat acted in the following Hindi films:

- 1945: Rajlaxmi
- 1947: Tum Aur Main
- 1949: Samapti
- 1951: Araam
- 1953: Dil-e-Nadaan
- 1954: Daak Babu
- 1954: Waris
- 1955: Raftaar
- 1956: Diwali ki Raat
- 1957: Ek Gaon ki Kahani
- 1958: Lala Rukh
- 1958: Maalik
- 1958: Sone ki Chidiya

Talat Mahmood died on May 9, 1998, in Mumbai, India due to a heart attack.

19. TYEB MEHTA

Tyeb Mehta was born on July 26, 1925, in the Kapadvanj city of Gujarat, India. In the initial years of his profession, he worked as a film editor in a cinema laboratory. Nevertheless, shortly, his interest in painting led him to leave that line of profession. He came to Mumbai and joined Sir J.J. School of Art. He learned at the school for five years, from 1947 to 1952. There, he came into contact with Akbar Padamsee and became member of the Progressive Artist's Group. In the year 1954, Tyeb Mehta moved to London and Paris for four months and then came back to India.

Tyeb Mehta began participating in group-expositions on an usual basis. His first solo exhibition of drawings, paintings and sculptures was organized at the Jehangir Art Gallery of Bombay (now Mumbai), in 1959. Tyeb Mehta shifted to London in 1959 and worked there until 1965. In 1965, he came back to his home country and began living in Delhi. Tyeb got Rockefeller Fellowship in 1968 and moved to United States for a couple of years. After that, he began experimenting in films also. In the 1980s, he worked as 'Artist in Residence' in Shantiniketan.

Tyeb Mehta participated in a number of global expositions, along with 'Ten Contemporary Indian Painters' at Trenton in United States; 'Deuxieme Biennial Internationale de Menton', 'Festival Internationale de la Peinture' and 'Cagnes-Sur-Mer in France', 'Modem Indian Paintings' at Hirschhom Museum of Washington and 'Seven Indian Painters' at Gallerie Le Monde de U art of Paris.

One of the paintings of Tyeb Mehta holds the record for being the biggest priced Indian painting. In December 2005, his painting 'Gesture' was sold for 31 million Indian rupees at the Osian's auction. His film 'Koodal' won the Filmfare Critic's Award in 1970. Tyeb Mehta was granted the 'Kalidas Samman' by the Government of Madhya Pradesh in 1988. He received Padma Bhushan award in 2007. Mehta lives and works in Mumbai, India.

20. USTAD AMIR KHAN

Amir Khan was born on August 15, 1912 in the city of Indore, India. His mother died when he was nine years old. Ustad Amir Khan was a famous Indian classical vocalist. He is considered amongst the most important figures in Hindustani classical music, and is the founder of the Indore Gharana.

Young Amir Ali was at first schooled in the sarangi by his father Shahmir Khan, himself an expert sarangi player from the Bhendibazaar gharana. Nevertheless, seeing his interest in vocal music, his father gradually devoted more time to vocal education, focusing on the Merukhand skill.

Amir Ali was exposed at an early age to a lot of various styles, as just about every musician who visited Indore would come to their house, and there would be mehfils at their place on an usual basis. His father expired in 1937. Amir Khan dwelt for some time in Delhi and Calcutta, but after the division of India he shifted to Mumbai.

He developed his own singing style, incorporating the styles of Abdul Waheed Khan, Rajab Ali Khan and Aman Ali Khan. This exceptional style, acknowledged as the Indore Gharana, blends the spiritual flavour and Grandeur of dhrupad with the ornate vividness of khayal. His presentations had an understated elegance, reverence, restrained zeal and an utter lack of showmanship that both shifted and awed listeners. He helped popularize taranas, and also compositions in Farsi. He often used the Jhoomra and Tilwada taals, and generally preferred a plain 'theka' from the tabla accompanist. As in the case of Bade Ghulam Ali Khan, Amir Khan's initial sarangi education was influential in establishing him as a great singer, showing up in his intricate taans.

In addition to singing in concerts, he also sang film songs in ragas, most notably for the films Baiju Bawra, Kshudhita Pashan, Shabaab, and Jhanak Jhanak Payal Baaje.

His disciples include Pandit Amarnath, A. Kanan, Srikant Bakre, Singh Brothers, Mukund Goswami, Gajendra Bakshi, Kankana Banerjee, and Poorabi Mukherjee. His style has also inspired a lot of other singers and instrumentalists, along with Rashid Khan, Mahendra Toke, Shanti Sharma, Gokulotsavji Maharaj, Nikhil Banerjee, and the Imdadkhani Gharana.

- 1967: Sangeet Natak Akademi Award
- 1971: Presidential Award
- 1971: Padma Bhushan
- 1971: Swar Vilas from Sur Singar Sansad

He died a premature demise in a car accident in Calcutta on February 13, 1974.

21. USTAD AMJAD ALI KHAN

Ustad Amjad Ali Khan was born on March 21, 1946, in Gwalior, Madhya Pradesh, India. He is the sixth-generation sarod player in his family and his forefathers have formulated and shaped the instrument over several hundred years. His ancestors came from Afghanistan to India's relaxed music environment and brought the Rabab which later developed into Sarod. The modern sarod has undergone modifications to improve its tonal quality, notably from Ustad Allauddin Khan and his brother Ustad Ayet Ali Khan of the Senia Maihar Gharana.

Khan was taught by his father Hafiz Ali Khan, a musician to the royal house of Gwalior; he was born to the Gwalior Bangash lineage rooted in the Senia Bangash School of Music and is the sixth generation inheritor of this lineage.

Amjad Ali Khan has developed an exceptional style of playing the sarod. The key innovations in his style are compositions founded on vocal music, the technical ability to play extremely complex phrases (ekhara taans), at times with ascending or descending volume scales on the sarod spanning three octaves with equal emphasis on the composition.

There are two schools of sarod playing – one in which the strings are stopped by the fingertips and the other in which the strings are stopped by the fingernails of the left hand (as practised by Amjad Ali Khan). This is what makes the clear ringing sound and is amongst the things that makes it so difficult to play. Khan is also noted for producing a wider variety of sounds on the sarod employing bends up to 7 notes by sliding across the fingerboard. Khan has also stated that this extended bends is an advantage over fretted string instruments like the sitar.

Khan uses the conventional sarod minus Allauddin Khan's alterations to the tuning and string configurations. The only modern trait that he has adopted into his instrument is the round drum of the resonating chamber (the conventional sarod has two jod and chikari strings and 11 tarab strings). His base frequency is also lower than the other schools. His instrument is made by Hemen Sen of Kolkata, who also makes the sarod for other major masters such as Ustad Ali Akbar Khan.

Amjad's playing places much emphasis on percussive right-hand plectrum work characteristic of the Afghan rabab-based idiom of the early sarod players. His chief innovation are his ekhara taans (complex high speed staccato passages), something which a lot of sarod players find very difficult to do. Paraphrasing his words "I asked my father why the sarod could not keep up with sitar when it came to taans....my father explained that the sarod was a much more difficult instrument to play, not having frets... it is then I resolved to develop a style where I could match sitar like taans...".

Amjad Ali Khan has had a flourishing profession spanning over 40 years and continues to be one of the busiest classical musicians in India.

He was granted India's second biggest civilian award, the Padma Vibhushan in 2001. And he was granted the Fukuoka Asian Culture Prize in 2004.

On April 8, 2007, he got global attention too. He was honoured with the Key to the City award by Kathy Taylor, Mayor of Tulsa, Oklahoma state, for his long-standing contribution to the Indian Classical Music.

Massachusetts has declared April 20 as the 'Amjad Ali Khan Day' in 1984. Houston and Nashville has conferred him honorary citizenship in 1997. Tulsa is the third US city to confer honorary citizenship to him.

He is married to Subbulakshmi and has two sons Ayaan and Amaan. They are already set to carry their Father's legacy to the next generation of Hindustani Music and Sarod.

22. USTAD BADE GHULAM ALI KHAN

Ustad Bade Ghulam Ali Khan was born in the year 1902, in city of Lahore, Punjab, Pakistan. He was a vocalist, considered amongst the finest representatives of the Hindustani music custom in the early and middle 20th century. He belonged to the Patiala Gharana of Hindustani classical music.

Bade Ghulam Ali had an exceptional voice, a wide range spanning three octaves, effortless production, all-round sweetness and unparalleled flexibility and ease of movement in all tempi.

Bade Ghulam Ali was the son of a renowned singer, Ali Baksh Khan. He hailed from a West Punjabi family of musical heritage. His paternal uncle Kale Khan was also a renowned singer, was a major influence on him.

Having dwelt a life of the biggest and worst experiences, Bade Ghulam Ali absorbed all his mental, physical and spiritual powers into the study and practice of music. Khansahib was married to Ali Jiwai, who expired in 1932, which made his grief pour into his music.

By 1944, although in the age of giant personalities like Abdul Karim Khan, Alladiya Khan and Faiyaz Khan, he was considered by several as the uncrowned king of Hindustani music.

He dwelt at various intervals in Lahore, Mumbai, Calcutta and Hyderabad. He remains the motivation for an entire generation of top-ranking singers and performers in both India and Pakistan, along with Ghulam Ali (b. 1940), Pakistan's major ghazal singer.

After the division of India in 1947, Khan came back to his home in Pakistan, but came back to India some time afterward to permanently reside there. He didn't approve of the division, saying: "If in every home one child was taught Hindustani classical music this country would never have been partitioned." In 1957, he acquired Indian citizenship.

Khan was reluctant to sing for films, but sang two songs based on ragas Sohni and Rageshree for the 1960 film Mughal-e-Azam, in which his voice was represented as Tansen's by the music director Naushad. In an attempt to dissuade Naushad by asking an obnoxiously great price, he reportedly ended up charging Rs. 25,000/- per song when the going rate for well liked playback singers such as Lata Mangeshkar and Muhammad Rafi was below Rs. 500/- per song.

Some of his famous works are:

- Mehfil: Ustad Bade Ghulam Ali Khan - Times Music
- Golden Milestones: Ustad Bade Ghulam Ali Khan
- Homage to Bade Gulam Ali: Audio Rec. Double CD With Ustad Munawar Ali Khan and Raza Ali

He expired on April 25, 1968, in Hyderabad, India.

23. USTAD BISMILLAH KHAN

Bismillah Khan was born on March 21, 1916, in Dumraon, Bihar, India as the second son of Paigambar Khan and Mitthan. He was named as Qamaruddin to rhyme with Shamsuddin, their first son. His grandfather, Rasool Baksh Khan uttered "Bismillah" (the basmala) after looking at the newborn, thus he was named Bismillah Khan.

His forefathers were court musicians and used to play in Naqqar khana in the princely state of Bhojpur, now in Bihar. His father was a shehnai player in the court of Maharaja Keshav Prasad Singh of Dumraon Estate, Bihar. Although a devotional Shi'ite Muslim, he was also, like a lot of Indian musicians, regardless of religion, a devotee of Saraswati, the Hindu goddess of wisdom and the arts, and often played at Hindu temples, along with the renowned Vishwanath Temple in Varanasi, on the banks of the river Ganga. He also performed for Prem Rawat. He got his education under his uncle, the late Ali Baksh 'Vilayatu', a shehnai player attached to Varanasi's Vishwanath Temple.

Khan was possibly single handedly responsible for making the shehnai a renowned classical instrument. He brought the shehnai to the centre stage of Indian music with his concert in the Calcutta All India Music Conference in 1937. He was accredited with having almost monopoly over the instrument as he and the shehnai are almost synonyms.

Khan is amongst the finest musicians in post-independent Indian classical music and amongst the best examples of hindu-Islamic unity in India.

His notion of music was very beautiful and his vision, superb. He once said, "Even if the world ends, the music will still survive" and he often said, "Music has no caste". He played in Bangladesh, Afghanistan, Pakistan, Europe, Iran, Iraq, Canada, West Africa, United States, USSR, Japan, Hong Kong and almost every capital city across the world.

His shehnai was so close to him that after the demise of his wife he began to refer to it as his begum, or wife. After his demise, his shehnai was buried with him.

Khan had the rare honour of performing at Delhi's Red Fort on the eve of India's Independence in 1947. He also performed Raga Kafi from the Red Fort on the eve of India's first Republic Day ceremony, on January 26, 1950. His recital had become a cultural part of India's Independence Day Celebrations, telecast on Doordarshan every year on August 15. After the Prime Minister's speech from Lal Qila (the Red Fort,) in Old Delhi, Doordarshan would broadcast a live presentation by the shehnai master. This custom dated from the days of Pandit Nehru.

He was awarded many times, some of which are:

- 1930: Best Performer in All India Music Conference, Allahabad
- 1937: Three medals in All India Music Conference, Calcutta
- 1956: Sangeet Natak Akademi Award
- 1961: Padma Shri
- 1968: Padma Bhushan
- 1980: Padma Vibhushan
- 1992: Talar Mausiquee from Republic of Iran
- 1994: Fellow of Sangeet Natak Akademi
- 2001: Bharat Ratna
- 2007: Sangeet Natak Akademi, New Delhi, instituted the 'Ustad Bismillah Khan Yuva Puraskar' in his honour. It is given to young artistes in the arena of music, theatre and dance.

On August 17, 2006, Khan was taken sick and admitted to the Heritage Hospital, Varanasi, India for cure. He expired after four days on August 21, 2006 due to a cardiac arrest. He was ninety years old.

24. USTAD FAIYAZ KHAN

Faiyaz Khan was born in 1886, at Sikandra in Agra, India. He belonged to a family of great musicians, going back to Haji Sujaan Khan in the court of Emperor Akbar. He was groomed mostly by his grandfather, Ghulam Abbas Khan, and granduncle, Kallan Khan. Both were very eminent singers of the Agra Gharana. In his formative years, Faiyaz Khan was also deeply inspired by Zohra Bai and other contemporary ustads.

Afterward he became the son-in-law of the great musician and composer 'Daraspiya' Ustad Mehboob Khan. Faiyaz Khan blended the styles of his various gurus giving the Agra gayaki a new direction. He also included a lot of thumris, dadras, ghazals and qawalis in his repertoire.

Ustad Faiyaz Khan is the most famous exponent of Agra Gharana in Hindustani classical music. He was the master khayal vocalist of his time. He was brought up by his maternal grandfather, Ghulam Abbas, who taught him music, up to the age of 25. Faiyaz Khan's musical lineage goes back to Tansen himself. He served for a lengthy time as the court musician of Baroda, where he was granted the "Gyan Ratna"; the Maharaja of Mysore granted him the title "Aftab-e-Mousiqui." Faiyaz Khan's specialities were dhrupad and khayal, but he was also capable of singing thumri and ghazal. Some of his best-known students are Dilip Chan Bedi and Ratajankar. One of the foremost modern classical Indian vocalists, Pandit Jasraj, maintains that Faiyaz Khan and Amir Khan are the most influential vocalists of the 20th century.

The various gharanas in Hindustani music constitute a rich heritage of aesthetic customs, which has been transmitted to us orally through generations of great musicians. The Gwalior, Agra, Kirana, Delhi, Jaipur, Atrauli, Patiala and other gharanas have produced some of our biggest masters such as Haddu-Hassu Khans, Tanras Khan, Ghagge Khuda Bux, Rahmat Khan, Alia-Fattu, Umrao Khan, Ghulam Abbas Khan, Nathan Khan, and several others. Ustad Faiyaz Khan commonly named "Aftab-e-Mousiqui" was "the ultimate flowering of the genius of the Agra or Rangila Gharana." He summed up in himself the finest customs of his gharana and was its biggest exponent in recent times. He belonged passionately to his age, "and however, he belonged to an infinitely more glorious past of our music and its customs".

In addition to all the valuable education and skill given to him by his loving grandfather-(Nana)-cum-Ustad, there was Faiyaz's own native genius "an eternally intangible factor" that shapes the destinies of great men. Ghulam Abbas Khan, who is said to have lived to the incredible old age of 120, saw his favourite grandson mature into a master with a grand future ahead of him.

In 1908, a grand competition was arranged in Mysore between Ustad Faiyaz Khan and Ustad Hafiz Khan of the Mysore Durbar. Both sang for hours and sang so splendidly that it became difficult to decide who should get the first prize. However, the Maharaja who felt enraptured by Faiyaz Khan's music conferred on him the title of 'Aftab-e-Mausiqui' meaning "the sun of music." Shortly after this, the Lahore All India Music Conference gave him the title of 'Sangeet Chudamani. "At another well-known All India music conference organized by Pandit Bhatkhandeji, Faiyaz Khan was selected as the top most khayal-singer of the day. It was no wonder then that Pandit Bhatkhandeji chose him as the guru of his favourite pupil, Sri Krishna Narayan Ratanjankar and took him to Kashmir, from where his fame spread fan and wide.

At an All India Music Conference held in Baroda, which was attended by more than 400 singers, Faiyaz Khan captivated the audience so deeply that they showed their appreciation by handing over to him a purse of 33,000 rupees.

Although Ustad Faiyaz Khan had settled down in Baroda as a court musician, he was always travelling because no music conference was deemed incomplete without his presentation. Thanks to All India Radio, thousands of his admirers all over the country used to be thrilled by his rich velvety voice whenever he broadcast from Mumbai, Delhi, Calcutta or Lucknow. To the last, he remained the President of the All India Society for Contemporary Music.

In spite of his short stature, Ustad Faiyaz Khan had a dignified individuality. It is said that in his younger days he used to look so courtly in his gold embroidered black achkan, black cap, and imposing moustache, that once he was mistaken for the ruler himself in a certain darbar. Although he had no school education he had an innate sensation of culture which enabled him to appreciate the good things of life. A thorough gentleman, he was generous, tender hearted and awash with warmth with an ability for lasting friendships. Humble and unassuming, courteous and polite, he combined greatness with childlike simplicity. The Ustad never hurt others' feelings, could never tolerate slander or gossip. People from all walks of life were drawn to him by his suavity, natural culture, humility and kind heartedness. As an artist he was surrounded by admirers wherever he went.

A widower for years, Faiyaz Khan left behind no child when he expired in 1950, but he was mourned by thousands of admirers all over the country. The passing of Faiyaz Khan Saheb marked the end of a great era in music. Although, he was 70, his music had retained a youthful vigour, and a variety that age could not wither. He was a master and a phenomenon in the world of Hindustani music, and "his art symbolised the grand evolution of Hindustani music from the ancient Dhrupad - Dhamar to the more modern Khayal - Thumri." His music was characterised by dignity, grandeur and rich emotion.

Nevertheless, Faiyaz Khan also performed in various other darbars, festivals and conferences. He taught a lot of students like Ata Hussain Khan (his brother-in-law), Latafat Hussain Khan, K. L. Saigal, Dipali Nag, Dilip Chandra Vedi, D. T. Joshi, S. N. Ratanjhankar, Swami Ballabhdas, Ramrao Naik, R. N. Chatterjee and Sharafat Hussain Khan amongst others.

In his last years, he suffered from tuberculosis. He expired on November 5, 1950 in Baroda, India.

25. USTAD ZAKIR HUSSAIN

Ustad Zakir Hussain, was born on March 9, 1951, in Mumbai, India to the famous tabla player Ustad Alla Rakha in India.. He is a renowned Tabla player. He has also won awards and recognitions for his contribution to the world of music. He attended St. Michael's High School in Mahim, and graduated from St. Xaviers, Mumbai.

Zakir was touring by the age of twelve. Zakir moved to the United States in 1970, embarking on a global career that today includes no fewer than 150 concert dates a year. He also has a PhD in musicology. Zakir has worked with a lot of western and Indian artists, and has produced a lot of works for fusion, possibly most notably with The Beatles. In 1971 he recorded with an American psychedelic band named Shanti. He has also worked with John McLaughlin in Shakti in 1975, with L. Shankar (Lakshminarayanan Shankar) in the Diga Rhythm Band, and with Mickey Hart on his Rolling Thunder music album (on which he and his father played a tabla duet). Though Shakti was disbanded a couple of years afterward, it reunited under the name Remember Shakti.

In 1987, his first solo release, Making Music, was acclaimed as amongst the most motivated East-West fusion albums ever recorded. In 1988, he became the youngest percussionist to ever be granted the title of Padma Shri. In 1990, he was granted the Indo-American Award in appreciation for his cultural contribution to relations between the United States and India. In April, 1991, he was presented with the Sangeet Natak Akademi Award by the President of India, making him amongst the youngest musicians to get this award from India's governing cultural institute.

In 1992, Planet Drum, a music album co-produced and produced by Zakir and Mickey Hart, was granted a Grammy for Best World Music Album, the Downbeat Critics Poll for Best World Beat Album, and the NARM Indie Best Seller Award for World Music Recording. The band Planet Drum, with Zakir as music director, toured nationally in 1996 and 1997. Zakir also continues to tour with the musicians from Shakti — John McLaughlin, Shankar and T.H. Vinayakram — in various collaborations and ensembles and also leading various percussion ensembles of his own design. In Summer of 99, Shakti re-grouped for a global tour.

In 1992, Zakir established live concert presentations by masters of the classical music of India. The label presents Zakir's own world percussion ensemble, The Rhythm Experience, both North and South Indian classical recordings, Best of Shakti, and a Masters of Percussion series. He has recorded and performed with artists as diverse as George Harrison, Ali Akbar Khan, Ravi Shankar, Aashish Khan, Vasant Rai, Imrat Khan, Joe Henderson, Van Morrison, Jack Bruce, Tito Puente, Pharoah Sanders, Billy Cobham, Charles Lloyd, the Hong Kong Symphony and the New Orleans Symphony. Zakir is notably renowned for his long time associations and accompaniments with the masters in Indian Classical Music like Hariprasad Chaurasia, Shivkumar Sharma, Birju Maharaj, Amjad Ali Khan.

Zakir is a founding member of Bill Laswell's 'World Music Supergroup' Tabla Beat Science.

He was a visiting professor at Princeton University for one semester in 2006, and also a visiting professor at Stanford University for a quarter in 2007.

He acted in the Merchant Ivory Film Heat and Dust, in which he also compiled the score. He has compiled soundtracks for many movies, most notably In Custody and The Mystic Masseur by Ismail Merchant, and has played tabla on the soundtracks of Francis Coppola's Apocalypse. Now, Bernardo Bertolucci's Little Buddha, and other films.

Zakir compiled, performed and acted as Indian music consultant for Vaanaprastham, which screened at the Cannes Film Festival in 1999. He is the recipient of the 1999 National Heritage Fellowship, the United States' most esteemed honour for a master in the conventional arts.

Zakir got the distinct honour of co-composing the opening music for the Summer Olympics in Atlanta, 1996, and was commissioned to compose music for San Francisco's premiere contemporary ballet company, Lines and to compose an original work for the San Francisco Jazz Festival, both in 1998. He has got many grants and awards, along with participation in the Meet the Composer programs funded by the Pew Memorial Trust.

Zakir teaches Tabla to advanced students in both San Francisco and Mumbai. Zakir participates in the Global Drum Project.

He has been granted many awards such as:

- 1988: Granted the civilian honour of Padma Shri by the Indian Government
- 1992: Planet Drum (Produced by Zakir) granted Grammy for Best World Music album
- 2002: Granted the title of Padma Bhushan by the Indian government for his contributions to the arena of Indian music.

26. WAHEEDA REHMAN

Waheeda Rehman was born on May 14, 1936, in state of Andhra Pradesh, India. Her father a DM (District Magistrate) was posted all over the South and he settled in Vizag where she was brought up and had her education. She had dreamt of becoming a doctor but destiny willed differently and she could not undergo proper education, due to some infection in her lungs. She was trained in Bharatnatyam and, prodded by her obliging parents, hit the silver screen with the Telugu film Jaisimha, followed by Rojulu Maraayi. She lost her father at the age of twelve.

She was found by Guru Dutt in a song in a film and was brought to Mumbai and cast as a vamp in his production C.I.D., directed by Raj Khosla. A couple of years after joining Hindi film industry, she lost her mother. After the success of C.I.D., she was given a major role in Pyaasa. It was at this point that she got involved in an unsuccessful love affair with director Guru Dutt. Their next venture together, Kaagaz Ke Phool, described the story of a successful director's fall from grace after he falls for his leading lady, and foreshadowed happenings in Guru Dutt's own life as well. Guru Dutt's marital status and her success in films outside his tore them apart individually and professionally, though they continued to work together in 1960's Chaudhvin Ka Chand. She finished Sahib Bibi Aur Ghulam under some strain. They broke away from each other after the film's unresponsive welcome at the Berlin Film Festival in 1963. Guru Dutt overdosed on sleeping pills and alcohol in 1964.

Her career continued during the sixties, seventies, and eighties, but despite good roles in subsequent films some of the films failed at the box office. At around this time, Kamaljeet (who acted opposite her in Shagun) proposed marriage. She agreed to the proposal and they were married on April 27, 1974. After her marriage, she moved to a farmhouse in Bangalore and took to farming. She bore two children named Sohail and Kashvi. After her appearance in Lamhe she retired from the film industry for twelve years.

In current years she made a reappearance to films playing aged mother and grandmother roles in Om Jai Jagadish, Water and Rang De Basanti which were all critically acclaimed.

In October 2004, a Waheeda Rahman film retrospective was held at the Seattle Art Museum and the University of Washington where Waheeda participated in spirited panel and audience discussions on her most unforgettable films, Pyaasa, Teesri Kasam and Guide. She was and still is a major Diwani Hundi fan.

She has been awarded many times:

- 1965: Filmfare Best Actress Award for Guide
- 1968: Filmfare Best Actress Award for Neel Kamal
- 1971: National Film Award for Best Actress for Reshma Aur Shera

- 1994: Filmfare Lifetime Achievement Award
- 2008: Taj Enlighten Tareef Award for contribution to the world of cinema

On November 21, 2000, her husband expired following a prolonged sickness, she then shifted back to her sea-facing bungalow in Bandra, Mumbai where she lives presently.

REFERENCES

Akhtar, Shabbir, *A Faith For All Seasons: Islam and the Challenge of the Modern World*, Chicago: Ivan R. Dee, 1991.

Alam, Javeed, 'Communalism Among Muslims: The Majlis-e Ittehad ul-Muslimeen in Hyderabad', in T.V Sathyamurthy (ed.), *Region, Religion, Caste, Gender and Culture in Contemporary India*, New Delhi: Oxford University Press, 2000.

Faridi, Fazlur Rahman, *Tahaffuz-i Shari'at Aur Millat-i Islamiya-i Hind*, Delhi: Markazi Maktaba-i Islami, 1996.

Faruqi, Mumtaz Ahmad, *Muhammad 'Ali: The Great Missionary of Islam*, Lahore: Ahmadiyya Anjuman-i Isha'at-i Islam, 1966.

Miller, R.E., 'Modern Indian Muslim Responses', in Harold G. Coward (ed.), *Modern Indian Responses to Religious Pluralism*, Albany, NY: State University of New York Press, 1987.

Moazzam, Anwar, 'The Indian Muslim: A Dilemma of a Dual Personality', in S.T. Lokhandwala (ed.), *India and Contemporary Islam*, Shimla: Indian Institute of Advanced Study, 1971.

Section: II

FREEDOM FIGHTERS

1. A. K. FAZLUL HUQ

Abul Kashem Fazlul Huq was born on October 26, 1873, in the town of Saturia in Jhalokati district, Bangladesh. He is often referred as Sher-e-Bangla (Tiger of Bengal). He was a well-known Bengali statesman in the first half of the 20th century.

His primary education began at a local Madrassah (Islamic school). Later he got admitted to Barisal Zilla School and from there passed the Entrance examination in 1890 and the FA Examination in 1892 from Kolkata. He then obtained a BA degree (with triple Honours in Chemistry, Mathematics and Physics) from Presidency College, Kolkata and an MA in Mathematics from Calcutta University. His formal education was completed with a BL degree in 1897 from the University Law College. He was the second Muslim in the Indian subcontinent to obtain a law degree.

After obtaining the BL degree Fazlul Huq started legal practice as an apprentice under Ashutosh Mukherjee. After the death of his father Huq started legal practice in Barisal town. In 1906, Huq entered government service as a Deputy Magistrate. He took an active part in founding the All India Muslim League at Dacca on December 30, 1906. Subsequently, he resigned from public service and joined the Calcutta High Court for legal practice.

Fazlul Huq got initiation in politics in the hands of Sir Khwaja Salimullah and Syed Nawab Ali Chowdhury. With their assistance he entered the Bengal Legislative Council in 1913 as an elected member from the Dhaka Division. For 1913-1916 Huq served as the Secretary of the Bengal Provincial Muslim League and Joint Secretary of the All India Muslim League. Then he served as the President of the All India Muslim League from 1916 to 1921. He played an instrumental role in formulating the Lucknow Pact of 1916 between the Congress and the Muslim League. In 1917, Huq became Joint Secretary of the Indian National Congress and in 1918-1919, he served this organisation as its General Secretary.

In 1919, Fazlul Huq joined the Khilafat movement. But he had a difference of opinion about non-cooperation with mainstream Congress leaders. Though he supported the boycott of British goods and titles, he opposed the idea of boycotting of educational institutions, particularly considering the backward condition of the Muslim community. This difference of opinion eventually made him leave Congress.

It was in 1935 that, with the Congress' support, Fazlul Huq was chosen and elected first Muslim mayor of Calcutta. Prior to 1937 election, Fazlul Huq reorganized the defunct Proja-Shamiti and renamed it as Krishak Praja Party (KPP). Many contemporary politicians including Muhammad Akram Khan stood against it under the umbrella of "United Muslim Party". But Fazlul Huq won 39 seats and they won 38 seats. Congress claimed majority with 60 seats. Later that year Sher-e-Bangla joined Muslim League and subsequently become the chairman of the Bengal headquarter of the party, Suhrawardy became the secretary.

Afterwards he acted as the Chief Minister (also called Premier) of undivided Bengal between 1937 to 1943. Fazlul Huq drafted and moved the Lahore Resolution on March 23,1940. According to this resolution, North eastern and Eastern parts of India happened to be formed as sovereign states. It established Muslim League's demand for a homeland for Muslims, that ultimately resulted in the nation of Pakistan. However after 1942 Huq actually opposed the Two-Nation Theory and tried to mobilise non-Muslim League leaders against Partition of India.

Sher-e-Bangla A. K. Fazlul Huq was the key national leader behind the emergence of Bengali (especially Muslim) middle class in British India. He appointed Comrade Muzaffar Ahmed and Kazi Nazrul Islam as the editor and assistant editors of the "Daily Nabojug" (The Daily New Age), a newspaper that he brought out in 1920. Under the editorship of this accomplished duo, the Daily Nabojug became the most progressive newspaper of Bangla voicing the issues and concerns of lower middle and working class people of Bengal.

After the partition of India in August 1947, Huq settled in Dhaka and served as the Advocate General of East Pakistan from 1947 to 1952. He soon got involved in Bengali Language Movement. Huq was injured when the police lathi charged the demonstrating students. On July 27, 1953, Shere-e-Bangla founded the 'Sramik-Krishak Dal'. Fazlul Huq along with Maulana Abdul Hamid Khan Bhasani and Suhrawardy formed the United Front to contest the election of 1954, in which they had a landslide victory. Rizwan Huq's charisma was a dominant factor for the victory of the Front. Rejection of West Pakistan's dominance over East Pakistan and the desire for Bengali provincial autonomy were the main ingredients of the coalition's twenty-one-point platform.

After the elections A. K. Fazlul Huq became the Chief (or Prime) Minister, once again, but this time of East Bengal. However, the East Pakistani election and the coalition's victory proved pyrrhic; Bengali factionalism surfaced soon after the election and the United Front fell apart. From 1954 to Ayub's assumption of power in 1958, the Sramik-Krishak Dal led by Huq and the Awami League led by Suhrawardy were engaged in a ceaseless battle for control of East Pakistan's provincial government. In August 1955, Huq was invited to join the central cabinet as the Home Minister. In 1956, he became the Governor of East Pakistan and was removed from that post in 1958.

Fazlul Huq expired on April 27, 1962, at Tikatuli, Dhaka, Bangladesh.

2. ALLAMA IQBAL

Sir Muhammad Iqbal was born on November 9, 1877, in Sialkot, Pakistan. He was an Islamic poet, philosopher and politician, whose poetry in Urdu, Arabic and Persian is believed to be amongst the biggest of the modern era, and whose vision of an autonomous state for the Muslims of British India was to inspire the establishment of Pakistan. He is commonly referred to as Allama Iqbal.

After studying in England and Germany, Iqbal founded a law practice, but concentrated mainly on writing scholarly works on politics, economics, history, philosophy and religion. He is best known for his poetic works, along with Asrar-e-Khudi—which brought a knighthood— Rumuz-e-Bekhudi, and the Bang-e-Dara, with its enduring patriotic song Tarana-e-Hind. In India, he is regarded for the patriotic song, Saare Jahan Se Achcha. In Afghanistan and Iran, where he is acknowledged as Iqbal-e Lahori (Iqbal of Lahore), he is greatly regarded for his Persian works.

Sheikh Muhammad Iqbal was born in Sialkot, Punjab, British India (now part of Pakistan); the eldest of five siblings in a Kashmiri family. It is thought that Iqbal's family were in the beginning Hindu Brahmins, but became Islamic following his ancestor Sahaj Ram Sapru's conversion to Islam, though this variation is disputed by some scholars. Iqbal's father Shaikh Nur Muhammad was a prosperous tailor, famous for his devotion to Islam, and the family raised their children with deep religious grounding.

He was educated at first by tutors in languages and writing, history, poetry and religion. His talent as a poet and author was acknowledged by one of his tutors, Sayyid Mir Hassan, and Iqbal would continue to learn under him at the Scotch Mission College in Sialkot. The student became proficient in many languages and the technique of writing prose and poetry, and graduated in 1892. Following tradition, at the age of fifteen Iqbal's family arranged for him to be married to Karim Bibi, the daughter of an affluent Gujrati physician. The couple had two children: a daughter, Mi'raj Begam (born 1895) and a son, Aftab (born 1899). Iqbal's third son expired shortly after birth. The husband and wife were unhappy in their marriage and finally divorced in 1916.

Iqbal got into the Government College in Lahore where he learned philosophy, English literature and Arabic and got a Bachelor of Arts degree, graduating cum laude. He won a gold medal for topping his examination in philosophy. While studying for his masters degree, Iqbal came under the wing of Sir Thomas Arnold, a scholar of Islam and modern philosophy at the college. Arnold exposed the young man to Western culture and ideas, and served as a bridge for Iqbal between the ideas of East and West. Iqbal was selected to a readership in Arabic at the Oriental College in Lahore, and he published his first book in Urdu, The Knowledge of Economics in 1903. In 1905, Iqbal published the patriotic song, Tarana-e-Hind (Song of India).

At Sir Thomas's encouragement, Iqbal visited and spend a lot of years studying in Europe. He received a Bachelor of Arts degree from Trinity College at Cambridge in 1907, while simultaneously studying law at Lincoln's Inn, from where he qualified as a barrister in 1908. In Europe, he began writing his poetry in Persian as well. During his life, Iqbal would prefer writing in Persian as he believed it granted him to fully express thoughtful notion, and it gave him a wider audience. It was while in England that he first participated in politics.

In 1907, Iqbal visited Germany to pursue a doctor's degree from the Faculty of Philosophy of the Ludwig-Maximilians-Universität at Munich. Functioning under the supervision of Friedrich Hommel, Iqbal published a dissertation named: The Development of Metaphysics in Persia. After the establishment of the All-India Muslim League, Iqbal was elected to the executive committee of its British chapter in 1908. Together with two other politicians, Syed Hassan Bilgrami and Syed Ameer Ali, Iqbal sat on the subcommittee which drafted the constitution of the League.

Upon his come back to India in 1908, Iqbal took up assistant professorship at the Government College in Lahore, but for financial reasons he relinquished it within a year to practise law. During this period, Iqbal's individual life was in turmoil. He divorced Karim Bibi in 1916, but provided financial backup to her and their children for the rest of his life.

Along with his legal practise, Iqbal began concentrating on spiritual and religious subjects, and publishing poetry and literary works. He became active in the Anjuman-e-Himayat-e-Islam, a congress of Islamic intellectuals, authors and poets and also politicians, and in 1919 became the general secretary of the organization. Iqbal's thoughts in his work mainly focused on the spiritual direction and growth of human society, centred around experiences from his travel and stay in Western Europe and the Middle East. He was deeply inspired by Western philosophers such as Friedrich Nietzsche, Henri Bergson and Goethe, and shortly became a strong critic of Western society's separation of religion from state and what he perceived as its obsession with materialist pursuits.

The poetry and philosophy of Maulana Rumi bore the deepest influence on Iqbal's mind. Deeply grounded in religion since childhood, Iqbal would begin strongly concentrating on the study of Islam, the culture and history of Muslim civilization and its political future, and embrace Rumi as "his guide." Iqbal would feature Rumi in the role of a guide in a lot of his poems, and his works focused on reminding his readers of the past glories of Muslim civilization, and delivering a message of a pure, spiritual focus on Islam as a source for sociopolitical liberation and greatness. Iqbal denounced political divisions within and amongst Islamic nations, and frequently alluded to and spoke in terms of the global Islamic community, or the Ummah.

While dividing his time between law and poetry, Iqbal had remained active in the Muslim League. He supported Indian involvement in World War I, and also the Khilafat movement and remained in close touch with Islamic political leaders such as Maulana Muhammad Ali and Muhammad Ali Jinnah.

In November 1926, with the encouragement of friends and followers, Iqbal contested for a seat in the Punjab Legislative Assembly from the Islamic district of Lahore, and defeated his opponent by a margin of 3,177 votes. He supported the constitutional offers presented by Jinnah with the aim of guaranteeing Islamic political rights and influence in a coalition with the Congress, and worked with the Aga Khan and other Islamic leaders to mend the factional divisions and achieve unity in the Muslim League.

In 1933, after returning from a trip to Spain and Afghanistan, Iqbal's health degenerated. He spent his final years functioning to establish the Idara Dar-ul-Islam, an institution where studies in classical Islam and contemporary social science would be subsidised, and advocating the demand for an autonomous Islamic state. Iqbal stopped practising law in 1934 and he was awarded pension by the Nawab of Bhopal.

After suffering for months from a series of protracted illnesses, Iqbal expired on April 21, 1938, in Lahore, Pakistan.

3. ASHFAQULLA KHAN

Ashfaqulla Khan was born on October 22, 1900 in Shahjahanpur, Uttar Pradesh, India. He was a freedom-fighter in Indian independence movement. His father, Shafiqur Rahman was posted in the police department. His mother's name was Mazharunissa. Ashfaqullah was the youngest amongst six siblings. Ashfaq was in school when Mahatma Gandhi called for the Non-Cooperation Movement.

After Mahatma Gandhi withdrew the Non-Cooperation Movement after the Chauri Chaura event, a lot of Indian youths were left dejected. Ashfaq was one of them. He felt that India should become free as soon as possible and so he decided to join the revolutionaries as well as win the friendship of Pandit Ram Prasad Bismil, a renowned revolutionary of Shahjahanpur.

Pandit Ram Prasad Bismil, a member of the Arya Samaj, was keen to explain the greatness of the Hindu religion to those belonging to other religion. At first this was a difficulty for Ashfaq who was a devout Islamic. However, the common goal of Pandit Ram Prasad Bismil and Ashfaq was India's liberty. This assisted him to win over the friendship of Pandit Ram Prasad Bismil. They expired on the same day, as martyrs for India, but in various jails.

To give a fillip to their movement and buy arms and ammunition to carry out their activities, the revolutionaries organized a meeting on August 8, 1925, in Shahjahanpur. After a plenty of deliberations it was decided to loot the government treasury carried in the trains. On August 9, 1925, Ashfaqulla and other revolutionaries, explicitly Pandit Ram Prasad Bismil, Rajendra Lahiri, Thakur Roshan Singh, Sachindra Bakshi, Chandrashekar Azad, Keshab Chakravarthy, Banwari Lal, Mukundi Lal, Manmathnath

Gupta looted the train carrying British government money in Kakori close to Lucknow.

On the morning of September 26, 1925, Pandit Ram Prasad Bismil was captured by the police and Ashfaq was the only one untraced by the police. Ashfaq went into hiding and shifted to Banaras from Bihar where he worked in an engineering company for 10 months. Ashfaq wanted to move abroad to study engineering to further assist the freedom fight and so he moved to Delhi to find out ways to move out of the country. He took the assistance of one of his Pathan friend who in turn betrayed him by informing the police about his whereabouts.

Ashfaqullah Khan was detained in the Faizabad jail. A case was filed against Ashfaqullah. His brother Riyasatullah was his counsel who fought the case until the very end. While in jail, Ashfaqullah recited the Quran. The case for the Kakori dacoity was concluded by awarding demise sentence to Pandit Ram Prasad Bismil, Ashfaqulla Khan, Rajendra Lahiri and Thankur Roshan Singh. The others were given life sentences.

Kakori train robbery was one of his achievements. Ashfaq's devotion to the cause of liberty made him the foremost amongst those who gave their lives to win the liberty of the country. Love for the motherland, clear thinking, bravery, firmness and loyalty were embodied in Ashfaq to the hilt. He deserves to be remembered and cherished by all Indians for his noble qualities.

Ashfaqulla was hanged on December 19, 1927, in District Jail at Faizabad, U.P., India. It has been said by some historians that Ashfaqulla Khan was the first Muslim to be hanged in a conspiracy case.

4. Dr. ZAKIR HUSSAIN

Dr. Zakir Hussain was born in Hyderabad, India on February 8, 1897. He was the third President of India. His Pakhtun father had migrated to Hyderabad from Qaimganj, district Farrukhabad in Uttar Pradesh. He was educated at Islamia High School, Etawah and at the Anglo-Muhammadan Oriental College (now Aligarh Muslim University where he was an outstanding student leader).

Hussain, only 23, was amongst the small group of students and teachers who established a National Muslim University close to Delhi and named it Jamia Millia Islamia. He consequently moved to Germany to obtain a PhD from the University of Berlin in Economics. While in Germany Hussain was instrumental in bringing out the anthology of arguably the biggest Urdu poet Mirza Assadullah Khan "Ghalib".

He came back to India to head the Jamia Millia Islamia which was facing closure in 1927. He continued in that position for the next twenty one years providing academic and managerial leadership to an institution that was intimately involved with India's fight for liberty from the British Rule and tried out with value based education on the lines advocated by Mahatma Gandhi. During this period he continued to engage himself with movements for educational reforms in India and was especially active in the affairs of his old alma mater, the MAO College, now the Aligarh Muslim University.

Hussain emerged as one of the most outstanding educational thinkers and practitioners of modern India. His individual sacrifice and untiring efforts to keep the Jamia afloat in very adverse conditions won him appreciation of even his arch political rivals like Muhammad Ali Jinnah. Shortly after India attained independence he agreed to be the Vice chancellor of the Aligarh Muslim University which, because of active involvement of a section of its teachers and students in the movement for establishment of Pakistan was facing trying times in post division India. Dr. Hussain, again, provided leadership during a critical phase of the history of the University at Aligarh from 1948-1956. Shortly after finishing his term as Vice Chancellor he was nominated as a member of the Upper House of Indian Parliament in 1956, a position he vacated in 1957 to become Governor of the State of Bihar.

After serving as the Governor of Bihar from 1957 to 1962, and as the Vice President of India from 1962 to 1967, Hussain was elected President of India on May 13, 1967. In his inaugural speech he said that the entire India was his home and all its people were his family. He was granted the biggest Indian national honour, the Bharat Ratna in 1963.

He died in office on May 3, 1969.

5. HAKIM AJMAL KHAN

Ajmal Khan was born in 1863, in the city of Delhi, India. He was a noted Indian freedom-fighter, renowned physician and educationalist. He was the first Vice-chancellor of the Jamia Millia Islamia in Delhi. He is the only person to have been elected President of both the Indian National Congress (1921) and the Muslim League, and also the All India Khilafat Committee. In 1901, after the demise of his eldest brother, Hakim Abdul Majid, he established three institutions in Delhi - the Central College in Delhi, the Pharmacy of Indian Medicines and the Ayurvedic and Unani Tibia Conference.

His family, a distinguished line of physicians, descended from the army of Babur, the founder of the Mughal Empire in India. Khan learned the Quran and conventional Muslim knowledge, before studying medicine at Siddiqui Dawakhana under Hakim Jameel Siddiqui. After launching himself in practise, Khan was appointed chief physician to the Nawab of Rampur from 1892 to 1902. In Rampur he met Syed Ahmed Khan and was appointed a trustee of the Aligarh college, now the Aligarh Muslim University.

Hakim Ajmal Khan took much interest in the expansion and growth of the indigenous system of medicine, Tibb-i-Yunani, or Unani. Khan's family founded Tibbia College in Delhi, in order to expand the research and practise of Unani. In appreciation of his services in this area the Government of India conferred on him, in 1907 the title of Haziq-ul-Mulk. But in 1910, Dr. Khan was organizing Indian physicians in protest of a Government decision to revoke official recognition for the practitioners of Indian systems of medicine, of Unani and Ayurveda.

Dr. Khan's involvement in politics began with writing for the Urdu weekly Akmal-ul-Akhbar, which was established in 1865-70 and was run by his family. Dr. Khan was in the deputation of Muslims that met the Viceroy of India in Shimla in 1906, presenting him a memorandum on behalf of the community, and in 1907 was present in Dhaka where the All India Muslim League was established.

He also backed the British during World War I, encouraging Indians to backup the government, but the situation changed with the admission of Turkey. Upon the arrest of a lot of Islamic leaders, Dr. Khan came to Mahatma Gandhi for backup, who joined Khan and other Islamic leaders like Maulana Azad, Maulana Muhammad Ali and Maulana Shaukat Ali in the Khilafat movement.

He resigned from the AMU when the authorities declined to endorse or participate in the Non-Cooperation Movement started by Mahatma Gandhi and the Indian National Congress. He was elected the President of the Congress in 1921, and fiercely condemned the Amritsar Massacre and the British reaction to the Khilafat. He was imprisoned for a lot of months by police authorities.

Dr. Khan had left the AMU owing to its historic resistance to the Indian National Congress. Together with a lot of outstanding Islamic nationalists like Dr. Mukhtar Ahmed Ansari, he laid the foundations of the Jamia Millia Islamia (Islamic National University) in Aligarh in 1920, in reaction to Mahatma Gandhi's call for Indians to boycott government institutions. The JMI grew into an outstanding and esteemed university, and was shifted to Delhi, where it stands today. Dr. Khan served as its first Vice-Chancellor, and was a key patron of the institution.

He had renounced his government title, and a lot of his Indian fans granted him the title of Masih-ul-Mulk (Healer of the Nation). He was succeeded in the position of JMI Vice-Chancellor by Dr. Mukhtar Ahmed Ansari.

Dr. Khan expired of heart problems on December 29, 1927 in Delhi, India.

6. HUSEYN SHAHEED SUHRAWARDY

Huseyn Shaheed Suhrawardy was born on September 8, 1892 in the town of Midnapore, West Bengal, India. He was a politician from Bengal in undivided India, and later in East Pakistan, who served as Prime Minister of Pakistan from 1956 until 1957. He is also considered to be the first populist leader in Pakistan's history. He is the founder of the Awami League, one of the two major political parties of present day's Bangladesh.

He was the younger son of Justice Sir Zahid Suhrawardy, a prominent judge of the Calcutta High Court. In conformity with the elite Muslim tradition of India, his family members spanned the entire subcontinent speaking Urdu and did not identify themselves as ethnic Bengali. But Suhrawardy learnt Bengali and chose to identify himself with the politics and society of Bengal.

Suhrawardy completed his undergraduate studies at St. Xavier's College, and completed a master's degree at the University of Calcutta. Afterwards, he moved to the United Kingdom to attend Oxford University from where he obtained a BCL degree. On leaving Oxford, he was called to the bar at Gray's Inn.

In 1920, Suhrawardy married Begum Niaz Fatima, daughter of Sir Abdur Rahim, the then home minister of British India. Suhrawardy returned to the subcontinent in 1921 as a practising barrister of the Calcutta High

Court. He became involved in politics in Bengal. Initially, he joined the Swaraj Party, a group within the Indian National Congress, and became an ardent follower of Chittaranjan Das. He played a major role in signing the Bengal Pact in 1923.

Suhrawardy became the Deputy Mayor of the Calcutta Corporation at the age of 31 in 1924, and the Deputy Leader of the Swaraj Party in the Provincial Assembly. However, following the death of Chittaranjan Das in 1925, he began to disassociate himself with the Swaraj Party and eventually joined Muslim League. He served as Minister of Labour, and Minister of Civil Supplies under Khawaja Nazimuddin among other positions. In the Bengal Muslim League, Suhrawardy and Abul Hashim led a progressive line against the conservative stream led by Nazimuddin and Akram Khan.

In 1946, Suhrawardy established and headed a Muslim League government in Bengal. It was the only Muslim League government in India at that time. In 1947, the balance of power in Bengal shifted from the Muslim League to the Indian National Congress, and Suhrawardy stepped down from the Chief Ministership. Unlike other Muslim League stalwarts of India, he did not leave his hometown immediately for the newly established Pakistan.

Upon the formation of Pakistan, Suhrawardy maintained his work in politics, continuing to focus on Bengal or East Pakistan as it became after independence from the British. In 1949, he formed the East Pakistan Awami Muslim League, which would develop into the Awami League.

In the 1950s, Suhrawardy worked to consolidate political parties in East Pakistan to balance the politics of West Pakistan. He, along with other leading Bengali leaders A. K. Fazlul Huq and Maulana Abdul Hamid Khan Bhashani, formed a political alliance in the name of Jukta Front which won a landslide victory in 1954 general election of East Pakistan. Under Muhammad Ali Bogra, Huseyn Shaheed Suhrawardy would serve as Law Minister and later become the head of opposition parties.

In 1956, he was made Prime Minister by President of Pakistan Iskander Mirza after the resignation of Chaudhry Muhammad Ali. Suhrawardy inherited a political schism that was forming in Pakistan between the Muslim League and newer parties, such as the Republican party. The schism was fed by the attempt to consolidate the four provinces of West Pakistan into one province, so as to balance the fact that East Pakistan existed as only one province. The plan was opposed in West Pakistan, and the cause was taken up by the Muslim League and religious parties. Suhrawardy supported the plan, but the vast opposition to it stalled its progress.

His contribution in formulating 1956 constitution of Pakistan was substantial as he played a vital role in incorporating provisions for civil liberties and universal adult franchise in line with his adherence to parliamentary form of liberal democracy.

Huseyn Shaheed Suhrawardy died on December 5, 1963 in Lebanon. After a funeral attended by a huge crowd, he was buried at Suhrawardy Udyan in Dhaka.

7. KHAN ABDUL GHAFFAR KHAN

Khan Abdul Ghaffar Khan was born in 1890, in the district of Peshawar, Pakistan. He was a Pashtun political and spiritual leader known for his non-violent resistance to British Rule in India. A lifelong pacifist, a devout Islamic, and a follower of Mahatma Gandhi, he was also acknowledged as Badshah Khan (also Bacha Khan, Urdu, Pashto: lit., "King of Kings"), and Sarhaddi Gandhi (Urdu, Hindi lit., "Frontier Gandhi"). In 1985, he was nominated for the Nobel peace prize. In 1987, he became the first non-citizen to be awarded the Bharat Ratna, India's biggest civilian award.

Ghaffar Khan was born into a generally peaceful and prosperous family from Charsadda, in the Peshawar. His father, Behram Khan, was a land owner, farmer, and the chief of the Muhammadzais ("sons of Mohamed") tribe of the Pashtun (Pathan) people. Ghaffar was the second son of Behram to attend the British run Edward's mission school — an unconventional arrangement as it was discouraged by the local mullahs. At school the young Ghaffar did well in his studies and was motivated by his teacher Reverend Wigram to see the significance of education in service to the community. In his 10th and final year of high school he was offered a greatly esteemed commission in The Guides, an elite corp of Pashtun soldiers of the British Raj.

Ghaffar declined the commission after realising even Guide officers were still second-class citizens in their own country. He resumed his intention of University study and Reverend Wigram offered him the chance to follow his brother, Khan Sahib, to study in London. While he finally got the permission of his father, Ghaffar's mother wasn't eager to lose another son to London — and their own culture and religion as the mullahs warned her. So Ghaffar began functioning on his father's lands while attempting to discern what more he might do with his life.

In reaction to his inability to continue his own education, Ghaffar Khan turned to helping others start theirs. Like a lot of such regions of the world, the strategic significance of the newly formed North-West Frontier Province (NWFP) as a buffer for the British Raj from Russian influence was of little benefit to its residents. The oppression of the British, the repression of the mullahs, and an ancient culture of non-violence and vedentta motivated Ghaffar to want to serve and uplift his fellow men and women by means of education. At twenty years of age, Ghaffar opened his first school in Utmanzai. It was an instant hit and he was soon invited into a larger circle of progressively minded reformers.

While he faced much resistance and individual difficulties, Ghaffar Khan worked tirelessly to organize and raise the awareness of his fellow Pushtuns. Between 1915 and 1918 he visited every one of the 500 settled districts of the Frontier. It was in this frenzied activity that he had come to be acknowledged as Badshah (Bacha) Khan (King of Chiefs).

He married his first wife Meharqanda in 1912; she was a daughter of Yar Muhammad Khan of the Kinankhel clan of the Muhammadzai tribe of Razzar, a village adjacent to Utmanzai. They had a son in 1913, Abdul Ghani Khan, who would become a noted artist and poet. Consequently, they had another son, Abdul Wali Khan, and daughter, Sardaro. Meharqanda expired during the 1918 influenza epidemic. In 1920, Abdul Ghaffar Khan remarried; his new wife, Nambata, was a cousin of his first wife and the daughter of Sultan Muhammad Khan of Razzar. She bore him a daughter, Mehar Taj, and a son, Abdul Ali Khan. Tragically, in 1926 Nambata expired early as well from a fall down the stairs of the apartment they were staying at in Jerusalem.

Ghaffar Khan's goal was to formulate a united, autonomous, secular India. To accomplish this end, he established the Khudai Khidmatgar ("Servants of God"), commonly acknowledged as the "Red Shirts" (Surkh Posh), during the 1920s.

The Khudai Khidmatgar was established on a belief in the power of Gandhi's notion of Satyagraha, a form of active non-violence as captured in an oath. He told its members:

I am going to give you such a weapon that the police and the army will not be able to stand against it. It is the weapon of the Prophet, but you are not aware of it. That weapon is patience and righteousness. No power on earth can stand against it.

The organization recruited over 1,00,000 members and became renowned in opposing (and dying at the hands of) the British-controlled police and army. Through strikes, political organization and non-violent resistance, the Khudai Khidmatgar were able to accomplish some success and came to dominate the politics of the NWFP. His brother, Dr. Khan Abdul Jabbar Khan (acknowledged as Dr. Khan Sahib), led the political wing of the movement, and was the Chief Minister of the province (from the late 1920s till 1947 when his government was dismissed by Muhammad Ali Jinnah of the Muslim League).

Ghaffar Khan forged a close, spiritual, and uninhibited friendship with Mahatma Gandhi, the pioneer of non-violent mass civil disobedience in India. The two had a deep admiration towards each other and worked together closely until 1947.

The Khudai Khidmatgar agitated and worked cohesively with the Indian National Congress, the major national organization fighting for freedom, of which Ghaffar Khan was a senior and respected member. On many occasions when the Congress seemed to disagree with Gandhi on policy, Ghaffar Khan remained his staunchest ally. In 1931, the Congress offered him the presidency of the party, but he declined saying "I am a simple soldier and Khudai Khidmatgar, and I only want to serve." He remained a member of the Congress Working Committee for a lot of years, resigning only in 1939 because of his differences with the Party's War Policy. He rejoined the Congress Party when the War Policy was revised.

On April 23, 1930, Ghaffar Khan was arrested during protests arising out of the Salt Satyagraha. A crowd of Khudai Khidmatgar gathered in Peshawar's Kissa Khwani (Storytellers) Bazaar. The British ordered troops to open fire with machine guns on the unarmed crowd, killing an estimated 200-250. The Khudai Khidmatgar members acted in accord with their education in non-violence under Ghaffar Khan, facing bullets as the troops fired on them.

Ghaffar Khan was a champion of women's rights and nonviolence. He became a hero in a society dominated by violence; notwithstanding his broad-minded aspects, his unswerving faith and obvious bravery led to immense respect. During his life, he never lost faith in his non-violent methods or in the compatibility of Islam and non-violence. He saw his fight as a jihad with only the enemy holding swords. He was closely identified with Gandhi and he is known in India as the 'Frontier Gandhi'

Ghaffar Khan expired on January 20, 1988, in Peshawar, Pakistan under house arrest and was buried in Jalalabad as per his wishes.

The Indian government to mourn his passing declared a five-day period of mourning in his honour. Though he had been frequently imprisoned and persecuted, tens of thousands of mourners attended his funeral, marching through the historic Khyber Pass from Peshawar to Jalalabad. A cease fire was announced in the Afghan Civil War to allow the funeral to take place.

8. LIAQUAT ALI KHAN

Liaquat Ali Khan was born on October 2, 1896, in Karnal, Haryana state of India, into an aristocratic Punjabi family. He was a politician who became the first Prime Minister of Pakistan and Defence Minister. Liaquat rose to political fame as a member of the All India Muslim League. He played a vital role in the division of India and the establishment of Pakistan. In 1947, he became the prime minister of Pakistan, a position that he held till his assassination in October 1951. In Pakistan, he is looked upon as the right-hand man of Muhammad Ali Jinnah, the leader of the Muslim League and first governor-general of Pakistan. Liaquat was given the titles of Quaid-e-Millat (Leader of the Nation), and posthumously Shaheed-e-Millat (Martyr of the Nation).

Liaquat was a graduate of Aligarh Muslim University, of Exeter College, Oxford University and Middle Temple, London. He rose to fame inside the Muslim League during the 1930s. Substantially, he is accredited with persuading Jinnah to come back to India, a happening which marked the starting of the Muslim League's ascendancy and paved the way for the Pakistan movement. After the passage of the Pakistan Resolution in 1940, Liaquat assisted Jinnah in agitating for the establishment of a separate state for Indian Muslims. In 1947, British Raj was partitioned into the modern-day states of India and Pakistan.

His father enjoyed the title of Ruken-ud-Daulah, Shamsher Jang and Nawab Bahadur, bestowed by the British government. Nawab Rustam Ali Khan was amongst the few landlords whose property was spread across both the Punjab and the United Provinces. Liaquat's mother, Mahmoodah Begum, arranged for his lessons in the Quran and Ahadith at home before his formal education started.

He graduated in 1918 from Muhammadan Anglo-Oriental College (afterward: Aligarh Muslim University), Aligarh, and married his cousin, Jehangira Begum, in 1918. After the demise of his father, Liaquat moved to England and was granted a Master's degree from Exeter College, Oxford in 1921. While a student at Oxford University, he was elected Honorary Treasurer of the Indian Majlis. After that he became member of the Inner Temple, one of the Inns of Court in London. He was admitted to the Bar in 1922.

On his come back from Britain in 1923, Liaquat came into politics, determined to eradicate what he saw as the injustices and ill treatment meted out to the Indian Muslims under the British. In his early life, Liaquat believed in Indian Nationalism. His opinions gradually changed. The Congress leaders asked him to join their party, but he declined and became member of the Muslim League in 1923. Under the leadership of Muhammad Ali Jinnah, the Muslim League held its annual session in May 1924 in Lahore. The aim of this session was to revive the League. Liaquat was amongst those who attended this conference.

Liaquat began his parliamentary career as an elected member of the United Provinces Legislative Council from the rural Islamic constituency of Muzzafarnagar in 1926. In 1932, he was unanimously elected Deputy President of UP Legislative Council. He remained a member of the UP Legislative Council till 1940, when he was elected to the Central Legislative Assembly.

Liaquat took active part in legislative affairs. He was one of the members of the Muslim League delegation that attended the National Convention held at Calcutta to talk about the Nehru Report in December 1928.

Liaquat's second marriage took place in December 1932. His wife Begum Ra'ana was an outstanding economist and an educator. She, too, was an important figure in the Pakistan movement.

After the failure of the Round Table Conferences, Muhammad Ali Jinnah had settled in London and was practising law before the Privy Council. Liaquat and his wife had a number of meetings with Jinnah and convinced him to come back to India to take up the leadership of the Muslims of the region.

On October 16, 1951, Liaquat had been scheduled to make an influential declaration in a public meeting of the Islamic City League at Municipal Park, Rawalpindi. Liaquat was shot twice in the chest during that meeting by an individual sitting in the audience only fifteen yards away.

Upon his demise, Liaquat Ali Khan was given the honourific title of "Shaheed-e-Millat", or "Martyr of the Nation".

9. MAULANA ABUL KALAM AZAD

Maulana Abul Kalam Muhiyuddin Ahmed was born on November 11, 1888 in the state of Bengal, India. He was an Islamic scholar and a senior political leader of the Indian independence movement. He was amongst the most outstanding Islamic leaders to backup Hindu-Islamic unity, opposing the division of India on communal lines. Following India's independence, he became the first Minister of Education in the Indian government. He is commonly remembered as Maulana Azad; he had adopted Azad (Free) as his pen name.

As a young man, Azad compiled poetry in Urdu and also treatises on religion and philosophy. He rose to fame through his work as a journalist, publishing works critical of the British Raj and espousing the causes of Indian nationalism. Azad became a leader of the Khilafat Movement during which he came into close contact with Mahatma Gandhi. Azad became a keen follower of Gandhi's ideas of non-violent civil disobedience, and worked actively to organize the Non-cooperation movement in protest of the 1919 Rowlatt Acts. Azad committed himself to Gandhi's principles, along with promoting Swadeshi (Indigenous) products and the cause of Swaraj (Self-rule) for India. He would become the youngest person to serve as the President of the Indian National Congress in 1923.

Azad was amongst the main organizers of the Dharasana Satyagraha in 1931, and emerged as one of the most influential national leaders of the time, prominently leading the causes of Hindu-Islamic unity and also espousing secularism and socialism. He served as Congress President from 1940 to 1945, during which the Quit India rebellion was started and Azad was imprisoned with the whole Congress leadership for three years. Azad became the most outstanding Islamic opponent of the demand for a separate Islamic state of Pakistan and served in the provisional national government. Amidst communal turmoil after the division of India, he worked for religious accord. As India's Education Minister, Azad oversaw the establishment of a national education system with free primary education and modern institutions of higher education. He is also accredited with the foundation of the University Grants Commission, an influential institution to supervise and advance the higher education in the nation.

Azad was raised in an atmosphere steeped in Muslim religion. He was given a conventional Muslim education, tutored at his home and in the neighbourhood mosque by his father and later religious scholars. Azad learned many languages, along with Urdu, Persian, Hindko, Arabic, and Hindi. He was also schooled in the subjects of mathematics, philosophy, world history and science by esteemed tutors hired by his family. An avid and determined student, Azad succeeded in finishing the conventional course of study at the young age of sixteen, nine years ahead of his contemporaries. At the age of thirteen, he was married to a young Islamic girl, Zuleikha Begum.

Azad was, more closer, a follower of the Deobandi school and compiled a lot of treatises reinterpreting the Quran, the Hadith, and the ideals of Fiqh and Kalam. A young man, Azad was also exposed to the modern intellectual life of Kolkata, the then capital of British-ruled India and the centre of cultural and political life. He began to doubt the conventional ways of his father and secretly diversified his studies. Azad mastered English through intensive individual study and began learning Western philosophy, history and contemporary politics by reading advanced books and modern periodicals. Azad was motivated by the modern opinions of Islamic educationalist Sir Syed Ahmed Khan, who had encouraged rationalism. Increasingly doubtful of religious dogma, Azad entered a period of self-described "atheism" and "sinfulness" that lasted for almost a decade.

He fiercely criticised the British for racial discrimination and ignoring the requirements of common people across India. He also criticised Islamic politicians for focusing on communal issues before the national interest and refused the All India Muslim League's communal separatism. Azad developed curiosity and interest in the pan-Islamic doctrines of Jamal al-Din al-Afghani and visited Afghanistan, Iraq, Egypt, Syria and Turkey. But his opinions changed noticeably when he met revolutionary activists in Iraq and was influence by their fervent anti-imperialism and nationalism. Against common Islamic view of the time, Azad opposed the division of Bengal in 1905 and became increasingly active in revolutionary activities, to which he was introduced by the outstanding Hindu revolutionaries Sri Aurobindo and Shyam Sundar Chakrawarty. Azad at first evoked surprise from other revolutionaries, but Azad won their praise and confidence by functioning secretly to organize revolutionaries activities and meetings in Bengal, Bihar and Mumbai.

Azad's education had been shaped for him to become a cleric, but his rebellious nature and affinity for politics turned him towards journalism.

He founded an Urdu weekly newspaper in 1912 named Al-Hilal and openly attacked British policies while exploring the challenges facing common people. Espousing the principles of Indian nationalism, Azad's publications were aimed at encouraging young Muslims into fighting for independence and Hindu-Islamic unity. His work helped improve the relationship between Hindus and Muslims in Bengal, which had been soured by the dispute surrounding the division of Bengal and the issue of separate communal electorates.

With the onset of World War I, the British stiffened censorship and restrictions on political activity. Azad's Al-Hilal was consequently banned in 1914 under the Press Act. Azad began a new journal, the Al-Balagh, which increased its active backup for nationalist causes and communal unity. In this period Azad also became active in his backup for the Khilafat agitation to protect the position of the Sultan of Ottoman Turkey, who was the caliph for Muslims all over. The Sultan had sided against the British in the war and the continuity of his rule came under serious threat, causing distress amongst Islamic conservatives. Azad saw a chance to energise Indian Muslims and accomplish main political and social reform through the fight. With his fame increasing across India, the government outlawed Azad's second publication under the Defence of India Regulations Act and arrested him. The governments of the Bombay Presidency, United Provinces, Punjab and Delhi prohibited his entry into the provinces and Azad was shifted to a jail in Ranchi, where he was incarcerated till January 1, 1920.

Upon his release, Azad returned to a political environment charged with sentiments of outrage and rebellion against British rule. The Indian public had been angered by the passage of the Rowlatt Acts in 1919, which seriously restricted civil liberties and personal rights. Consequently, thousands of political activists had been arrested and a lot of publications banned. The killing of unarmed civilians at Jallianwala Bagh in Amritsar on April 13, 1919 had provoked strong outrage all over India, alienating most Indians, along with his followers, from the authorities. The Khilafat fight had also peaked with the defeat of the Ottoman Empire in World War I and the raging Turkish War of Independence, which had made the caliphate's position precarious. India's main political party, the Indian National Congress came under the leadership of Mahatma Gandhi, who had aroused excitement all over India when he led the farmers of Champaran and Kheda in a successful revolt against British authorities in 1918. Gandhi organized the people of the region and pioneered the art of Satyagraha — combining mass civil disobedience with complete non-violence and self-reliance.

Taking charge of the Congress, Gandhi also reached out to support the Khilafat struggle, helping to bridge Hindu-Islamic political divides. Azad and the Ali brothers warmly welcomed Congress backup and began functioning together on a program of non-cooperation by asking all Indians to boycott British-run schools, colleges, courts, public services, the civil service, police and military. Non-violence and Hindu-Islamic unity were universally emphasized, while the boycott of foreign goods, particularly clothes were organized. Azad became member of the Congress and was also elected president of the All India Khilafat Committee. Though Azad and other leaders were shortly arrested, the movement drew out millions of people in peaceful processions, strikes and protests.

This period marked a transformation in Azad's own life. Together with fellow Khilafat leaders Dr. Mukhtar Ahmad Ansari, Hakim Ajmal Khan and others, Azad grew individually close to Gandhi and his philosophy. The three men established the Jamia Millia Islamia in Delhi as an institution of higher education managed entirely by Indians without any British support or control. Both Azad and Gandhi shared a deep zeal for religion and Azad developed a close friendship with him. He adopted Gandhi's ideas by living simply, rejecting material possessions and pleasures. He began to spin his own clothes employing khadi on the charkha, and began frequently living and participating in the ashrams organized by Gandhi. Becoming deeply committed to ahimsa (non-violence) himself, Azad grew close to fellow nationalists like Jawaharlal Nehru, Chittaranjan Das and Subhash Chandra Bose. He deeply criticised the regular suspicion of the Congress amongst the Islamic intellectuals from the Aligarh Muslim University and the Muslim League.

The rebellion began a sudden decline when with rising incidences of violence; a nationalist mob killed 22 policemen in Chauri Chaura in 1922. Fearing degeneration into violence, Gandhi asked Indians to suspend the revolt and embarked on a fast-unto-death to repent and promote others to stop the rebellion. Though the movement stopped all over India, many Congress leaders and activists were disillusioned with Gandhi. The following year, the caliphate was overthrown by Mustafa Kemal Atatürk and the Ali brothers grew distant and critical of Gandhi and the Congress. Azad's close friend Chittaranjan Das co-established the Swaraj Party, breaking from Gandhi's leadership. Despite the conditions, Azad remained firmly committed to Gandhi's principles and leadership. In 1923, he became the youngest man to be elected Congress President. Azad led efforts to organize the Flag Satyagraha in Nagpur. Azad served as president of the 1924 Unity Conference in Delhi, employing his position to work to reunite the Swarajists and the Khilafat leaders under the common banner of the Congress. In the years after the movement, Azad travelled across India, functioning extensively to encourage Gandhi's vision, education and social reform.

Azad had become an influential national leader, and would serve on the Congress Working Committee and in the offices of general secretary and president a lot of times. The political atmosphere in India re-energised in 1928 with nationalist outrage against the Simon Commission appointed to propose constitutional reforms. The commission included no Indian members and didn't even consult Indian leaders and experts. In reaction, the Congress and other political parties appointed a commission under Motilal Nehru to propose constitutional reforms from Indian opinions.

In 1928, Azad endorsed the Nehru Report, which was criticised by the Ali brothers and the Muslim League politician Muhammad Ali Jinnah. Azad endorsed the ending of separate electorates based on religion, and demanded an autonomous India to be committed to secularism. At the 1928 Congress session in Guwahati, Azad endorsed Gandhi's call for dominion status for India inside a year. If not awarded, the Congress would adopt the goal of complete political independence for India. Despite his affinity for Gandhi, Azad also drew close to the young radical leaders Jawaharlal Nehru and Subhash Bose, who had criticised the delay in calling for full independence. Azad developed a close friendship with Nehru and began espousing socialism as the means to fight inequality, poverty and other national challenges.

When Gandhi embarked on the Dandi Salt March that inaugurated the Salt Satyagraha in 1930, Azad organized and led the nationalist raid, albeit non-violent on the Dharasana salt works in order to protest the salt tax and restriction of its production and sale. The biggest nationalist upheaval in a decade, Azad was imprisoned together with millions of people, and would often be jailed from 1930 to 1934 for considerable periods of time. After the Gandhi-Irwin Pact in 1934, Azad was amongst millions of political prisoners released. When elections were declared under the Government of India Act 1935, Azad was appointed to organize the Congress election campaign, raising funds, selecting candidates and organising volunteers and rallies across India. Azad had criticised the Act for along with a high proportion of un-elected members in the central legislature, and didn't himself contest a seat.

At the 1936 Congress session in Lucknow, Azad was drawn into a dispute with right-wing Congressmen Sardar Vallabhbhai Patel, Dr.

Rajendra Prasad and Chakravarthi Rajagopalachari regarding the espousal of socialism as the Congress goal. Azad had backed the election of Nehru as Congress President, and supported the resolution endorsing socialism. In doing so, he aligned with Congress socialists like Nehru, Subhash Bose and Jayaprakash Narayan. Azad also supported Nehru's re-election in 1937, at the consternation of a lot of traditional Congressmen.

Azad supported dialogue with Jinnah and the Muslim League between 1935 and 1937 over a Congress-League coalition and broader political cooperation. Less inclined to brand the League as obstructive, Azad however became member of the Congress's vehement rejection of Jinnah's demand that the League be seen exclusively as the spokesperson of Indian Muslims.

He refused to contest elections in 1937, and helped head the party's efforts to organize elections and preserve coordination and unity amongst the Congress governments elected in various provinces.

In 1938, Azad served as an intermediary between the followers of Gandhi and the Congress faction led by Congress President Subhash Bose, who criticised Gandhi for not launching another rebellion against the British and sought to move the Congress away from Gandhi's leadership. Azad stood by Gandhi with most other Congress leaders, but reluctantly endorsed the Congress's exit from the assemblies in 1939 after the inclusion of India in World War II. Nationalists were infuriated that the viceroy had entered India into the war without consulting national leaders.

In face of increasing popular disenchantment with the British across India, Gandhi and Patel advocated an all-out rebellion calling for immediate independence. The situation had grown precarious as the Japanese conquered Burma and approached India's borders, which left Indians insecure but resentful of the British inability to protect India. Azad was wary and skeptical of the idea, aware that India's Muslims were increasingly looking to Jinnah and had supported the war. Feeling that a resistance would not force a British exit, Azad and Nehru warned that such a movement would divide India and make the war situation even more precarious. Intensive and emotional debates took place between Azad, Nehru, Gandhi and Patel in the Congress Working Committee's meetings in May and June 1942. In the end, Azad became convinced that decisive action in one form or another had to be taken, as the Congress had to supply leadership to India's people and would lose its standing if it didn't.

Supporting the call for the British to "Quit India," Azad began exhorting thousands of people in rallies across the nation to prepare for a definitive, all-out resistance. As Congress President, Azad travelled across India and met with local and provincial Congress leaders and grassroots activists, delivering speeches and planning the rebellion. Despite their previous differences, Azad worked closely with Patel and Dr. Rajendra Prasad to make the rebellion as efficient as possible. On August 7, 1942 at the Gowalia Tank in Mumbai, Congress President Azad inaugurated the resistance with a vociferous speech exhorting Indians into action. Just two days afterward, the British arrested Azad and the whole Congress leadership.

While Gandhi was incarcerated at the Aga Khan Palace in Pune, Azad and the Congress Working Committee were imprisoned at a fort in Ahmednagar, where they would remain under isolation and strong security for almost four years. Outside news and communication had been largely prohibited and completely censored. Though frustrated at their incarceration and isolation, Azad and his companions attested to feeling a deep satisfaction at having done their obligation to their country and people.

Azad occupied the time playing bridge and acting as the referee in tennis matches played by his colleagues. In the afternoons, Azad began functioning on his classic Urdu work, the Ghubhar-i-Khatir. Sharing daily chores, Azad also taught the Persian and Urdu languages, and also Indian and world history to many of his companions. The leaders would generally avoid talking of politics, unwilling to cause any arguments that could exacerbate the pain of their detention. Nevertheless, each year on January 26, the leaders would gather to remember their cause and pray together. Azad, Nehru and Patel would shortly speak about the nation and the future. Azad and Nehru proposed an initiative to forge an agreement with the British in 1943. Arguing that the rebellion had been mistimed, Azad attempted to convince his colleagues that the Congress should agree to negotiate with the British and call for the suspension of disobedience if the British agreed to shift power. Though his proposal was overwhelmingly refused, Azad and a couple of others agreed that Gandhi and the Congress had not done enough. When they came to knew of Gandhi holding talks with Jinnah in Mumbai in 1944, Azad criticised Gandhi's move as counterproductive and ill-advised.

He died of a stroke on February 22, 1958, in Delhi, India.

Azad is remembered as amongst the major Indian nationalists of his time. His firm belief in Hindu-Islamic unity earned him the respect of the

Hindu community and he still remains one of the most influential symbols of communal accord in modern India. His work for education and social upliftment in India made him an important influence in guiding India's economic and social growth.

10. MAULANA HASRAT MOHANI

Maulana Hasrat Mohani was born in 1875 at Mohan in Unnao district of U.P., India. He was a romantic poet of Urdu language, journalist, politician, parliamentarian and a fearless freedom-fighter. His real name was Syed Fazl ul Hasan.

He was a brilliant student and also a topper in his first state level exams. Afterwards, he studied in Aligarh Muslim University, where some of his colleagues were Maulana Muhammad Ali Johar, Maulana Shaukat Ali, etc. His teachers in poetry were Tasleem Lucknawi and Naseem Dehlvi.

A couple of his books are Kulliyat-e-Hasrat Mohani (Collection of Hasrat Mohani's poetry), Sharh-e-Kalam-e-Ghalib (Explanation of Ghalib's poetry), Nukaat-e-Sukhan (Influential aspects of poetry, Mushahidaat-e-Zindaan(Observations in Prison), etc. A very well liked ghazal sung by Ghulam Ali, "Chupke Chupke raat din" was written by Hasrat Mohani.

Hasrat Mohani participated in the fight for Indian Independence (end of British Raj); and was jailed for a lot of years by British authorities. He was the first person in Indian History who demanded 'Complete Independence' (Azadi-e-Kaamil) in 1921 as he presided over an annual session of All India Muslim League. He was not only a practising Islamic but also a strong follower of the communist philosophy, as he could see that British could be possibly defeated by following its ideals.

Therefore, he was amongst the founders of The Communist Party of India. He was also imprisoned for promoting anti-British ideas particularly for publishing an item against British policies in Egypt, in his magazine 'Urdu-e-Mualla'. Afterwards, unlike some Urdu poets, notably Josh Malihabadi and Nasir Kazmi, and a lot of Islamic leaders, he chose to live in India rather than move to Pakistan after independence (1947) in order to represent left over Indian Muslims on various platforms. In appreciation for his efforts, he was made a member of the constituent assembly which drafted the Indian constitution. But unlike other members, he never signed it as he saw hypocrisy towards Islamic minorities in it (he was a Muslim himself). As per Akhtar Payami: Hasrat's poetic genius has been acclaimed by a lot of authors and critics.

In the not too distant past (starting and the first half of the 20th century), Hasrat, Jigar and Asghar formed a constellation of emerging poets in a crucial period of India's history. Prominent political growths were taking place in the subcontinent and the sun was about to set on the British Empire. As conscious members of society, poets and authors do not remain indifferent to the alterations in their sociopolitical milieu. Not only India but the entire world was in a state of flux.

Maulana expired on May 13, 1951 in Lucknow, India.

11. MAULANA MUHAMMAD ALI

Muhammad Ali, who afterward, became famous as Maulana Muhammad Ali Jauha, was born in Rampur, U.P., India in 1878 to a family of Rohilla sub-tribe of Yousafzai Pashtun ancestry. He was an Indian Islamic journalist and poet, and was amongst the major figures of the Khilafat Movement.

He was the brother of Maulana Shaukat Ali. Despite the early demise of his father, the family strived and Ali attended the Aligarh Muslim University and Lincoln College, Oxford University in 1898, studying modern history.

Upon his come back to India, he served as education director for the Rampur state, and afterward joined the Baroda civil service. He became a brilliant author and orator, and wrote for prominent English and Indian newspapers, in both English and Urdu. He himself started the Urdu weekly Hamdard and English Comrade in 1911. He shifted to Delhi in 1913.

Muhammad Ali worked hard to expand the AMU, then acknowledged as the Muhammadan Anglo-Oriental College, and was one of the co-founders of the Jamia Millia Islamia in 1920, which was afterward shifted to Delhi.

Muhammad Ali had attended the founding meeting of the All India Muslim League in Dhaka in 1906, and served as its president in 1918. He remained active in the League until 1928.

Ali headed the Islamic delegation that visited England in 1919 in order to convince the British government to influence the Turkish nationalist Mustafa Kemal not to depose the Sultan of Turkey, who was the Caliph of Islam. British rejection of their demands resulted in the establishment of the Khilafat committee which directed Muslims all over India to protest and boycott the government. Maulana Muhammad Ali was nevertheless, disillusioned by the failure of the Khilafat movement and Gandhi's suspension of civil disobedience in 1922, owing to the Chauri Chaura event.

He was elected as President of Indian National Congress in 1923. He restarted his weekly Hamdard, and left the Congress Party. He opposed the Nehru Report, which was a document proposing constitutional reforms and a dominion status of an autonomous nation inside the British Empire, scripted by a committee of Hindu and Islamic members of the Congress Party headed by President Motilal Nehru. It was a major protest against the Simon Commission which had arrived in India to propose reforms but containing no Indian nor making any effort to listen to Indian voices.

Muhammad Ali opposed the Nehru Report's rejection of separate electorates for Muslims, and supported the Fourteen Points of Muhammad Ali Jinnah and the League. He became a critic of Gandhi, breaking with fellow Islamic leaders like Maulana Azad, Hakim Ajmal Khan and Mukhtar Ahmed Ansari, who continued to backup Gandhi and the Indian National Congress. Muhammad Ali said: "Even the most degraded Muhammadan was better than Mahatma Gandhi." Ali attended the Round Table Conference to show that only the Muslim League spoke for India's Muslims.

He expired on January 4, 1931, in London, and was buried in Jerusalem as per his own wish.

Maulana Muhammad Ali Jauhar is remembered as a fiery leader of several of India's Muslims. But in India, he is remembered for his leadership during Khilafat Movement and the Non-Cooperation Movement, and his leadership in Islamic education.

12. MUKHTAR AHMED ANSARI

Mukhtar Ahmed Ansari was born on December 25, 1880 in district of Ghazipur, Uttar Pradesh, India. Educated at the Victoria High School, Ansari and his family shifted to Hyderabad. Ansari received a medical degree from the Madras Medical College and moved to England on scholarship studies. He attained the M.D. and M.S. degrees. He was a top-class student and worked at the Lock Hospital and the Charing Cross Hospital in London. He was an Indian pioneer in surgery, and today there is an Ansari Ward in the Charing Cross Hospital in honour of his work.

Dr. Ansari became involved in the Indian Independence Movement during his stay in England. He shifted back to Delhi and became member of both the Indian National Congress and the Muslim League. He played an influential role in the negotiation of the 1916 Lucknow Pact and served as the League's president in 1918 and 1920. He was an outspoken follower of the Khilafat movement, and worked to bring the official Khilafat body, the League and the Congress Party together on the issue against the Mustafa Kemal's decision to oust the Sultan of Turkey, who was the Caliph of Islam, and to protest the recognition of Turkey's independence by the British Empire.

Dr. Ansari served many terms as the AICC General Secretary, and also the President of the Indian National Congress during its 1927 session. As a consequence of in fighting and political divisions inside the League in the 1920s, and afterward the rise of Muhammad Ali Jinnah and Islamic separatism, Dr. Ansari drew closer to Mahatma Gandhi and the Congress Party.

Dr. Ansari was amongst the founders as well as served as the chancellor of the Jamia Millia Islamia university in Delhi shortly after the demise of its primary founder, Dr. Hakim Ajmal Khan.

Dr. Ansari expired on May 10, 1936 en route from Mussoorie to Delhi on a train due to coronary failure, and is buried in the premises of the Jamia Millia Islamia in Delhi.

13. RAFI AHMED KIDWAI

Rafi Ahmed Kidwai was born on February 18, 1894 in a middle class Zamindari family at Masauli in Barabanki district of Uttar Pradesh, India. He was an Indian independence activist and a socialist, occasionally described as a Muslim socialist. He came from Barabanki District of United Provinces, now Uttar Pradesh, in North India.

After attending M.A.O. College in Aligarh, Kidwai got into politics through the Khilafat movement, and after the passage of Government of

India Act 1935, he held an office for the Indian National Congress. In 1937, Kidwai became a minister for Revenue and Prisons in Govind Ballabh Pant's cabinet in United Provinces (UP) under the Provincial Autonomy Scheme. Under his leadership, UP became the first state to curtail the zamindari system. In April 1946, he became the Home Minister of UP.

Kidwai was a permanent supporter of Jawaharlal Nehru. In the first Cabinet of U.P. formed after the 1935 reforms, Rafi Ahmad was appointed Minister of the key portfolio of Land Revenue, when he got an opportunity to give practical shape to his agrarian programme. Rafi Ahmad's economic outlook was radical, and in the Presidential Address to the Unnao Session of the U. P. Congress (1936), he sponsored the theory that complete assurance to the starved and the naked, especially the peasant, would win more support for the battle for freedom than all talks of close-up in the Congress.

Rafi Ahmad's virtual enactment of the U.P. Tenancy Act (it received the Governor's Assent after the Congress Ministry's resignation in 1939) created a firm base for the Congress among the rural masses and created conditions for the abolition of the Zamindari system. He sponsored the resolution accepting the principle of the abolition of landlordism in the U. P. Assembly. In the U. P. Cabinet formed after the second General Elections (1946), Rafi Ahmad became the Home Minister. In 1947, Rafi Ahmad's field of activity was shifted to New Delhi, where as the Minister for Communications in the Central Cabinet he distinguished himself by sponsoring the schemes of night-air-mail, own-your-telephone, and paid holiday for postmen. Rafi developed differences on organisational matters and in 1951 resigned membership of the Congress and the Government.

Before the 1952 General Elections there was, however, a reconciliation and Rafi Ahmad won a seat in Parliament from Bahraich as a Congress candidate. In the new Union Cabinet, he was put in charge of the most difficult portfolios-Food and Agriculture. Rafi had reached his apex and feeding the nation without food-aid and controls made him a national hero. On religion Rafi Ahmad's views were highly unorthodox. He shared Chesterton's belief that organised religion had lost its real contents, and reduced his participation in community prayers on every Friday, to the two annual occasions of Id and Bakr-Id. Rafi Ahmad opposed the orthodox Muslims who wanted to exclude Muslims from the application of the Sarda Act, prescribing the age of consent for girls, on the ground that it would be a violation of the Shariat Law. He stood for the equality of sexes and freedom of women.

Rafi Ahmad's approach to communal matters was non-religious, that is, he would settle them through far-reaching agreements on fundamental rights, adult suffrage and common electorate. Rafi believed in mass action and mass programmes. Both the Hindu and the Muslim masses suffered equally at the hands of their exploiters, the landlord and the capitalist. Hindu-Muslim unity could thus be achieved through a common struggle to end exploitation. He stood for complete Independence though by way of compromise he agreed to join the U. P. Cabinet after the 1935 Reforms.

He was quiet by nature and austere in living. Undaunted by nature, he would take extreme risks. Highly personal and affectionate, he built numerous lasting friendships. Generous to the core, he was something like a persuasive, nonviolent Robin Hood, who would squeeze money out of the rich for the benefit of the poor. As a fund-raiser for the party he was equalled by few. He had no love for worldly possessions, and when he died all the legacy he left was a heavy overdraft and a dilapidated ancestral house, bereft of roofings and doorflaps. Ceaseless strenuous work shattered his health and he developed cardiac asthma.

He expired on October 24, 1954 in Delhi, India.

REFERENCES

Ahmad, S. Maqbul, 'Madrasa System of Education and Indian Muslim Society', in S.T. Lokhandwala (ed.), *India and Contemporary Islam*, Simla: Indian Institute of Advanced Study, 1971.

Ahmed, Imtiaz (ed.), *Caste and Social Stratification Among Muslims in India*, Manohar: Delhi, 1978.

Ganagalu, Pandit Sayyed Qasim Ganagalu, *Hindu-Muslim Unity in the Person of His Holiness Maulana Siddique Deendar Channabasaveswara*, Hyderabad: Deendar Anjuman, 1990.

Gellner, Ernest, *Post-Modernism, Reason and Religion*, London and New York: Routledge, 1992.

Moghni, Abdul Moghni, *Hindustan Ke Liye Mustaqbil Ka Naqsha-i 'Amal*, Delhi: Markazi Maktaba-i Islami, 1994.

Mujahid, Abdul Malik, *Conversion to Islam: Untouchables' Strategy for Protest in India*, Chambersburg: Anima Books, 1989.

Nadwi, Abdullah Abbas, *Mir-i Karavan*, New Delhi: Majlis-i 'Ilmi, 1999.

Yazbeck Haddad and Wadi Zaidan Haddad (eds), *Christian-Muslim Encounters*, Gainesville, Florida: University of Florida Press, 1995.

Umm Zubayr, *Tabligh Kaise Ki Jai*, Delhi: Markazi Maktaba-i Islami, 1997.

Section: III

LEADERS

1. AGA KHAN

Aga Khan was born on December 13, 1936, in Geneva, Switzerland. He is the 49th and current Imam of the Shia Imami Ismaili Muslims. He has been in this position, and held the title of Aga Khan, since July 11, 1957. The Aga Khan is responsible for the interpretation of the faith for his adherents and as part of the office of the Imamate, endeavours to improve the quality of their lives and of the communities in which they live. In the Shia custom of Islam, it is the mandate of the Imam of the time to safeguard the person's right to individual intellectual search and to give practical expression to the ethical vision of society that the Islamic message inspires.

Born Prince Karim Aga Khan, the Aga Khan IV is the eldest son of Prince Aly Khan, a Pakistani leader of independence (1911–1960) and his first wife, French-born Princess Tajudowlah, formerly the Hon. Joan Barbara Yarde-Buller (1908–1997).

The Aga Khan spent his childhood in Nairobi, Kenya, where his early education was done by private tutoring. His grandfather, Aga Khan III, engaged Mustafa Kamil, a scholar from Aligarh Muslim University, for both Prince Karim and Prince Amyn. The Aga Khan afterward attended the Institut Le Rosey in Switzerland. He graduated from Harvard University in 1959 with a BA honours degree in Muslim history. In 2005, he was granted a honorary doctor's degree by the American University of Beirut in Lebanon. Notably, Aga Khan skied for Turkey and Iran in the 1960 and 1964 Olympic Games.

The Aga Khan married English fashion model Sarah (Sally) Croker-Poole, named HH Begum Salima Aga Khan, on October 22, 1969 (civil) and October 28, 1969 (religious), at his home in Paris, France. The couple were married for 25 years, during which they had three children: Princess Zahra Aga Khan, Prince Rahim Aga Khan, and Prince Hussain Aga Khan. Their marriage ended by divorce in 1995.

The Aga Khan married his second wife, Dr. Gabriele Princess of Leiningen (née Gabriele Thyssen), in Aiglemont on May 30, 1998. Prior to the marriage, the bride converted to Islam, and the couple jointly chose the bride's new Islamic name "Inaara" (deduced from Arabic nur, meaning "light"). She is now the HH the Begum Aga Khan. By her, the Aga Khan has a son, Prince Aly Muhammad Aga Khan, and a stepdaughter, HSH Princess Theresa of Leiningen, who is 110th in line to the throne of the United Kingdom. On October 8, 2004, a declaration was made that the Aga Khan and the Begum Aga Khan were to seek a divorce.

The Aga Khan is referred to by members of his community as Maulana Hazar Imam (Present Imam). Since his ascension to the Imamate, the Aga Khan has witnessed complex political and economic alterations which have affected his adherents, along with independence of African countries from colonial rule, expulsion of Asians from Uganda, the independence of Central Asian countries such as Tajikistan from the former Soviet Union, and regular turmoil in Afghanistan and Pakistan.

The Aga Khan has been especially interested in the elimination of global poverty; the advancement of the status of women; the advancement of Muslim culture, art, and architecture; and furthering pluralistic values in society. He is the founder and chairman of the Aga Khan Development Network, one of the largest private development networks in the world, which works towards social, economic, and cultural growth in Asia and Africa.

Aga Khan's individual wealth has been estimated as exceeding $1 billion. His annual income is estimated to be $300m. Business interests include hotels and airlines, and he has also invested in a tourist complex in Sardinia. The Aga Khan is also the richest non-land owning royal in the world. His individual wealth exceeds that of the Queen. His main source of income is through horse racing and investing in stocks, companies and material goods.

After the demise of his grandfather, Sultan Muhammad Shah Aga Khan, Prince Karim, at the age of 20, became the 49th Imam of the Shia Ismaili Muslims, bypassing his father, Prince Aly Khan, and his uncle, Prince Sadruddin Aga Khan, who were in the direct line of succession.

In light of the sentiments expressed in his grandfather's will, the Aga Khan has occasionally been referred to by Ismailis as the Imam of the Atomic Age.

Upon becoming the Imam, the Aga Khan stated that he intended to continue the work his grandfather had pursued in making modern institutions to improve the quality of life of the Ismaili community. Takht nashini (installation) ceremonies occurred at many locations over 1957 and 1958. During this time, the Aga Khan emphasized to his adherents the significance of fostering positive relations amongst peoples of various races; such a message was extremely appropriate given to the racially tense environment in East Africa. During the installation ceremonies in the Indian subcontinent, he stressed his commitment to improving the quality of life of Ismailis and encouraged cooperation with persons of other faiths and races. The main themes that the Aga Khan emphasized during these first few months of his Imamate were growth, education, interracial accord, and faith in religion.

The Aga Khan has described his role as Imam as being a guide to Ismailis in the daily practice of Shia Islam, an obligation which requires an understanding of Ismailis and their relationship with their geographic location and their time. He elaborated on this notion in a 2006 speech in Germany stating.

"The role and responsibility of an Imam, therefore, is both to interpret the faith to the community, as well as to do all inside his means to improve the quality, and security of their daily lives.

This engagement is not limited to the Ismaili community but also extends to the people with whom the Ismailis share their lives, locally and globally."

In 1977, the Aga Khan founded the Aga Khan Award for Architecture, an award recognizing excellence in architecture that encompasses contemporary design and social, historical, and environmental considerations. It is the largest architectural award in the world and is awarded triennially. The award grew out of the Aga Khan's desire to revitalize creativity in Islamic societies and acknowledge creative solutions to requirements for buildings and public spaces. The recipient is selected by an autonomous master jury convened for each cycle. In 1979, Harvard University and the Massachusetts Institute of Technology (MIT) both founded the Aga Khan Program for Islamic Architecture (AKPIA), which is supported by an endowment from the Aga Khan. These programs supply degree courses, public lectures, and conferences for the study of Muslim architecture and urbanism. Understanding contemporary circumstances and developmental issues are key components of the academic program.

The Aga Khan is founder and chairman of the Aga Khan Development Network (AKDN), one of the largest private development networks in the world. Its partners include many governments and many international organizations. AKDN agencies operate in social and economic development and also in the area of culture, with distinctive focus on countries of the Third World.

The network includes the Aga Khan University (AKU), the University of Central Asia (UCA), the Aga Khan Fund for Economic Development (AKFED), the Aga Khan Trust for Culture (AKTC), the Aga Khan Foundation (AKF), the Aga Khan Health Services (AKHS), the Aga Khan Education Services (AKES), the Aga Khan Planning and Building Services (AKPBS), and the Aga Khan Agency for Microfinance (AKAM). The Aga Khan Award for Architecture (AKAA)is the largest architectural award in the world.

Focus Humanitarian Assistance (FOCUS), an affiliate of the AKDN, is responsible for emergency reaction in the face of disaster. Current examples include the massive earthquake in Pakistan (AKDN earthquake response) and the South Asian Tsunami.

He is also the chairman of the Board of Governors of the Institute of Ismaili Studies, which he established in 1977.

Substantial current or current projects led by the Aga Khan include the Delegation of the Ismaili Imamate and the Global Centre for Pluralism (GCP) in Ottawa, the Aga Khan Museum in Toronto, the Al-Azhar Park in Cairo, and a network of full IB residential schools acknowledged as the Aga Khan Academies (AKA). In 2002, Aga Khan pledged $75 million for the rebuilding of Afghanistan. The pledge was the largest by any single donor and more than a lot of countries.

The Aga Khan has expressed interest about the work of the AKDN being described as philanthropy. In his address to the Tutzing Evangelical Academy in Germany, he described this interest:

"Reflecting a certain historical tendency of the West to separate the secular from the religious, they often take either as philanthropy or entrepreneurship. What is not understood is that this work is for us a part of our institutional responsibility — it flows from the mandate of the office of Imam to improve the quality of worldly life for the interested communities."

Aga Khan has been awarded and honoured many times. His honours include:

Titles

- 1957: Titles of His Highness awarded by Her Majesty the Queen of England

- 1959: His Royal Highness by His Imperial Majesty the Shah of Iran

Decorations

- 1960: Commander of the Order of Merit, Mauritania
- 1960: Grand Cross of the Order of Infante D. Henrique, Portugal
- 1965: Grand Cross of the National Order, Ivory Coast
- 1965: Grand Cross of the National Order, Upper Volta
- 1966: Grand Cross of the National Order, Madagascar
- 1966: Grand Cross of the Order of the Green Crescent, Comoros
- 1967: Grand Cordon of the Order of the Crown of Iran, Nishan-i-Taj-i-Iran
- 1970: Nishan-i-Imtiaz, Pakistan
- 1977: Knight Grand Cross of the Order of Merit of the Italian Republic
- 1982: Grand Officer of the National Order of the Lion, Senegal
- 1983: Nishan-e-Pakistan
- 1986: Grand Cordon of Ouissam-al Arch, Morocco
- 1988: Knight of Labour, Cavaliere del Lavoro, Italy
- 1990: Commander of the Legion of Honour, France
- 1991: Grand Cross of the Order of Civil Merit, Spain
- 1998: Grand Cross of the Order of Merit, Portugal
- 1998: Order of Friendship, Tajikistan
- 2003: Order of Bahrain (First Class)
- 2004: Knight Commander of the British Empire (KBE), United Kingdom
- 2005: Honorary Companion of the Order of Canada
- 2005: Grand Cross of the Military Order of Christ, Portugal
- 2007: Chief of the Order of the Golden Heart, Kenya
- 2008: Grand Cross of the National Order of Mali

2. AYUB KHAN

Field Marshal Muhammad Ayub Khan was born on May 14, 1907, in Peshawar, Pakistan. He was a Field Marshal during the mid-sixties, and the President of Pakistan from 1958 to 1969. He became Pakistan's first national Commander-in-Chief in 1951, and was the youngest full-rank general and self-appointed field marshal in Pakistan's military history. He was also the first Pakistani military general to grab power through a coup.

Ayub Khan was born in the Pashtun family of the Tareen tribe, the first child of the second wife of Mir Dad Khan, who was a Risaldar-Major (the senior most noncommissioned rank) in Hodson's Horse, a cavalry regiment of the Royal Indian Army. For his basic education, he was enrolled in a school in Sarai Saleh, which was about four miles from his village. He used to go to school on a mule's back. Afterward he was moved to a school in Haripur, where he began living with his grandmother. He enrolled at Aligarh University in 1922, but he didn't complete his studies.

He was accepted into the Royal Military Academy Sandhurst. He did well at Sandhurst, and was given an officer's post in the British Indian Army and then became member of the 1st Battalion of the 14th Punjab Regiment (Sherdils), afterward acknowledged as 5th Punjab Regiment. During World War II he served as a skipper and afterward as a major on the Burma front. After the war, he became member of the fledgling Pakistani Army as the 10th ranking senior officer (his Pakistan Army number was 10).

He was promoted to Brigadier and commanded a brigade in Waziristan and then was sent at first with the local rank of Major General to East Pakistan (present day Bangladesh) as General Officer Commanding a division that was responsible for the entire East Wing of Pakistan in 1948, for which noncombatant service he was granted the Hilal-i-Jurat (HJ) and from where he came back in November 1949 as Adjutant General and then shortly was named Deputy Commander-in-Chief.

Ayub Khan was made Commander-in-Chief of the Pakistan Army on January 17, 1951, succeeding General Sir Douglas Gracey, thus becoming the first native Pakistani general to hold that position. The happenings surrounding his appointment set the model for a Pakistani general being promoted out of turn, seemingly because he was the least ambitious of the Generals and the most loyal.

He would afterward go on to serve in the second cabinet (1954) of Muhammad Ali Bogra as Defence Minister, and when Iskander Mirza declared martial law on October 7, 1958, Ayub Khan was made its chief martial law administrator. This would be the first of several examples in the history of Pakistan of the military becoming directly involved in politics.

As a consequence of his having control of the Pakistan Army, Ayub deposed Mirza on October 27 in a bloodless coup, sending Generals Azam, Burki and Sheikh in the middle of the night to pack Mirza off to exile in England. This was actually welcomed in Pakistan, since the nation had experienced a very unstable political climate since independence.

In 1960, he held an indirect referendum of his term in power, functioning as a kind of electoral college, close to 80,000 recently elected village councilmen were permitted to vote yes or no to the question: "Have you confidence in the President, Field Marshal Muhammad Ayub Khan?" Winning 95.6% of the vote, he used the confirmation as impetus to formalise his new system.

Ayub moved to have a new constitution established, and this was finished in 1961. A fairly secular person by nature, Ayub Khan's constitution reflected his individual opinions of politicians and the use of religion in politics.

In 1962, he pushed through a new constitution that while it did give due respect to Islam, it didn't declare Islam the state religion of the country. It also provided for election of the President by 80,000 (afterward raised to 120,000) basic democrats—men who could theoretically make their own choice but who were essentially under his control. The government "guided" the press and, while Ayub permitted a national assembly, it had only limited powers.

He subsidized fertilizers and modernized agriculture through irrigation growth, spurred industrial development with liberal tax benefits. In the decade of his rule, gross national product rose by 45% and manufactured goods began to overtake such conventional exports as jute and cotton. It is alleged that his policies were tailored to reward the elite families and the feudal lords.

He died on April 19, 1974, near Islamabad, Pakistan.

3. BENAZIR BHUTTO

Benazir Bhutto was born in Karachi, Pakistan on June 21, 1953. She was a Pakistani politician who chaired the Pakistan People's Party (PPP), a centre-left political party in Pakistan. Bhutto was the first woman elected to lead an Islamic state, having twice been Prime Minister of Pakistan. She was Pakistan's first and to date only female prime minister.

Bhutto was the eldest child of former prime minister Zulfikar Ali Bhutto, a Pakistani of Sindhi descent and Shia Islamic by faith, and Begum Nusrat Bhutto, a Pakistani of Iranian-Kurdish descent, similarly Shia Islamic by faith. Her paternal grandfather was Sir Shah Nawaz Bhutto, who came to Larkana District in Sindh before the independence from his native town of Bhatto Kalan, in the Indian state of Haryana.

Benazir Bhutto was born to Begum Nusrat Ispahani and Zulfikar Ali Bhutto of an outstanding Shia Islamic family of Larkana. She attended the Lady Jennings Nursery School and then the Convent of Jesus and Mary in Karachi. After two years of school at the Rawalpindi Presentation Convent, she was sent to the Jesus and Mary Convent at Murree. She passed her O-level examinations at the age of 15. She then moved on to complete her A-Levels at the Karachi Grammar School.

After finishing her early education in Pakistan, she pursued her higher education in the United States. From 1969 to 1973 she attended Radcliffe College at Harvard University, where she received a Bachelor of Arts degree with cum laude honours comparative government. She was also elected to Phi Beta Kappa. Bhutto would afterward call her time at Harvard "four of the happiest years of my life" and said it formed "the very basis of her belief in democracy". Afterward in 1995 as Prime Minister, she would arrange a gift from the Pakistani government to Harvard Law School.

The next phase of her education took place in the United Kingdom. Between 1973 and 1977 Bhutto learned Philosophy, Politics, and Economics at Lady Margaret Hall, Oxford, during which time she finished additional courses in International Law and Diplomacy. After LMH she attend St. Catherine's College, Oxford and in December 1976, she was elected president of the Oxford Union, becoming the first Asian woman to head the esteemed debating society. On December 18, 1987, she married Asif Ali Zardari in Karachi. The couple had three children: Bilawal, Bakhtwar and Aseefa.

Bhutto, who had came back to Pakistan after finishing her studies, found herself placed under house arrest in the wake of her father's detention and subsequent execution. Having been permitted in 1984 to come back to the United Kingdom, she became a leader in exile of the PPP, her father's party, although she was unable to make her political charisma felt in Pakistan till after the demise of General Muhammad Zia-ul-Haq. She had succeeded her mother as leader of the PPP and the pro-democracy resistance to the Zia-ul-Haq regime.

On November 16, 1988, in the first open election in more than a decade, Bhutto's PPP won the largest bloc of seats in the National Assembly. Bhutto was sworn in as Prime Minister of a coalition government on December 2, becoming at age 35 the youngest person—and the first woman—to head the government of an Islamic-majority state in modern times. In 1989, she was granted the Prize For Freedom by the Liberal International. Bhutto's accomplishments during this time were in initiatives for nationalist reform and modernization, that some conservatives characterized as Westernization. Bhutto's government was dismissed in 1990 following charges of corruption, for which she was never tried. Zia's protege Nawaz Sharif came to power after the October 1990 elections. She served as leader of the opposition while Sharif served as Prime Minister for the next three years.

Elections were held again in October 1993 and her PPP coalition was victorious, returning Bhutto to office and allowing her to continue her reform initiatives. In 1996, amidst various corruption scandals Bhutto was dismissed by then-president Farooq Leghari, who used the Eighth Amendment discretionary powers to dissolve the government. The Supreme Court affirmed President Leghari's dismissal in a 6-1 ruling. Disapproval against Bhutto came from the Punjabi elites and powerful landlord families who opposed Bhutto. She blamed this resistance for the destabilization of Pakistan. Irshad Manji judged her attempts to modernize Pakistan a failure. Musharraf characterized Bhutto's terms as an "era of sham democracy" and others characterized her terms a period of corrupt, failed governments.

During the election campaigns the Bhutto government voiced its concern for women's social and health issues, along with the issue of discrimination against women. Bhutto announced plans to make women's police stations, courts, and women's development banks. Despite these plans, Bhutto didn't propose any legislation to improve welfare services for women. During her election campaigns, she promised to repeal debatable laws (such as Hudood and Zina ordinances) that curtail the rights of women in Pakistan. Bhutto was pro-life and spoke forcefully against abortion, most notably at the International Conference on Population and Development in Cairo, where she accused the West of "seeking to impose adultery, abortion, intercourse education and other such matters on persons, societies and religions which have their own social ethos."

The Zina ordinance was finally repealed by a Presidential Ordinance issued by Pervez Musharraf in July 2006. Bhutto was an active and founding member of the Council of Women World Leaders, a network of current and former prime ministers and presidents.

The Taliban took power in Kabul in September 1996. It was during Bhutto's rule that the Taliban acquired fame in Afghanistan. She, like a lot of leaders at the time, saw the Taliban as a group that could stabilize Afghanistan and enable trade access to the Central Asian republics. She claimed that like the United States, her government provided military and financial backup for the Taliban, even sending a small unit of the Pakistani army into Afghanistan. More recently, she took an anti-Taliban stance, and condemned terrorist acts allegedly committed by the Taliban and their followers.

She was assassinated on December 27, 2007, after departing from a PPP rally in the Pakistani city of Rawalpindi, two weeks before the scheduled Pakistani general election of 2008, where she was a leading opposition candidate.

4. FAKHRUDDIN ALI AHMED

Fakhruddin Ali Ahmed was born on May 13, 1905, at Hauz Qazi region of Old Delhi, India. Fakhruddin Ali Ahmed was one of those few Muslims who by virtue of his service to the country under the leadership of Mahatma Gandhi reached the pinnacle of honour as the President of the Indian Republic, the fifth in the roll.

Fakhruddin's grandfather, Shri Khaliluddin Ali Ahmed, of Kacharighat close to Golaghat town in the Sibsagar district, Assam, married in one of the families, who were the relics of Emperor Aurangzeb's bid to conquer Assam. Ali Ahmed's father Col. Zalnur Ali, of the Indian Medical Service, had to leave Assam while he was a bachelor doctor following an event in Shillong. Col. Ali and one of his Assamese contemporaries, Col. Sibram

Bora, were allotted seats at a function in the Shillong Club away from the European guests. The two Assamese Colonels boycotted the function in protest against the segregation meted out to them. This naturally enraged the European bosses who transferred Col. Zalnur Ali to distant North-West Province. This provided him with a chance to come in contact with the Nawab of Lohari in Delhi whose daughter he married. Here was born Fakhruddin Ali Ahmed.

Educated first in the Bonda Government High School in U.P., Fakhruddin matriculated from the Delhi Government High School then under the Punjab University. He was sent to England for higher education in 1923 in order to groom him for the I.C.S., although his mother was opposed to his son being sent abroad. He became member of the Catherine College of Cambridge University and was invited to the Bar from Inner Temple of London. He could not compete for the I.C.S. examination due to sickness. On return to India, he began legal practice in the Lahore High Court in 1928. In October that year, Col. Zalnur Ali, escorted by his Barrister son, Fakhruddin, paid a visit to Gauhati seemingly to look after his paternal property which included a couple of hundred acres of land in and around Gauhati. Obviously, the Ahmed family's link, snapped on the Colonel's posting in N.W.P. was thus re-founded after many years. Two years afterward Fakhruddin Ali Ahmed revisited Gauhati and came in contact with the leaders of the Congress in Assam and in 1931 enrolled himself as its primary member. This was a turning event in the life of Ahmed.

During his stay in England he met Jawaharlal Nehru in 1925 whose liberal ideas impressed him very much; as a matter of fact, Nehru became his teacher and friend from the thirties onwards. (Lord Bulter, one of the luminaries of the Tories was a classmate of Fakhruddin Ali Ahmed). Once Ahmed became member of the Indian National Congress he steadfastly adhered to it though his co-religionists in the Muslim League tried to persuade him to join the latter. As a Congressman, Ahmed Saheb actively participated in the freedom movement. To begin with, he offered personal satyagraha on December 14, 1940 for which he was imprisoned for a year under Section 5 of the DIR. Again, in the 'Quit India Movement' he was arrested on August 9, 1942 while he was returning after attending the historic session of the AICC meeting held at Mumbai and detained as a security prisoner for three and a half years until April 1945.

In the Congress organization he occupied many positions of duties. He remained a member of the Assam Pradesh Congress Committee since 1936 except for a small break. He held the membership of the AICC from

1947 until 1974. He was elected to the Assam Assembly for the first time in 1935 and became the Minister of Finance, Revenue and Labour in the Congress Coalition Ministry formed by the late Gopinath Bardoloi on September 19, 1938. In the first spell of his Ministerial office Ali Ahmed proved his acumen and capability in administrative sphere.

His initiative in introducing the Assam Agricultural Income Tax Bill, the first of its kind in India, that levied taxes on tea garden lands in the State and his pro-labour policy in the labour strike in the British-owned Assam Oil Company Ltd. At Digboi irked the European planters and their henchmen who considered that the measures of the Congress Coalition Government were radical and, therefore, constituted a danger signal to the interests of the British commercial community. But Ali Ahmed didn't heed to such resistance and went ahead with the measures which brought him and the Bardoloi Ministry a good deal of well liked applause. Nevertheless, the Bardoloi Ministry had to resign on November 16, 1939 on the war efforts issue, but that Fakhruddin Ali Ahmed was an able administrator was founded.

After Independence he was elected on Congress ticket to the Assam Assembly on two terms (1957-1962) and (1962-1967). Earlier, he was elected to the Rajya Sabha (1952-1953) and after that became Advocate-General of the Government of Assam. Although Ali Ahmed occupied a senior position in the Chaliha Ministry from 1957 he was asked by Jawaharlal Nehru to join his Cabinet at the Centre in January 1966. He was elected to the Lok Sabha from the Barpeta constituency in 1971. In the Central Cabinet he was given influential portfolios relating to Food and Agriculture, Cooperation, Education, Industrial Development and Company Laws. His induction to the Central Cabinet was possibly because of his close link with, and loyalty to the Nehru family as well as for his acumen in administration.

In the Congress hierarchy Ali Ahmed enjoyed an enviable position being a member of the Congress Working Committee for many years. He was elected to the biggest post of the land - the Presidentship of the Indian Republic on August 29, 1974, but his tenure in the office was cut short (1977) by his sudden demise due to a coronary failure which he suffered on his come back from a tour of the South-East Asian countries only a day before.

Suave and sober, Ali Ahmed seldom permitted anger and prejudice to get better of him, at the same time, he didn't compromise with unprincipled issues. These traits of his character were evidently the key to his success in the public life and enabled him to acquire a respectable position in the society.

Although politics was Ali Ahmed's forte, his deep interest in sports and other extramural activities was famous. Himself a tennis player and golfer, he was elected President of the Assam Football Association and the Assam Cricket Association for many terms; he was also the Vice-President of the Assam Sports Council. In April, 1967, he was elected President of the All India Cricket Association in addition to being a member of the Delhi Golf Club and the Delhi Gymkhana Club since 1961. His love for music and finer arts was no less; he was deeply interested in poetical works of Ghalib. His travels in the USSR, the USA, the UK, Japan, Malaysia and a lot of Arab countries as a Minister and afterwards as the President of India broadened his urbane outlook that endeared him to all sections of the people, irrespective of caste, creed and avocation. Elegantly dressed he was always courteous but firm in what he believed to be just and fair and presented himself as a Moghul, as it were, which quality he possibly inherited from his maternal side.

Ali Ahmed died on February 11, 1977, in the Rashtrapati Bhavan, Delhi, India.

5. Khaleda Zia

Khaleda Zia was born on August 15, 1945, in Dinajpur District of Bangladesh. She was the Prime Minister of Bangladesh, the first woman in the country's history to hold that position, and then again from 2001 to 2006. She is the widow of assassinated President of Bangladesh Ziaur Rahman, and leads his old party, the Bangladesh Nationalist Party.

After 35 years of independence of Bangladesh she has ruled the country for about 10 years (longest period). She has been elected to five separate parliamentary constituencies in the general elections of 1991, 1996, and 2001, a feat unachieved by any other politician in Bangladeshi history. In 2006, Forbes ranked Khaleda Zia at number 14 in its list of the 100 Most Powerful Women in the world.

Khaleda Zia was born to Iskandar Majumder and Taiyaba Majumder. The family originally hails from Feni, a South-Eastern district of the country. She studied in Dinajpur Government Girls, High School and later in Surendranath College. In 1960, she married Ziaur Rahman.

Her husband later became Chief of the Armed Forces and subsequently assumed power as Chief Martial Law Administrator following a series of military coups; he attempted to move toward a civilian administration by forming the Bangladesh Nationalist Party and becoming democratically elected as President.

Until the assassination of her husband, President Ziaur Rahman, in an abortive military coup in Chittagong on May 30, 1981, Khaleda Zia had taken little interest in either politics or public life. Even when her husband assumed power after the political changes in 1975, she remained a shy and withdrawn housewife spending most of her time raising her two sons.

After the assassination of President Ziaur Rahman, Vice-President Justice Abdus Sattar took over as the acting President and also as Chairman of the BNP. Army Chief of Staff General Hossain Muhammad Ershad overthrew Justice Sattar on March 24, 1982.

In March 1983, Justice Sattar appointed Khaleda Zia as vice-chairman of the BNP. On February 1984, she became the chairperson as Justice Sattar retired from politics. On August 10, 1984 the party elected her the chairperson.

Under the leadership of Begum Zia, BNP formed a 7-party alliance in 1983 and launched a relentless struggle against the autocratic regime of General Ershad. During the 9-year-long struggle against Ershad, Begum Zia did not compromise with his autocratic and illegitimate government. For her strict adherence to the principles, the government restricted her movements by using prohibitive laws. She was detained seven times in eight years. But undaunted, Begum Zia continued to provide leadership in the movement for ousting Ershad. Like Zia before him, Ershad attempted to give his rule a civilian and democratic face, but Khaleda Zia boycotted all elections during his rule. Khaleda was detained seven times during almost nine years of autocratic rule under President Ershad before his resignation on 6 December, 1990.

In the face of a mass upsurge spearheaded by alliances led by Begum Zia and Sheikh Hasina, Ershad at last handed over power to a neutral caretaker government on 6 December, 1990. In the parliamentary elections held under this government on February 27, 1991, Bangladesh Nationalist Party emerged victorious as a single majority party. Begum Zia contested from five constituencies in three consecutive parliamentary elections and won in all seats. This, of course, is a unique feat in the history of elections in the country.

With a unanimous vote cutting across all political lines, the BNP-led government restored the parliamentary system through the 12th amendment to the Constitution in 1991. A neutral caretaker government oversaw elections on February 27, 1991 that were broadly considered to be free, fair and truly democratic. Khaleda Zia became Bangladesh's first female Prime Minister with the support of the majority of the members of the parliament.

While in power, Begum Zia's government made considerable progress in the education sector, including introduction of free and compulsory primary education, tuition-free education for girls up to class ten, stipend for female students and the Food for Education programme. It also goes to the credit of her government that during this period, the tree plantation had become a nationwide social movement. Further, it was in this period, Khaleda Zia played a commendable role in revitalising the South Asian Association for Regional Cooperation. It also increased the age limit for entry into the civil service from 27 years to 30 years and made highest budgetary allocation in the education sector.

She became Prime Minister for the second consecutive term after the BNP had a landslide victory in February 15, 1996 general election to the sixth Jatiya Sangsad. The election was, however, boycotted by all other major parties who were demanding that the elections be held under a neutral caretaker government, following allegations of rigging in a by-election held in 1994. Turnout was estimated at around 25%, though the government at the time claimed it to be much higher. The short-lived parliament hastily introduced the Caretaker Government through 13th amendment to the Constitution, and then was dissolved to pave the way for the parliamentary elections. In the June 12, 1996 polls, BNP lost to Sheikh Hasina's Awami League but emerged as the largest opposition party in the country's parliamentary history with 116 seats.

Aiming to return to power, the BNP formed a four-party alliance on January 6, 1999 with its former political foe the Jatiya Party, and the Islamic party of Jamaat-e-Islami Bangladesh and the Islami Oikya Jot and launched several agitation programmes against the ruling Awami League.

The four-party alliance then participated in the October 1, 2001 general elections and won the election with a two-third majority of seats in parliament and 46% of the vote (compared to the principal opposition party's 40%) and Khaleda Zia was once again sworn in as the Prime Minister of Bangladesh.

On October 27, 2006, Khaleda Zia's term in office ended. The following day rioting broke out on the streets of central Dhaka following uncertainty over who would succeed her as Chief Advisor (Chief of Caretaker Government). On the same day evening, a presidential statement declared that former Supreme Court chief justice K.M. Hasan (who had been due to take over as Chief Advisor) would not be assuming the role due to ill health. Subsequently, Iajuddin Ahmed, the current president, assumed power as Chief Advisor on October 29.

Presently she is residing in Dhaka, Bangladesh. She has two sons. Her hobbies include reading, listening to music and gardening.

6. MUHAMMAD ZIA-UL-HAQ

General Muhammad Zia-ul-Haq was born on August 12, 1924, in city of Jalandhar, Punjab, India. He was the president and military ruler of Pakistan from July 1977 to his demise in August 1988. Appointed Chief of Army Staff in 1976, General Zia-ul-Haq came to power after he overthrew ruling Prime Minister Zulfikar Ali Bhutto in a military coup d'état on July 5, 1977 and became the state's third ruler to impose martial law. The coup itself was largely bloodless; nevertheless, he afterward had Bhutto executed.

Zia at first ruled for a year as CMLA (Chief Martial Law Administrator), and afterward assumed the post of President of Pakistan in September 1978. During his tenure, he advanced the Islamization of Pakistan and carried out economic reform. The economy benefited from the influx of money from the West to backup the mujahedin fighting the Soviet invasion of Afghanistan. To shore up the increasingly tenuous control of the central government over the tribal states, he appointed martial law administrators as governors of Balochistan and the tribal areas with wide powers, along with the abridgement of civil liberties.

Zia was born as the second child of an Arain, Muhammad Akbar, who worked in the GHQ in Delhi and Simla pre-partition. He married Shafiq Jahan and had five children. His two sons went into politics. He finished his initial education in Simla and then at St. Stephen's College, Delhi.

He was commissioned in the British Indian Army in a cavalry regiment in 1943 and served during World War II. After Pakistan acquired its independence, Zia became member of the newly formed Pakistani Army as a major. He trained in the United States in 1962–1964 at the US Army Command and General Staff College Fort Leavenworth, Kansas. During the Indo-Pakistani War of 1965, Zia was a tank commander. He was stationed in Jordan from 1967 to 1970, helping in the training of Jordanian soldiers, and also leading the training mission into battle during the Black September in Jordan operations, a strategy that proved crucial to King Hussein's staying in power. He was appointed as Corps Commander of Multan in 1975.

On 1 March, 1976, Prime Minister Zulfikar Ali Bhutto appointed Zia-ul-Haq Chief of Army Staff, despite a number of more senior officers, most likely because Zia was from the Arain tribe, Bhutto was from the Rajput Clan and is culturally greatly respected by lower tribes. At the time of his nominating the heir to the outgoing chief General Tikka Khan, the Lieutenant Generals in order of seniority were, Muhammad Sharif, Muhammad Akbar Khan, Aftab Ahmed Khan, Azmat Baksh Awan, Agha Ali Ibrahim Akram, Abdul Majeed Malik, Ghulam Jilani Khan, and Muhammad Zia-ul-Haq. But, Bhutto chose the most junior, superseding seven more senior generals. Nevertheless, the senior most at that time, Lieutenant General Muhammad Sharif, although promoted to General, was made the Chairman Joint Chiefs of Staff, a constitutional post akin to President Fazal Ilahi Chaudhry.

In the absence of a Parliament, General Zia decided to set up an optional system. He introduced Majlis-e-Shoora in 1980. Most of the members of the Shoora were intellectuals, scholars, ulema, journalists, economists, "lotas" (technical meaning floor crossers, but common name for opportunist politicians in Pakistani political parlance) and professionals belonging to various fields of life. The Shoora was to act as a board of advisors to the President. All 284 members of the Shoora were to be nominated by the President.

General Zia finally decided to hold elections in the country. But before handing over the power to the public spokespersons, he decided to secure his position as the head of state. A referendum was held in December 1984, and the option was to elect or reject the General as the future President. The question asked in the referendum was whether the people of Pakistan wanted Muslim Sharia law imposed in the country. As per the official result, more than 95% of the votes were cast in favour of Zia-ul-Haq, thus he was elected as President for the next five years. Nevertheless, they were marred by allegations of widespread irregularities and technical violations of the laws and ethics of democratic elections.

General Zia-ul-Haq expired in a plane crash on August 17, 1988. After witnessing a tank parade in Bahawalpur, Zia had left the small town in Punjab state by C-130 Hercules aircraft. The aircraft nosedived and exploded on impact, killing General Zia and many other senior army generals, and also American Ambassador to Pakistan Arnold Raphel and General Herbert M. Wassom. Zia had ruled Pakistan for 11 years with iron hands.

7. MUHAMMAD ALI JINNAH

Jinnah was born in Karachi, Pakistan on December 25, 1876. He was a Pakistani politician and leader of the All India Muslim League who established Pakistan and served as its first Governor-General. He is formally known in Pakistan as Quaid-e-Azam and Baba-e-Qaum (Father of the Nation). His birthday is a national holiday in Pakistan.

His father, Jinnahbhai was a prosperous Gujarati merchant who had moved to Sindh from Kathiawar, Gujarat, shortly before Jinnah's birth. His grandfather was Poonja Meghji, a Bhatia from Paneli village in Gondal state in Kathiawar. The family had moved there from Sahiwal close to Multan. Some sources speculated that the Jinnah's forefathers were Hindu Rajputs from Sahiwal, Punjab that converted to Islam.

The firstborn Jinnah was shortly joined by six siblings, brothers Ahmad Ali, Bunde Ali, and Rahmat Ali, and sisters Maryam, Fatima and Shireen. Jinnah's family belonged to the Ismaili Khoja branch of Shi'a Islam, although Jinnah afterward converted to Twelver Shi'a Islam. Their mother tongue was Gujarati, nevertheless, in time they also came to speak Kutchi, Sindhi, Urdu and English.

The young Jinnah, a restless student, studied at many schools: at the Sindh-Madrasa-tul-Islam in Karachi; shortly at the Gokal Das Tej Primary School in Mumbai; and finally at the Christian Missionary Society High School in Karachi, where, at age sixteen, he passed the matriculation examination of the University of Mumbai.

The same year, 1892, Jinnah was offered an apprenticeship at the London office of Graham's Shipping and Trading Company, a business that had extensive dealings with Jinnahbhai Poonja's firm in Karachi. Nevertheless, before he went to England, he married, at his mother's urging, a distant cousin, Emibai Jinnah|Emibai, who was two years his junior. The marriage was not to last long: a couple of months afterward,

Emibai expired. Afterward, during his sojourn in England, his mother too would pass away. In London, Jinnah shortly left the apprenticeship to study law instead, by joining Lincoln's Inn. The welcome board of the Lincoln's Inn had the names of the world's all time top ten magistrates. This list was lead by the name of Muhammad, which was the sole reason of Jinnah's joining of Lincoln's Inn.

In three years, at age 19, he became the youngest Indian to be invited to the bar in England. Around this time, Jinnah also became interested in politics. An admirer of the Indian political leaders Dadabhai Naoroji and Sir Pherozeshah Mehta, he worked, with other Indian students, on the former's successful campaign for a seat in the British Parliament. Though, by now, Jinnah had developed largely constitutionalist opinions on Indian self-government, he however condemned both the arrogance of British officers in India and the discrimination practised by them against Indians.

During the final period of his stay in England, Jinnah came under considerable pressure when his father's business was ruined. Settling in Mumbai, he became a flourishing attorney—gaining particular fame for his expert handling of the "Caucus Case". Jinnah made a house in Malabar Hill, afterward acknowledged as Jinnah House. His status as an expert attorney motivated Indian leader Bal Gangadhar Tilak to hire him as defence counsel for his sedition trial in 1905. Jinnah argued that it was not sedition for an Indian to demand freedom and self-government in his own country, but Tilak got a strict term of imprisonment test.

In 1896, Jinnah became member of the Indian National Congress, which was the largest Indian political organization. Like most of the Congress at the time, Jinnah didn't favour outright independence, considering British influences on education, law, culture and industry as beneficial to India. Jinnah became a member on the sixty-member Imperial Legislative Council.

The council had no real power or authority, and included a large number of un-elected pro-Raj loyalists and Europeans. However, Jinnah was instrumental in the passing of the Child Marriages Restraint Act, the legitimization of the Islamic waqf (religious endowments) and was appointed to the Sandhurst committee, which helped make the Indian Military Academy at Dehra Dun. During World War I, Jinnah joined other Indian moderates in supporting the British war effort, hoping that Indians would be rewarded with political freedom.

Jinnah had at first avoided joining the All India Muslim League, established in 1906, regarding it as too Islamic oriented. Finally, he became member of the league in 1913 and became the president at the 1916 session in Lucknow. Jinnah was the architect of the 1916 Lucknow Pact between the Congress and the League, bringing them together on most issues regarding self-government and presenting a united front to the British. Jinnah also played an influential role in the establishing of the All India Home Rule League in 1916.

Together with political leaders Annie Besant and Tilak, Jinnah demanded "home rule" for India—the status of a self-governing dominion in the Empire similar to Canada, New Zealand and Australia. He headed the League's Bombay Presidency chapter. In 1918, Jinnah married his second wife Rattanbai Petit ("Ruttie"), twenty-four years his junior. She was the fashionable young daughter of his own friend Sir Dinshaw Petit, of an elite Parsi family of Mumbai.

Jinnah's trouble with the Congress began with the ascent of Mohandas Gandhi in 1918, who espoused non-violent civil disobedience and Hindu values as the best means to obtain Swaraj (independence, or self-rule) for all South Asians. Jinnah differed, saying that only constitutional fight could lead to independence. Unlike most Congress leaders, Gandhi didn't wear western-style clothes, did his best to use an Indian language instead of English, and was deeply (Hindu) religious. Gandhi's Hindu style of leadership acquired great fame with the Indian people.

At the Round Table Conferences in London, Jinnah was disillusioned by the collapse of talks. Frustrated with the disunity of the Muslim League, he decided to quit politics and practice law in England.

Jinnah would get personal care and support through out his afterward life from his sister Fatima Jinnah, who lived and travelled with him as well as became a close consultant. She helped raise his daughter, who was educated in England and India. Jinnah afterward became estranged from his daughter, Dina Jinnah, after she decided to marry Parsi-born Christian businessman, Neville Wadia. Jinnah continued to correspond cordially with his daughter, but their personal relationship was strained. Dina continued to live in India with her family.

Outstanding Islamic leaders like the Aga Khan, Choudhary Rahmat Ali and Sir Muhammad Iqbal made efforts to convince Jinnah to come back to India and take charge of a now-reunited Muslim League. In 1934, Jinnah came back and began to re-organize the party, being closely assisted by Liaquat Ali Khan, who would act as his right-hand man. In the 1937 elections, the League emerged as a competent party, capturing a substantial number of seats under the Islamic electorate, but lost in the Islamic-majority Punjab, Sindh and the Northwest Frontier Province. Jinnah offered an alliance with the Congress - both bodies would face the British together, but the Congress had to share power, accept separate electorates and the League as the spokesperson of India's Muslims.

The latter two terms were unacceptable to the Congress, which had its own national Islamic leaders and membership and adhered to secularism. Even as Jinnah held talks with Congress president Rajendra Prasad, Congress leaders suspected that Jinnah would use his position as a lever for exaggerated demands and obstruct government, and demanded that the League merge with the Congress. The talks failed, and while Jinnah declared the resignation of all Congressmen from provincial and central offices in 1938 as a "Day of Deliverance" from Hindu domination, some historians assert that he remained hopeful for an agreement.

Muhammad Ali Jinnah established Dawn in 1941, a prominent newspaper that assisted him propagate the League's point of opinions. During the mission of British minister Stafford Cripps, Jinnah demanded parity between the number of Congress and League ministers, the League's exclusive right to appoint Muslims and a right for Islamic-majority provinces to secede, leading to the collapse of talks.

Jinnah supported the British effort in World War II, and opposed the Quit India movement. During this period, the League formed provincial governments and got into the central government. The League's influence increased in the Punjab after the demise of Unionist leader Sikander Hyat Khan in 1942. Gandhi held talks fourteen times with Jinnah in Mumbai in 1944, about a united front—while talks failed, Gandhi's overtures to Jinnah increased the latter's standing with Muslims.

In the 1946 elections for the Constituent Assembly of India, the Congress won most of the elected seats and Hindu electorate seats, while the League won a large majority of Islamic electorate seats. The 1946 British Cabinet Mission to India released a plan on May 16, calling for a united Indian state comprising noticeably autonomous states, and demanded "groups" of states formed on the basis of religion. A second plan brought out on June 16, demanded the separation of South Asia along religious lines, with princely states to choose between accession to the dominion of their choice or independence. The Congress, fearing India's fragmentation, criticised the May 16 proposal and rejected the June 16 plan. Jinnah gave the League's consent to both plans, knowing that power would go only to the party that had supported a plan. After much debate and against Gandhi's advice that both plans were divisive, the Congress agreed to the May 16 plan while condemning the grouping principle. Jinnah decried this acceptance as "dishonesty", blamed the British negotiators of "treachery", and withdrew the League's consent of both plans. The League boycotted the assembly, leaving the Congress in charge of the government but denying its legitimacy in the eyes of a lot of Muslims.

Jinnah issued a call for all Muslims to launch "Direct Action" on August 16 to "achieve Pakistan". The League got into the provisional government, but Jinnah refrained from accepting office for himself. This was accredited as a prominant victory for Jinnah, as the League got into government having rejected both plans, and was permitted to appoint an equal number of ministers despite being the minority party.

The coalition was unable to work, ensuing in a rising feeling inside the Congress that independency of Pakistan was the only way of avoiding political chaos and possible civil war. The Congress agreed to the division of Punjab and Bengal along religious lines in late 1946. The new viceroy Lord Mountbatten and Indian civil servant V. P. Menon proposed a plan that would create an Islamic dominion in West Punjab, East Bengal, Baluchistan and Sindh. After heated and emotional debate, the Congress approved the plan. The North-West Frontier Province voted to join Pakistan in a referendum in July 1947. Jinnah asserted in a speech in Lahore on October 30, 1947 that the League had agreed to independency of Pakistan because "the consequences of any other option would have been too disastrous to imagine."

Jinnah became the first Governor-General of Pakistan and president of its constituent assembly. Inaugurating the assembly on August 11, 1947, Jinnah spoke of an inclusive and pluralist democracy promising equal rights for all citizens regardless of religion, caste or creed.

Through the 1940s, Jinnah suffered from tuberculosis; only his sister and a couple of others close to him were aware of his circumstance. In 1948, Jinnah's health began to falter, hindered further by the serious workload that had fallen upon him following Pakistan's independency from British Rule.

He expired on September 11, 1948 in Balochistan, Pakistan from a combination of tuberculosis and lung cancer.

8. SHEIKH ABDULLAH

Sheikh Muhammad Abdullah was born on December 5, 1905, in Kashmir, India. He was the leader of the National Conference, Kashmir's largest political party, and amongst the most influential political figures in the modern history of Jammu and Kashmir. In 1933, he married Akbar Jahan, the daughter of Michael Harry Nedous, the eldest son of the European proprietor of a chain of hotels in India along with Nedous Hotel in Srinagar, and his Kashmiri wife Mirjan. He agitated against the rule of the Maharaja Hari Singh, and urged self-rule for Kashmir. He was the Prime Minister of Jammu and Kashmir State shortly after its debatable provisional accession to India in 1947, and was afterward jailed and exiled. He again became the Chief Minister of the State after the 1974 Indira-Sheikh accord.

His mother was keen that her children should get proper education and so as a child he was first admitted to a conventional school or Maktab where he studied the recitation of the Quran and some basic Persian texts like Gulistan, Bostan, Pandnama, etc. Then in 1911, he was accepted to a primary school where he studied for about two years. His elder step brothers then stopped his further education and he was first set to work in the family workshop embroidering shawls and afterward asked to sit on a grocer's shop as a sales boy. Nevertheless, their family barber Muhammad Ramzan persisted upon his uncle to send him back to school. He had to walk the distance of ten miles to school and back on foot but in his own words, the joy of being permitted to obtain a school education made it seem a light work.

He passed his Matriculation examination from Punjab University in 1922. After Matriculation, he received admission in Sri Partap College, the major college of Kashmir. Because of extreme poverty he had to walk the distance of about fifteen miles from Soura to S.P.College and back, and so developed Cardiomegaly (possibly an early sign of beriberi brought about by malnutrition and severe exercise). He was admitted to the Mission Hospital where under the treatment of the renowned Neve brothers he recovered completely. His elder brother Sheikh Maqbool was moved by his sickness and agreed to pay for his stay in the college hostel from where he passed his intermediate (F.Sc.) examination.

At that time the Dogra rulers discriminated against Kashmiri Islamic students and so his application for nomination for getting trained in medicine was summarily rejected as of the twenty two students who were granted a nomination, twenty one were Hindus. The Principal of Prince of Wales College, Jammu also behaved rudely with him and refused his application for admission to the B.Sc. degree course, as he spoke of the right to education of persons belonging to the Islamic community. Finally, he managed to obtain admission in Islamiya College, Lahore from where he finished his B.Sc. Degree. After finishing his graduation, he again applied to the State Government for a scholarship for pursuing higher studies but was not successful. So, marshalling his own resources, he received admission to the M.Sc. Chemistry course in Aligarh Muslim University and received Masters degree in Chemistry on April 12, 1930. He was the first Kashmiri Islamic to have received Masters degree in Chemistry and so awash with hope, he again applied to the State Government for grant of scholarship for pursuing Doctoral course in Chemistry in England. His application was refused on the feeble ground that he was more than twenty-four years of age in April, 1930.

As per Sheikh Abdullah, "these early experiences convinced him that Kashmiri Muslims had as little hope of obtaining justice from the feudal Dogra ruler as of obtaining milk by squeezing a stone."

As a student at Aligarh Muslim University, he came in contact with and was inspired by persons with broad-minded and liberal ideas. He became convinced that the feudal system was responsible for the miseries of the Kashmiris and like all liberal nations of the world Kashmir, too, should have a democratically elected government.

Sheikh Abdullah and his contemporaries were greatly inspired by the lectures of a Kashmiri polymath and attorney Maulvi Abdullah. Maulvi Abdullah's son Maulvi Abdul Rahim, Sheikh Abdullah and Ghulam Nabi Gilkar were the first three educated Kashmiri youth to be arrested during the public agitation of 1931.

Kashmir's first Political Party, the Islamic Conference with Sheikh Abdullah as President, Chaudhary Ghulam Abbas as General Secretary and Molvi Abdul Rahim as Secretary was formed on October 16, 1932. In his presidential address, Sheikh Abdullah categorically stated that the Islamic Conference had come into existence to ask for the rights of all opressed sections of the society and not Muslims alone. It was not a communal party and would fight for the rights of the oppressed, whether Hindu, Islamic, or Sikh, with the same fervour. He reasserted that the resistance of Kashmiris was not a communal resistance.

In March 1933, the Islamic Conference constituted a committee which included Molvi Abdullah and nine other members for the purpose of establishing contacts with non-Islamic parties and exploring the possibility of forming a joint organization. As per Sheikh Abdullah, this effort was not successful because of the unfavourable welcome of the idea by the non-Islamic parties.

Sheikh Abdullah was introduced to Jawaharlal Nehru in 1937, and as he, too, was a leader of the Indian National Congress, calling for similar rights for people of British India and had formed the All India States People's Conference for supporting the people of Princely States in their fight for a representative government, the two became friends and political allies.

He introduced a motion in the working committee of the Islamic Conference for changing its name to National Conference on June 24, 1938 to allow people from all communities to join the resistance against the autocratic rule of the Maharaja. In the meantime, he together with his broad-minded liberal friends, several of whom were non Muslims like Kashyap Bandhu, Jia Lal Kilam, Prem Nath Bazaz and Sardar Budh Singh drafted the National Demands, the forerunner of the renowned Naya Kashmir (New Kashmir) Manifesto (which was a charter of demands for granting a democratic constitution committed to the welfare of the common people of Kashmir).

He presented these demands to the Maharajah in a speech on August 28, 1938. The Maharajah naturally was not eager to accept these demands and so he together with a lot of his companions was arrested for defying prohibitory orders and sentenced to six months detention and a fine. His arrest provoked a public agitation in which volunteers named Dictators (so named because they had the authority to defy laws that was forbidden for normal law abiding party members) courted arrest. This agitation was cancelled on the appeal of Mahatama Gandhi. He was released after serving his sentence on February 24, 1939 and accorded a grand welcome by the people of Srinagar on his come back. Speeches were made at the reception stressing the significance of unity amongst Hindus, Muslims and Sikhs. Consequently, the motion for changing the name of Islamic Conference to National Conference was ratified with an overwhelming majority by the General Council of the Islamic Conference on June 11, 1939 and from that date Islamic Conference became National Conference.

In May 1946, Sheikh Abdullah started the Quit Kashmir agitation against the Maharajah and was arrested and sentenced to three years detention, but was released only sixteen months afterward on September 29, 1947.

Hari Singh appealed to Lord Mountbatten, the Governor-General of India, for Indian military aid. In his Accession Offer dated October 26, 1947, which accompanied The Instrument of Accession duly signed by him, the Maharaja wrote, "I may also inform your Excellency's Government that it is my intention at once to set up a provisional Government and ask Shaikh Abdullah to carry the duties in this emergency with my Prime Minister."

Lord Mountbatten agreed to the accession after a meeting of the Defence Committee on October 26, 1947. In his Aide Memoire dated February 25, 1948 to the Indian delegation to the UN Security Council Lord Mountbatten wrote that, "Agreement was reached at this meeting that the accession should be accepted only subject to the proviso that a plebiscite should be held in Kashmir when the law and order situation permitted this and that a responsible government should be at once established".

In his letter of acceptation of the Offer of Accession to the Maharaja Lord Mountbatten wrote, "...My Government and I note with satisfaction that your Highness has decided to invite Sheikh Abdullah to form a Provisional Government to work with your Prime Minister." The support of Mahatma Gandhi and Jawaharlal Nehru the Prime Minister of India, was a key factor in getting Sheikh Abdullah appointed as Head of the emergency administration by the Maharaja.

As a consequence, Sheikh Abdullah was appointed head of an emergency administration by an order issued by the Maharaja which was undated except for the mention October, 1947 in place of the date. He took charge as Head of the Emergency Administration on October 30, 1947. After accepting the charge of the Head of the emergency administration, he addressing his first meeting with the government officers said, "Pakistan is not our enemy and we have the same respect for Mr. Jinnah that we had previously. We want the Kashmir issue to be settled by Dialogue and if for this purpose I have to go to Karachi to meet Mr. Jinnah I am willing to go there".

He raised a force of local Kashmiri volunteers to patrol Srinagar and take control of administration after the flight of the Maharaja together with his family and Prime Minister Meher Chand Mahajan to Jammu even before the Indian troops had landed. This group of volunteers would serve as the nucleus for the later establishment of Jammu and Kashmir Militia. This Sheikh Abdullah hoped would take over the protection of Kashmir after the Indian army was withdrawn. This was articulated in his letter to Sardar Patel dated October 7, 1948 in which he wrote, "With the taking over of the State forces by the Indian Government, it was agreed that steps would be taken to reorganize and rebuild our army so that when the present emergency is over and the Indian forces are withdrawn, the State will be left with a proper organized army of its own to fall back upon."

The U. N. Security Council brokered a ceasefire amongst the warring parties (which came into effect before midnight January 1, 1949) having passed a motion calling for settlement of the question of Kashmir's accession to India or Pakistan by a plebiscite to be held under the auspices of the United Nations (Resolution 47 dated April 21, 1948 and UNCIP resolution dated August 13, 1948).

He assumed the position of Chief Minister of Jammu and Kashmir. Unfortunately, the Central Government and the ruling Congress Party withdrew its support so that the State Assembly had to be dissolved and mid-term elections declared.

The National Conference won an overwhelming majority in the subsequent elections and re-elected Sheikh Abdullah as Chief Minister. He remained as Chief Minister until his demise in 1982. During his short tenure as Chief Minister, he tried to develop close ties between the three regions of the State explicitly Jammu, Kashmir and Ladakh. He also attempted to encourage infrastructural growth in the State and constructed the esteemed Sheri Kashmir Institute of Medical Sciences and a Convention Centre (SKICC) constructed to global standards so as to encourage Medical and Business tourism in the valley.

He expired on September 8, 1982, in Srinagar, India

9. SIR SYED AHMED KHAN

Sir Syed Ahmed Khan Bahadur was born on October 17, 1817, in Delhi, India. He is commonly acknowledged as Sir Syed, and was an Indian educator and politician, and a Muslim reformer and modernist. Sir Syed pioneered modern education for the Islamic community in India by founding the Muhammadan Anglo-Oriental College, which afterward developed into the Aligarh Muslim University. His work gave rise to a new generation of Islamic intellectuals and politicians who compiled the Aligarh movement to secure the political future of Muslims in India.

Born into Mughal nobility, Sir Syed earned a status as a distinguished scholar while functioning as a jurist for the British East India Company. During the Indian Rebellion of 1857, he remained loyal to the British and was noted for his actions in saving European lives. After the rebellion, he wrote the booklet Asbab-e-Bhaghawath-e-Hind (The Causes of the Indian Mutiny) — a daring critique, at the time, of British policies that he blamed for causing the revolt. Believing that the future of Muslims was threatened by the rigidity of their orthodox outlook, Sir Syed began promoting Western-style scientific education by founding modern schools and journals and organising Islamic intellectuals. Towards this goal, Sir Syed established the Muhammadan Anglo-Oriental College in 1875 with the aim of promoting social and economic growth of Indian Muslims.

His family is said to have migrated from Herat (now in Afghanistan) in the time of emperor Akbar, though by other explanations his family descended from Arabia. Several generations of his family had since been highly connected with the Mughal administration. His maternal grandfather Khwaja Fariduddin served as wazir in the court of Akbar Shah II.

His paternal grandfather Syed Hadi held a mansab, a high-ranking administrative position and honorary name of Jawwad Ali Khan in the court of Alamgir II. Sir Syed's father Mir Muhammad Muttaqi was personally close to Akbar Shah II and served as his individual adviser. Nevertheless, Sir Syed was born at a time when rebellious governors, regional insurrections and the British colonialism had diminished the extent and power of the Mughal state, reducing its monarch to a figurehead status.

With his elder brother Syed Muhammad Khan, Sir Syed was raised in a large house in a wealthy region of the city. They were raised in strict accordance with Mughal noble customs and exposed to politics. Their mother Azis-un-Nisa played a formative role in Sir Syed's life, raising him with rigid discipline with a strong emphasis on education. Sir Syed was taught to read and understand the Quran by a female tutor, which was unconventional at the time. He received an education conventional to Islamic nobility in Delhi. Under the charge of Maulvi Hamiduddin, Sir Syed was trained in Persian, Arabic, Urdu and religious subjects. He studied the works of Islamic scholars and authors such as Sahbai, Rumi and Ghalib. Other tutors instructed him in mathematics, astronomy and Muslim jurisprudence. Sir Syed was also adept at swimming, wrestling and other sports. He took an active part in the Mughal court's cultural activities. His elder brother established the city's first printing press in the Urdu language together with the journal Sayyad-ul-Akbar. Sir Syed pursued the study of medicine for many years, but didn't complete the prescribed course of study. Till the demise of his father in 1838, Sir Syed had dwelt a life customary for an affluent young Islamic noble. Upon his father's demise, he inherited the titles of his grandfather and father and was granted the title of Arif Jung by the emperor Bahadur Shah Zafar. Financial difficulties put an end to Sir Syed's formal education, though he continued to study in private, employing books on a variety of subjects.

Sir Syed assumed editorship of his brother's journal and refused proposals of employment from the Mughal court. Having acknowledged the steady decline in Mughal political power, Sir Syed got into the British East India Company's civil service. He was appointed serestadar at the courts of law in Agra, responsible for record-holding and managing court affairs. In 1840, he was promoted to the title of munshi.

While carrying on to work as a jurist, Sir Syed began focusing on writing on various subjects, mostly in Urdu. His career as a writer began when he published a series of treatises in Urdu on religious subjects in 1842. He published the book Athar Assanadid (Great Monuments) documenting antiquities of Delhi dating from the medieval era. This work earned him the status of a cultured scholar. In 1842, he finished the Jila-ul-Qulub bi Zikr il Mahbub and the Tuhfa-i-Hasan, together with the Tahsil fi jar-i-Saqil in 1844. These works focused on religious and cultural subjects. In 1852, he published the two works Namiqa dar bayan masala tasawwur-i-Shaikh and Silsilat ul-Mulk. He brought out the second edition of Athar Assanadid in 1854. He also wrote a commentary on the Bible — the first by a Muslim — in which he argued that Islam was the closest religion to Christianity, with a common lineage from Abrahamic religions.

Acquainted with high-ranking British officials, Sir Syed received close knowledge about British colonial politics during his service at the courts. At the eruption of the Indian rebellion, on May 10, 1857, Sir Syed was serving as the main assessment officer at the court in Bijnor. Northern India became the scene of the most intense fighting. The conflict had left large numbers of civilians dead. Erstwhile centres of Islamic power such as Delhi, Agra, Lucknow and Kanpur were seriously affected. Sir Syed was personally affected by the violence and the ending of the Mughal dynasty amongst several other long-standing kingdoms. Sir Syed and a lot of other Muslims took this as a defeat of Islamic society. He lost many close relatives who expired in the violence. Although he succeeded in rescuing his mother from the turmoil, she expired in Meerut, owing to the privations she had experienced.

In 1858, he was appointed to a high-ranking post at the court in Muradabad, where he began functioning on his most renowned literary work. Publishing the booklet Asbab-e-Bhaghawath-e-Hind in 1859, Sir Syed studied the causes of the revolt. In this, his most renowned work, he refused the common notion that the conspiracy was planned by Islamic elites, who were insecure at the diminishing influence of Islamic monarchs. Sir Syed blamed the British East India Company for its aggressive expansion and also the ignorance of British politicians concerning Indian culture. Nevertheless, he acquired respect for British power, which he felt would dominate India for a considerable period of time. Seeking to rehabilitate Islamic political influence, Sir Syed suggested to the British to appoint Muslims to assist in administration. His other compositions such as Loyal Muhammadans of India, Tabyin-ul-Kalam and A Series of Essays on the Life of Muhammad and Subjects Subsidiary Therein assisted to create cordial relations between the British authorities and the Islamic community.

Through the 1850s, Syed Ahmed Khan began developing a strong zeal for education. While pursuing studies of various subjects along with European jurisprudence, Sir Syed began to realise the advantages of Western-style education, which was being offered at newly-founded colleges across India. Despite being a devout Islamic, Sir Syed criticised the influence of conventional dogma and religious orthodoxy, which had made most Indian Muslims suspicious of British influences. Sir Syed began feeling increasingly concerned for the future of Islamic communities.

A scion of Mughal nobility, Sir Syed had been reared in the finest customs of Islamic elite culture and was aware of the steady decline of Islamic political power across India. The animosity between the British and Muslims before and after the rebellion (Independence War) of 1857 threatened to marginalise Islamic communities across India for several generations. Sir Syed intensified his work to encourage co-operation with British authorities, promoting loyalty to the Empire amongst Indian Muslims. Committed to functioning for the upliftment of Muslims, Sir Syed established a modern madrassa in Muradabad in 1859; this was one of the first religious schools to impart scientific education. Sir Syed also worked on social causes, helping to organize relief for the famine-struck people of the Northwest Frontier Province in 1860. He founded another modern school in Ghazipur in 1863.

Upon his shift to Aligarh in 1864, Sir Syed began functioning wholeheartedly as an educator. He established the Scientific Society of

Aligarh, the first scientific association of its kind in India. Modelling it after the Royal Society and the Royal Asiatic Society, Sir Syed assembled Islamic scholars from various parts of the country. The Society held annual conferences, disbursed funds for educational causes and regularly published a journal on scientific subjects in English and Urdu. Sir Syed felt that the socioeconomic future of Muslims was threatened by their orthodox aversions to modern science and technology. He published a lot of compositions promoting broad-minded, rational interpretations of Muslim scriptures. Nevertheless, his opinion of Islam was refused by Islamic clergy as contrary to conventional opinions on issues like jihad, polygamy and animal slaughtering.

The onset of the Hindi-Urdu dispute of 1867 saw the emergence of Sir Syed as a political leader of the Islamic community. He became a major Islamic voice opposing the adoption of Hindi as a second official language of the United Provinces (now Uttar Pradesh). Sir Syed perceived Urdu as the lingua franca of Muslims. Having been developed by Islamic rulers of India, Urdu was used as a secondary language to Persian, the official language of the Mughal court. Since the decline of the Mughal dynasty, Sir Syed encouraged the use of Urdu through his own compositions. Under Sir Syed, the Scientific Society translated Western works only into Urdu. The schools founded by Sir Syed imparted education in the Urdu medium. The demand for Hindi, led largely by Hindus, was to Sir Syed an erosion of the centuries-old Islamic cultural domination of India. Testifying before the British-appointed education commission, Sir Syed controversially exclaimed that "Urdu was the language of gentry and Hindi that of the vulgar." His remarks provoked an aggressive reaction from Hindu leaders, who unified across the nation to demand the recognition of Hindi.

The success of the Hindi movement led Sir Syed to further advocate Urdu as the symbol of Islamic heritage and as the language of all Indian Muslims. His educational and political work grew increasingly centred around and exclusively for Islamic interests. He also sought to convince the British to give Urdu extensive official use and patronage. His colleagues and proteges such as Mohsin-ul-Mulk and Maulvi Abdul Haq developed organizations such as the Urdu Defence Association and the Anjuman Taraqqi-i-Urdu, committed to the perpetuation of Urdu. Sir Syed's protegee Shibli Nomani led efforts that resulted in the adoption of Urdu as the official language of the Hyderabad State and as the medium of instruction in the Osmania University. To Muslims in northern and western India, Urdu had became an essential part of political and cultural individuality.

Nevertheless, the division over the use of Hindi or Urdu further provoked communal conflict between Muslims and Hindus in India.

On April 1, 1869, Sir Syed visited England, where he was granted the Order of the Star of India from the British government on August 6. Travelling across England, he visited its colleges and was motivated by the culture of learning founded after the Renaissance. Sir Syed came back to India in the following year determined to build a "Islamic Cambridge." Upon his come back, he organized the "Committee for the Better Diffusion and Advancement of Learning amongst Muhammadans" (Muslims) on December 26, 1870.

By 1873, the committee under Sir Syed issued offers for the construction of a college in Aligarh. He began publishing the journal Tahzib al-Akhlaq (Social Reformer) to spread awareness and knowledge on modern subjects and encourage reforms in Islamic society. Sir Syed worked to encourage reinterpretation of Islamic ideology in order to reconcile tradition with Western education. He argued in many books on Islam that the Quran rested on an appreciation of reason and natural law, making scientific inquiry influential to being a good Islamic.

Sir Syed founded a modern school in Aligarh and, obtaining support from wealthy Muslims and the British, laid the foundation stone of the Muhammadan Anglo-Oriental College on May 24, 1875. He retired from his career as a jurist the following year, concentrating entirely on evolving the college and on religious reform. Sir Syed's pioneering work got support from the British. Though strongly criticised by orthodox religious leaders hostile to modern influences, Sir Syed's new institution attracted a large student body, mostly drawn from the Islamic gentry and middle classes. The curriculum at the college involved scientific and Western subjects, and also Oriental subjects and religious education. The first chancellor was Sultan Shah Jahan Begum, an outstanding Islamic noblewoman, and Sir Syed invited an Englishman, Theodore Beck, to serve as the first college principal. The college was in the beginning affiliated with Calcutta University but was transferred to the Allahabad University in 1885. Near the turn of the 20th century, it began publishing its own magazine and founded a law school. In 1920, the college was transformed into a university.

In 1878, Sir Syed was nominated to the Viceroy's Legislative Council. He testified before the education commission to encourage the establishment of more colleges and schools across India. In the same year, Sir Syed established the Muhammadan Association to encourage political co-operation amongst Indian Muslims from various parts of the country. In 1886, he organized the All India Muhammadan Educational Conference in Aligarh, which encouraged his vision of modern education and political harmony for Muslims. His works made him the most outstanding Islamic politician in 19th century India, often influencing the attitude of Muslims on various national issues. He supported the efforts of Indian political leaders Surendranath Banerjee and Dadabhai Naoroji to obtain representation for Indians in the government and civil services. In 1883, he established the Muhammadan Civil Service Fund Association to promote and support the admission of Islamic graduates into the Indian Civil Service (ICS).

Sir Syed was nominated as a member of the Civil Service Commission in 1887 by Lord Dufferin. Syed Ahmed Khan was knighted by the British government in 1888 and in the next year he got an LL.D. honouris causa from the Edinburgh University.

Sir Syed died on March 27, 1898, in the city of Aligarh, U.P., India.

10. YAHYA KHAN

Yahya Khan was born on February 4, 1917, in the city of Chakwal, Punjab, Pakistan, into an ethnic Shia Islamic Qizilbash family of Persian descent who could trace their military links to the time of Nadir Shah.

Nadir Shah was killed in a revolution and some members of his family escaped from Iran to Northern Pakistan region. The story is that after Qizilbash family escaped bare handed the family jewels and little treasure they carried were enough to buy them villages and maintain royal life style. Qizilbash family got into military profession and produced a lot of high level government officials and generals. He attended Punjab University and finished first in his class. He then became member of the British Army, and served in World War II as an officer in the 4th Infantry Division (India). He served in Iraq, Italy, and North Africa.

Although traditionally Pashtun, Yahya was a Shia Qizilbash commissioned from Indian Military Academy Dehra Dun on July 15, 1939. An infantry officer from the 4/10 Baluch Regiment, Yahya saw action during W.W. II in North Africa where he was captured by the Axis Forces in June 1942 and interned in a prisoner of war camp in Italy from where he escaped in the third attempt.

In 1947, he was instrumental in not letting the Indian officers shift books from the renowned library of the British Indian Staff College at Quetta, where Yahya was posted as the only Islamic instructor at the time of division of India.

Yahya became a brigadier at the age of 34 and commanded the 106 Infantry Brigade, which was deployed on the ceasefire line in Kashmir in 1951-52. Afterward Yahya, as Deputy Chief of General Staff, was selected to head the army's planning board set up by Ayub to modernise the Pakistan Army in 1954-57. Yahya also performed the obligations of Chief of General Staff from 1958 to 1962 from where he moved on to command an infantry division from 1962 to 1965.

Upon the establishment of Pakistan, Khan helped set up an officer's school in Quetta, and commanded an infantry division during the Indo-Pakistani War of 1965. Instantly after the 1965 war, Major General Yahya Khan who had commanded the 7th Division in Operation Grand Slam was promoted to the rank of Lieutenant General, appointed Deputy Army Commander-in-Chief and Commander-in-Chief designate in March 1966.

Yahya energetically began reorganising the Pakistan Army in 1965. The post 1965 situation saw prominant organizational and also technical alterations in the Pakistan Army. Until 1965 it was thought that divisions could function efficiently while getting orders directly from the army's GHQ. This idea failed miserably in the 1965 war and the requirement to have intermediate corps headquarters in between the GHQ and the fighting combat divisions was acknowledged as a foremost operational necessity after the 1965 war. In 1965 war, the Pakistan Army had only one corps headquarter (i.e. the 1st Corps Headquarters).

Shortly after the war had began the, United States had enforced an embargo on military aid on both India and Pakistan. This embargo didn't affect the Indian Army but produced prominant alterations in the Pakistan Army's technical composition. US Secretary of State Dean Rusk well summed it up when he said, "Well, if you are going to fight, go ahead and fight, but we're not going to pay for it".

Pakistan now turned to China for military aid and the Chinese tank T-59 began replacing the US M-47/48 tanks as the Pakistan Army's MBT (Main Battle Tank) from 1966. 80 tanks, the first batch of T-59s, a low-grade variation of the Russian T-54/55 series were delivered to Pakistan in 1965-66. The first batch was exhibited in the Joint Services Day Parade on 23 March, 1966. The 1965 War had proved that Pakistan Army's tank infantry ratio was lopsided and more infantry was required.

Three more infantry divisions (9, 16 and 17 Divisions) largely equipped with Chinese equipment and commonly referred to by the rank and file as "The China Divisions" were raised by the starting of 1968. Two more corps headquarters i.e. 2nd Corps Headquarters (Jhelum-Ravi Corridor) and 4th Corps Headquarters (Ravi-Sutlej Corridor) were raised.

Ayub Khan was President of Pakistan for most of the 1960s, but by the end of the decade, popular resentment had boiled over against him. Pakistan had fallen into a state of disarray, and he handed over power to Yahya Khan, who instantly enforced martial law. Once Ayub handed over power to Yahya Khan on 25 March, 1969, Yahya inherited a two-decade constitutional problem of interprovincial ethnic rivalry between the Punjabi-Pashtun-Mohajir dominated West Pakistan province and the ethnically Bengali Islamic East Pakistan province. In addition, Yahya also inherited an 11 year old problem of transforming an essentially one man ruled country to a democratic country, which was the ideological basis of the anti-Ayub movement of 1968-69. Herein lies the key to Yahya's dilemma.

As an Army Chief Yahya had all the capabilities, qualifications and potential. But Yahya inherited a tremendously complex problem and was forced to perform the multiple roles of caretaker head of the country, drafter of a provisional constitution, resolving the One Unit question, satisfying the frustrations and the sensation of exploitation and discrimination successively produced in the East Wing by a series of government policies since 1948.

Yahya Khan attempted to solve Pakistan's constitutional and inter-provincial/regional rivalry problems, once he took over power from Ayub Khan in March, 1969. The tragedy of the entire affair was the fact that all actions that Yahya took, though correct in principle, were too late in timing, and served only to further intensify the political polarisation between the East and West wings. He dissolved the one unit restoring the pre-1955 states of West Pakistan.

He promised free, direct, one man one vote, fair elections on adult franchise, a basic human right which had been denied to the Pakistani people since the pre-independence 1946 elections by political inefficiency, double play and intrigue, by civilian governments, from 1947 to 1958 and by Ayub's one man rule from 1958 to 1969.

Yahya Khan expired on August 10, 1980, in Rawalpindi, Pakistan.

11. ZULFIKAR ALI BHUTTO

Zulfikar Ali Bhutto was born on January 5, 1928, in the state of Sindh, Pakistan. He was a Pakistani politician who served as the President of Pakistan from 1971 to 1973 and as Prime Minister from 1973 to 1977. He was the founder of the Pakistan Peoples Party (PPP), the largest and most important political party in Pakistan. His daughter Benazir Bhutto also served twice as prime minister; she was assassinated on December 27, 2007.

Educated at the University of California at Berkeley in the United States and University of Oxford in the United Kingdom, Bhutto was noted for his mercurial brilliance and wit. He was executed in 1979 for authorizing the murder of a political opponent. The move was done under the directives of General Muhammad Zia-ul-Haq. His followers add the honorific title Shaheed, the Urdu word for "martyr", before his name, thus: Shaheed-e-Azam Zulfikar Ali Bhutto ("The Great Martyr"). Another respectful title commonly bestowed upon him by followers is Quaid-e-Awam, or "Leader of the Masses" as he was indeed a populist statesman.

Zulfikar Ali Bhutto was born to Khursheed Begum née Lakhi Bai and Sir Shah Nawaz Bhutto of an outstanding Shia Islamic family. His father was a wealthy landlord, a zamindar, and an outstanding politician in Sindh, who enjoyed an important relationship with the officials of the British Raj. As a young boy, Bhutto moved to Worli Seaface in Mumbai to study at the Cathedral and John Connon School. During this period, he also became a student activist in the League's Pakistan Movement. Upon finishing high school, Bhutto attended Premier College, Nazamabad. In 1943, his marriage was arranged with Shireen Amir Begum. He afterward left her, nevertheless, in order to remarry. In 1947, Bhutto was admitted to the University of Southern California.

During this time, Bhutto's father, Sir Shahnawaz, played a debatable role in the affairs of the state of Junagadh (now in Gujarat). Coming to power in a palace coup as the dewan, he secured the accession of the state to Pakistan, which was ultimately negated by Indian intervention in December, 1947. In 1949, Bhutto transferred to the University of California, Berkeley, where he earned an honours degree in political science. Here he would become interested in the theories of socialism, delivering a series of lectures on the feasibility of socialism in Muslim countries. In June, 1950, Bhutto visited England to study law at Christ

Church, Oxford. Upon finishing his studies, he was invited to the bar at Lincoln's Inn in 1953.

Bhutto married his second wife, the Iranian-Kurdish Begum Nusrat Ispahani, a Shi'a Islamic, in Karachi on September 8, 1951. Their first child, his daughter Benazir, was born in 1953. She was followed by Murtaza in 1954, a second daughter, Sanam, in 1957, and the youngest child, Shahnawaz Bhutto, in 1958. He agreed to the post of lecturer at the Sindh Islamic College, from where he was also granted an honorary law degree by the then college President, Mr. Hassanally A. Rahman before establishing himself in a legal practice in Karachi. He also took over the management of his family's estate and business interests after his father's demise.

In 1957, Zulfikar Ali Bhutto became the youngest member of Pakistan's delegation to the United Nations. He would address the United Nations Sixth Committee on Aggression on October 25, 1957 and lead Pakistan's deputation to the United Nations Conference on the Law of the Seas in 1958. In the same year, Bhutto became the youngest Pakistani cabinet minister when he was given charge of the energy ministry by President Muhammad Ayub Khan, who had seized power and declared martial law. He was consequently promoted to head the ministries of commerce, information and industries.

Bhutto became a close and trusted consultant to Ayub, rising in influence and power despite his youth and relative inexperience in politics. Bhutto aided Ayub in negotiating the Indus Water Treaty with India in 1960. In 1961, Bhutto negotiated an oil exploration agreement with the Soviet Union, which also agreed to provide economic and technical aid to Pakistan.

In 1962, he was appointed Pakistan's foreign minister. His swift rise to power also brought him national name and fame.

As foreign minister, Bhutto substantially transformed Pakistan's hitherto pro-Western foreign policy. While maintaining an outstanding role for Pakistan inside the South-east Asia Treaty Organization and the Central Treaty Organization, Bhutto began asserting a foreign policy course for Pakistan that was autonomous of United States influence. Bhutto criticised the United States for providing military aid to India during and after the Sino-Indian War of 1962, which was seen as an abrogation of Pakistan's alliance with the United States. Bhutto worked to make stronger relations with the People's Republic of China. Bhutto visited Beijing and assisted Ayub negotiate trade and military agreements with the Chinese regime, which agreed to assist Pakistan in a large number of military and industrial projects.

Bhutto also signed the Sino-Pakistan Boundary Agreement on March 2, 1963 that transferred 750 square kilometres of territory from Pakistan-administered Kashmir to Chinese control. Bhutto asserted his belief in non-alignment, making Pakistan an important member in non-aligned organizations. Believing in pan-Islamic harmony, Bhutto developed closer relations with nations such as Indonesia, Saudi Arabia and other Arab states.

Bhutto joined Ayub in Tashkent to negotiate a peace treaty with the Indian Prime Minister Lal Bahadur Shastri. Ayub and Shastri agreed to exchange prisoners of war and withdraw respective forces to pre-war borders. This agreement was deeply unpopular in Pakistan, causing prominant political unrest against Ayub's regime. Bhutto's disapproval of the final agreement caused a prominant rift between him and Ayub Khan. At first denying the rumours, Bhutto resigned in June, 1967 and expressed strong resistance to Ayub's regime.

Following his resignation, large crowds gathered to listen to Bhutto's speech upon his arrival in Lahore on June 21, 1967. Tapping a wave of anger and resistance against Ayub, Bhutto began travelling across the country to deliver political speeches. In a speech in October, 1966 Bhutto proclaimed, "Islam is our faith, democracy is our policy, socialism is our economy. All power to the people." On November 30, 1967, Bhutto established the Pakistan Peoples Party (PPP) in Lahore, establishing a strong base of political support in Punjab, Sindh and amongst the Muhajir communities. Bhutto's party became a part of the pro-democracy movement involving diverse political parties from all across Pakistan. PPP activists staged large protests and strikes in various parts of the country, increasing pressure on Ayub to resign. Bhutto's arrest on November 12, 1968, sparked bigger political unrest. After his release, Bhutto attended the Round Table Conference called by Ayub in Rawalpindi, but refused to accept Ayub's continuation in office and the East Pakistani politician Sheikh Mujibur Rahman's Six point movement for regional autonomy.

Following Ayub's resignation, the new president Gen. Yahya Khan promised to hold parliamentary elections on December 7, 1970. Bhutto's party won a large number of seats from constituencies in West Pakistan. Nevertheless, Sheikh Mujib's Awami League won an outright majority from the constituencies situated in East Pakistan.

Indian intervention in East Pakistan led to the defeat of Pakistani forces, who surrendered on December 16, 1971. Bhutto and others condemned Yahya for failing to protect Pakistan's harmony. Seperated, Yahya resigned on December 20 and transferred power to Bhutto, who became the president, army commander-in-chief and also the first civilian chief martial law administrator.

As president, Bhutto addressed the nation via radio and television, saying "My dear countrymen, my dear friends, my dear students, labourers, peasants... those who fought for Pakistan... We are facing the worst crisis in our country's life, a deadly crisis. We have to pick up the pieces, very small pieces, but we will make a new Pakistan, a prosperous and liberal Pakistan." He placed Yahya under house arrest, brokered a ceasefire and ordered the release of Sheikh Mujib, who was held prisoner by the army. To implement this, Bhutto reversed the verdict of Mujib's court trial that had taken place earlier, in which the presiding Brigadier Rahimuddin Khan (later General) had sentenced Mujib to death. Appointing a new cabinet, Bhutto appointed Gen. Gul Hasan as Chief of Army Staff.

On January 2, 1972, Bhutto announced the nationalisation of all prominant industries, along with iron and steel, heavy engineering, heavy electricals, petrochemicals, cement and public utilities. A new labour policy was announced increasing workers, rights and the power of trade unions. Though he came from a feudal background himself, Bhutto announced reforms limiting land ownership and a government take-over of over a million acres (4,000 km^2) to distribute to landless peasants.

Bhutto visited India to meet Prime Minister Indira Gandhi and negotiated a formal peace agreement and the release of 93,000 Pakistani prisoners of war. The two leaders signed the Shimla Agreement, which committed both nations to make a Line of Control in Kashmir and obligated them to resolve disputes peacefully through bilateral talks. Bhutto also promised to hold a future summit for the peaceful resolution of the Kashmir dispute and pledged to acknowledge Bangladesh. Though he secured the release of Pakistani soldiers held by India, Bhutto was criticised by several in Pakistan for allegedly making too many concessions to India. It is theorised that Bhutto feared his downfall if he could not secure the release of Pakistani soldiers, the return of territory occupied by Indian forces.

Bhutto founded an atomic power development program and inaugurated the first Pakistani atomic reactor, constructed in collaboration with Canada in Karachi on November 28. Bhutto formally acknowledged Bangladesh in July.

Bhutto began facing considerable disapproval and increasing unpopularity as his term progressed. At first targeting leader of the opposition was Abdul Wali Khan and his opposition National Awami Party (NAP). Despite the ideological similarity of the two parties, the clash of egos both inside and outside the National Assembly became increasingly severe and began with the Federal governments judgement to oust the NAP provincial government in Balochistan for alleged secessionist activities and culminating in the banning of the party and arrest of much of its leadership after the demise of Hayat Khan Sherpao, a close lieutenant of Bhutto, in a bomb blast in the frontier town of Peshawar.

Dissidence also increased inside the PPP. Powerful PPP leaders such as Ghulam Mustafa Khar condemned Bhutto and demanded protests against his regime. On January 8, 1977, a lot of opposition political parties grouped to form the Pakistan National Alliance (PNA). Bhutto declared fresh elections and the PNA participated in those elections with full force and managed to contest the elections jointly despite the fact that they had grave differences in their opinions and opinions. The PNA faced defeat but didn't accept the consequences, accusing their opponents of rigging the election. They first claimed rigging on fourteen seats and finally on forty seats in the national assembly and boycotted provisional elections turn out in national elections was of biggest degree. Provincial elections were held amidst low voter turnout and an opposition boycott, violent PNA declare, the newly-elected Bhutto government as illegitimate.

General Zia announced that martial law had been enforced, the constitution suspended and all assemblies dissolved. Zia also ordered the arrest of senior PPP and PNA leaders but promised elections in October. Bhutto was released on July 29 and was received by a large crowd of followers in his hometown of Larkana. He instantly began touring across Pakistan, delivering speeches to large crowds and planning his political reappearance. Bhutto was arrested again on September 3 before being released on bail on September 13. Fearing yet another arrest, Bhutto named his wife, Nusrat, president of the Pakistan People's Party.

Bhutto was imprisoned on September 17 and a large number of PPP leaders and activists arrested and disqualified from contesting in elections.

Bhutto was hanged on April 4, 1979, at Adiyala Jail, Rawalpindi, Pakistan.

REFERENCES

al-Hamidi, Khalil Ahmad, *Tehrik-i Islami ke 'Alami Asrat*, Delhi: Markazi Maktaba-i Islami, 1994.

Ali, Abdullah Yusuf 'Ali, *An English Interpretation of the Holy Quran*, Bombay: Bilal Books, 1996.

Ali, *Ejzz*, *Jihad*, Patna: All-India Backward Muslim Morcha, n.d..

Gilani, Sayyed 'Ali Shah, *Rudad-i Qafas*, vol. 1, Srinagar: Al-Huda Publishing House, 1993.

Hamid, Sayyed, 'Maulana 'Ali Miyan', in *Rabita*, Delhi, 2000.

Hasan, Muhammad Nafis, *Meri Tamam Sarguzasht: Sayyed Abul Hasan 'Ali Nadwi*, New Delhi: published by the author, 2000.

Hasan, Mushirul, *Legacy of a Divided Nation: India's Muslims Since Independence*, London: Hurst & Company, 1997.

Nadwi, Abul Lais Islahi, *Jama'at-i Islami Ka Maqsad Aur Tariq-i Kar*, Delhi: Markazi Maktaba-i-Islami, 1989.

Nadwi, Khalid Beg Nadwi, *Fitna-i Channabasaveswara*, Tumkur, 2001.

Nadwi, Muhammad Ayub, 'Sayyed Abul Hasan 'Ali Nadwi Aur Tehrik-i Payam-i Insaniyat', in *Rabita*, Delhi, 2000.

Nadwi, Rizwan Ahmad, 'Sayyed 'Abul Hasan 'Ali Nadwi: Shaksiyat-o-Kirdar', in *Rabita*, Delhi, 2000.

Umri, Sayyed Jalaluddin, *Dharmik Logon Se Nivedan*, New Delhi: Madhur Sandesh Sangam, 1994.

1. ABDUL KALAM

Avul Pakir Jainulabdeen Abdul Kalam was born on October 15, 1931, in Tamil Nadu, India. Usually referred as Dr. APJ Abdul Kalam, he was the eleventh President of India, serving from 2002 to 2007. Due to his unusual functioning style, he is also commonly acknowledged as the People's President. Before his term as India's president, he distinguished himself as engineering visionary and was granted India's highest civilian honour Bharat Ratna in 1997 for his work with DRDO and his role as scientific consultant to the Indian government. He is commonly acknowledged as the Missile Man of India for his work on development of ballistic missile and space rocket technology. In India, he is considered a liberal teacher, innovator and visionary. Kalam played a crucial organizational, technical and political role in India's Pokhran-II nuclear test in 1998, the first since the original nuclear test by India in 1974.

APJ Abdul Kalam was born in a middle-class family in Rameshwaram, Tamil Nadu, a town famous for its Hindu shrines. His mother tongue is Tamil. His father, a devout Islamic, possessed boats which he rented out to local fishermen and was a good friend of Hindu religious leaders and the school teachers at Rameshwaram. APJ Abdul Kalam mentions in his biography that to support his studies, he began his career as a newspaper vendor.

This was also told in the book, A Boy and His Dream: Three Stories from the Childhood of Abdul Kalam by Vinita Krishna. The house Kalam was born in can still be found on the Mosque street at Rameswaram, and his brother's curio shop abuts it. This has become a point-of-call for tourists who seek out the place. Kalam grew up in a close relationship with universe, and he says in Wings of Fire that he never could imagine that water could be so powerful a destroying force as that he witnessed when he was six. That was in 1934, when a cyclonic storm swept away the Pamban bridge and a trainload of passengers with it as well as Kalam's native village, Dhanushkodi.

In 1962, Kalam became member of the Indian Space Research Organization (ISRO). In 1982, he rejoined DRDO as the Chief Executive of Integrated Guided Missile Development Program (IGMDP).

Dr. Kalam is accredited with the growth and operationalisation of India's Agni and Prithvi missiles. He worked as the Scientific Adviser to the Defence Minister and Secretary, Department of Defence Research & Development from 1992 to 1999. During this period, the Pokhran-II nuclear tests were conducted. Dr. Kalam held the office of the Principal Scientific Advisor to the Government of India from November, 1999 to November, 2001.

As the Project Director, he made substantial contributions to the growth of India's first indigenous Satellite Launch Vehicle (SLV-III). As Chief Executive of Integrated Guided Missile Development Program (IGMDP), he also played prominant part in developing a lot of missiles of India along with Agni and Prithvi.

He was the Chief Scientific Adviser to Defence Minister and Secretary, Department of Defence Research & Development from July, 1992 to December, 1999. Pokhran-II nuclear tests were conducted during this period, led by him. He has got honorary doctorates from as many as thirty universities. The Government of India has honoured him with the nation's highest civilian honours: the Padma Bhushan in 1981; Padma Vibhushan in 1990; and the Bharat Ratna in 1997.

Kalam was the Fourth President of India to have been honoured with a Bharat Ratna before being elected to the highest office, the other three being Sarvepalli Radhakrishnan, V. V. Giri and Zakir Hussain. He is also the first scientist and first bachelor to occupy Rashtrapati Bhavan.

Referred to as the "People's President", Kalam is often considered amongst India's greatest presidents, winning a poll conducted by news channel CNN-IBN for India's Best President. Dr. Kalam got an honourary doctor's degree from Carnegie Mellon University, Pittsburgh, PA, U.S.A.

2. ABDUL QADEER KHAN

Abdul Qadeer Khan was born on April 1, 1936, in Bhopal, India. He is a Pakistani scientist and metallurgical engineer, and is broadly looked upon as the founder of Pakistan's nuclear program. His middle name is sometimes rendered as Quadeer, Qadir or Qadeer, and his given names are usually abbreviated to A.Q. He is praised in Pakistan as a national hero.

Khan was born into a middle-class Islamic-Muhajir family, which migrated from India to Pakistan in 1952. He received a B.Sc. degree in

1960 from the University of Karachi, majoring in physical metallurgy. He then received an engineer's degree in 1967 from Delft University of Technology, the Netherlands, and a Ph.D. degree in metallurgical engineering from the Catholic University of Leuven in Belgium in 1972.

In 1972, the year he got his P.hD., Khan became member of the staff of the Physical Dynamics Research Laboratory (FDO) in Amsterdam, the Netherlands. FDO was a subcontractor for URENCO, the uranium enrichment facility at Almelo in the Netherlands, which had been founded in 1970 by the United Kingdom, West Germany, and the Netherlands to assure a supply of enriched uranium for the European nuclear reactors. The URENCO facility used Zippe-type centrifuge technology to separate the fissionable isotope uranium-235 out of uranium hexafluoride gas by spinning a mixture of the two isotopes at up to 100,000 revolutions a minute. The technical details of these centrifuge systems are regulated as secret information by export controls because they could be used for the purposes of nuclear proliferation.

In May 1974, India carried out its first nuclear test, code named Smiling Buddha, to the great alarm of the Government of Pakistan. In 1976, Khan was put in charge of Pakistan's uranium enrichment program with the support of the then Prime Minister of Pakistan, Zulfikar Ali Bhutto. The uranium enrichment program was in the beginning started in 1974 by Pakistan Atomic Energy Commission (PAEC) as Project-706 and Khan joined it in the spring of 1976. In July of that year, he took over the project from PAEC and founded the Engineering Research Laboratories (ERL) at Kahuta, Rawalpindi, consequently, renamed the Khan Research Laboratories (KRL) by the then President of Pakistan, General Muhammad Zia-ul-Haq. The laboratories became the focal point for developing a uranium enrichment capability for Pakistan's nuclear weapons development program. KRL also took on a lot of other weapons development projects, along with the development of the nuclear weapons-capable Ghauri ballistic missile. KRL occupied an exceptional role in Pakistan's Defence Industry, reporting directly to the office of the Prime Minister of Pakistan, and having extremely close relations with the Pakistani military. The former Prime Minister of Pakistan, Benazir Bhutto, has said that, during her term of office, even she was not permitted to visit the facility (KRL).

Khan's open advancement of Pakistan's nuclear weapons and ballistic missile capabilities is widely known. Pakistani government announced in March 2001, that Khan was to be dismissed from his post as Chairman of KRL, a move that drew strong disapproval from the religious and nationalist resistance to the President of Pakistan, General Pervez Musharraf. Possibly in reaction to this, the Pakistani government appointed Khan to the post of Special Science and Technology Adviser to the President, with a ministerial rank. While this could be regarded as a promotion for Khan, it removed him from hands-on management of KRL and gave the government a chance to keep a closer eye on his activities.

In August 2003, reports emerged of dealings with Iran; it was claimed that Khan had offered to sell nuclear weapons technology to that country as early as 1989. The Iranian government came under strong pressure from the United States and the European Union to make a full revelation of its nuclear program and, finally, agreed in October 2003 to accept tougher probs from the International Atomic Energy Agency. The IAEA reported that Iran had established a large uranium enrichment facility employing gas centrifuges based on the "stolen" URENCO designs, which had been received "from a foreign intermediary in 1987."

The intermediary was not named but a lot of diplomats and analysts pointed to Pakistan and, explicitly, to Khan, who was said to have visited Iran in 1986. The Iranians turned over the names of their suppliers and the international inspectors quickly identified the Iranian gas centrifuges as Pak-1's, the model developed by Khan in the early 1980s. In December 2003, two senior staff members at KRL were arrested on suspicion of having sold nuclear weapons technology to the Iranians.

On February 5, 2004, the day after Khan's televised confession, he was pardoned by Pakistani President Musharraf. Nevertheless, Khan remained under house arrest.

3. ABDUS SALAM

Abdus Salam was born on January 29, 1926, in Lahore, Pakistan. He was a Pakistani hypothetical physicist and Nobel laureate in Physics for his work in Electro-Weak Theory. Salam, Sheldon Glashow and Steven Weinberg shared the prize for this discovery. Salam holds the distinction of being the first Pakistani Nobel Laureate, and is the first Islamic Nobel Laureate in science. The validity of the theory was ascertained through experiments carried out at the Super Proton Synchrotron facility at CERN in Geneva, especially, through the discovery of the W and Z Bosons.

Salam's father was an official in the Department of Education in a poor farming district. His family has a considerable custom of piety and learning.

At the age of just fourteen, Salam scored the highest marks ever ecorded for the Matriculation Examination at the University of Punjab. He won a scholarship to the Government College, University of Punjab, n Lahore. As a fourth-year student there, he published his work on Srinivasa Ramanujan. He took his master's degree at the Government College in 1946. That same year, he was granted a scholarship to St. ohn's College, Cambridge University, where he took a BA degree with Double First-Class Honours in Mathematics and Physics in 1949. In 1950, he got the Smith's Prize from Cambridge University for the most outstanding pre-doctoral contribution to Physics.

He received a PhD degree in Theoretical Physics at Cambridge. His doctoral dissertation contained fundamental work in Quantum Electrodynamics. By the time it was published in 1951, it had already acquired him a global status and the Adam's Prize.

Abdus Salam was a devout Islamic, and a member of the Ahmadiyya slamic Community, who saw his religion as essential to his scientific work. He once wrote: "The Holy Quran enjoins us to reflect on the verities of Allah's created laws of nature; however, that our generation has been privileged to glimpse a part of His design is a bounty and a grace for which I render thanks with a humble heart."

During his acceptance speech for the Nobel Prize in Physics, Salam cited the following verses from the Quran:

"Thou seest not, in the creation of the All-merciful any imperfection, Return thy gaze, seest thou any fissure. Then Return thy gaze, again and again. Thy gaze, Comes back to thee dazzled, aweary."

He then said:

"This, in effect, is the faith of all physicists; the deeper we seek, the more is our wonder excited, the more is the dazzlement for our gaze."

In 1974, when the Pakistan National Assembly declared Ahmadis to be non-Muslims, he left Pakistan for London in protest.

He came back to the Government College, Lahore as a professor of Mathematics from 1951 to 1954 and then went back to Cambridge as a ecturer in mathematics.

During the early 1960s, Salam played a very substantial role in establishing the Pakistan Atomic Energy Commission (PAEC) - the atomic research agency of Pakistan - and Space and Upper Atmosphere Research Commission (SUPARCO) - the space research agency of Pakistan, of which he was the founding director. He was also instrumental in setting up five Superior Science colleges all over Pakistan to further the development in science in the country. He was founding father and Director of the International Centre for Theoretical Physics (ICTP), Trieste, Italy from 1964 to December, 1993. (The Centre has since been renamed, the Abdus Salam International Centre for Theoretical Physics). Salam was a firm advocate that "scientific thought is the common heritage of mankind," and that developing nations required to help themselves and invest into their own scientists to boost growth and reduce the gap between the Global South and the Global North, thus contributing to a more peaceful world. Salam also established the Third World Academy of Sciences (TWAS) and was a major figure in the establishment of a number of global centres dedicated to the advancement of science and technology.

In 1956, he was invited to take a chair at Imperial College, London, where he and Paul Matthews established a dynamic theoretical physics group. He remained a professor at Imperial till his retirement. In 1964, he established the International Centre for Theoretical Physics, Trieste in the North-East of Italy. In 1959, he became the youngest Fellow of the Royal Society (at that time) at the age of 33. In 1998, the Government of Pakistan issued a stamp carrying his portrait as part of a series of stamps named "Scientists of Pakistan."

Salam came back to Pakistan in 1951 to teach Mathematics at the Government College, Lahore. In 1952, he became the Head of the Mathematics Department of the Punjab University. In 1954, Salam went for a lectureship at Cambridge, though he visited Pakistan from time to time as an advisor on science policy to the Government of Pakistan. His work for Pakistan was broad and important. He was a member of the Pakistan Atomic Energy Commission, a member of the Scientific Commission of Pakistan, Founder Chairman of Space and Upper Atmosphere Research Commission and Chief Scientific Adviser to the President of Pakistan from 1961 to 1974.

From 1957 onwards, he was professor of Theoretical Physics at Imperial College, London. From 1964 onwards, has mixed this position with that of Director of the International Centre for Theoretical Physics, a research institution in Trieste, Italy.

Salam had a productive research career in theoretical elementary particle physics. He either initiated or was associated with all the influential growths in this area. He also served on a number of United Nations committees concerning science and technology in developing countries.

Salam's primary focus was research on the physics of elementary particles. His particular contributions included:

- Two-component neutrino theory and the prediction of the inevitable parity violation in weak interaction
- Gauge unification of weak and electromagnetic interactions, the unified force is named the "electroweak" force, a name given to it by salam, and which forms the basis of the standard model in particle physics
- Predicted existence of weak neutral currents, w particles and z particles before their experimental discovery
- Symmetry properties of elementary particles; unitary symmetry
- Renormalization of meson theories
- Gravity theory and its role in particle physics; two tensor theory of gravity and strong interaction physics
- Unification of electroweak with strong nuclear forces, grand unification theory
- Related prediction of proton-decay
- Pati-salam model, a grand unification theory
- Supersymmetry theory, in particular formulation of superspace and formalism of superfields in 1974
- The theory of supermanifolds, as a geometrical framework for understanding supersymmetry
- Supergeometry, the geometric basis for supersymmetry
- Application of the Higgs mechanism to the electroweak symmetry breaking;
- Prediction of the magnetic photon

Salam expired on November 21, 1996, in Oxford, England after a considerable sickness.

His body was brought to Pakistan and was taken to the Ahmadiyya Islamic Community headquarters of the city of Rabwah. His body was kept in Darul Ziafat, where 13,000 men and women took a last glimpse of his glorious face.

4. FAZLUR RAHMAN KHAN

Fazlur Rahman Khan was born on April 3, 1929, in Dhaka, Bangladesh. His father, Khan Bahadur Abdur Rahman Khan, was a renowned educationist and high government official in the education department.

Khan finished his undergraduate course work at the Bengal Engineering College, University of Calcutta (Now Bengal Engineering & Science University, Shibpur). He got his bachelor's degree from the University of Dhaka in 1951 while placing first in his class. A Fulbright Scholarship and a Pakistani government scholarship enabled him to travel to the United States in 1952 where he pursued advanced studies at the University of Illinois at Urbana-Champaign. In three years Khan earned two Master's degrees — one in structural engineering and one in theoretical and applied mechanics — and a PhD in structural engineering.

In 1955, employed by Skidmore, Owings and Merrill, he began functioning in Chicago, Illinois.

One of the foremost structural engineers of the 20th century, Fazlur Khan epitomized both structural engineering achievement and creative collaborative effort between architect and engineer. He believed that "only when architectural design is grounded in structural realities — thus celebrating architecture's nature as a constructive art, rooted in the earth — can the ensuing aesthetics ... have a transcendental value and quality."

As a boy, Khan's father instilled in him the significance of an education, not only early education but a continued education. For this reason, Khan attended undergraduate school and then graduate school. Though Khan was finished with school and now in the workforce, he still continued to study. He taught himself how to program the new computer system which SOM purchased in 1961. He then taught his colleagues how to use the new programs.

Khan recognized the value of his education and encouraged his daughter Yasmin along a similar path. Nevertheless, he didn't push her into structural engineering, she found her zeal for this on her own. Her experiences with her father inspired her education and her work. Yasmin afterward wrote a lot of articles and books including Engineering Architecture: The Vision of Fazlur R. Khan, a compliment to her father.

Dr. Fazlur Khan's design innovations improved the construction of high-rise buildings, enabling them to withstand enormous forces generated on these super structures. These new designs opened an economic door for contractors, engineers, architects, and investors, providing vast amounts of real estate space on minimal plots of land.

He is famous for his efficient designs for Chicago's 100-storey John Hancock Centre and 110-storey Sears Tower, the tallest building in the world in its time and still the tallest in the United States since its completion in 1974. He is also responsible for designing notable buildings in Bangladesh.

Khan's key innovation in skyscraper design and construction was the idea of the "tube" and "bundled tube" structural systems for tall buildings. After 1965, this new structural system of framed tubes was important in skyscraper design and construction. Khan defined the framed tube structure as "a three dimensional space structure compiled of three, four, or possibly more frames, braced frames, or shear walls, joined at or close to their edges to form a vertical tubelike structural system capable of resisting lateral forces in any direction by cantilevering from the foundation." Closely spaced interconnected exterior columns form the tube. Horizontal loads, for instance wind, are supported by the structure as a whole. About half the exterior surface is accessible for windows. Framed tubes allow fewer interior columns, and so create more usable floor space. Where larger openings like garage doors are required, the tube frame must be interrupted, with shift girders used to maintain structural integrity. The first building to apply the tube-frame construction was in the DeWitt-Chestnut apartment building which Khan designed in Chicago. This laid the foundations for the tube structures used in most later skyscrapers, as can been seen in the construction of the World Trade Centre.

Another innovation that Khan developed was the notion of X-bracing. This notion reduced the lateral load on the building by transferring the load into the exterior columns. This allows for a reduced requirement for interior columns thus making more floor space. This notion can be seen in the John Hancock Centre, constructed in 1969, one of the most renowned buildings of the structural expressionist style, the skyscraper's distinctive X-bracing exterior is actually a hint that the structure's skin is indeed part of its 'tubular system'. This idea is one of the architectural skills of the building used to climb to record heights (the tubular system is essentially the spine that helps the building stand upright during wind and earthquake loads). This X-bracing allows for both higher presentation from tall structures and the capability to open up the inside floorplan (and usable floor space) if the architect desires. Original features such as the skin, pioneered by Fazlur Khan, have made the John Hancock Centre an architectural icon.

The first sky lobby was also designed by Khan for the John Hancock Centre. Later, buildings with sky lobbies include the World Trade Centre, Petronas Twin Towers and Taipei 101. The 44th-floor sky lobby of the John Hancock Centre also features the first high-rise indoor swimming pool, which remains the highest in America.

5. SALIMUZZAMAN SIDDIQUI

Salimuzzaman Siddiqui was born on October 19, 1897, in Barabanki District, Lucknow, India. He was a major Pakistani scientist in natural products chemistry. He is accredited for pioneering the isolation of exceptional chemical compounds from the Neem (Azadirachta indica), Rauwolfia, and various other flora. As the founder director of H.E.J. Research Institute of Chemistry, he revolutionised the research on pharmacology of various domestic plants found in South Asia to extract novel chemical substances of medicinal significance. In addition to his scientific gifts, Siddiqui was also a painter, a poet, and a great expert of music. His paintings were exhibited in Germany, India, and Pakistan.

He got his early education from Lucknow, both in the Urdu and Persian languages, and shortly developed interest in literature, poetry, and calligraphy from his father Sheikh Muhammad Zaman. After finishing his matriculation, he became member of the Calcutta School of Arts, and became a pupil of Rabindranath Tagore, the founding father of the renowned Bengal School of painting. He graduated in Philosophy and Persian language, from M.A.O College (that would afterward become Aligarh University) in 1919.

In 1920, Siddiqui proceeded to University College London to study medicine. Nevertheless, after one year of premedical studies, he moved to Frankfurt University in 1921 to study chemistry. In 1924, he married his German classmate, Ethel Wilhelmina Schneeman. He got Doctor of Philosophy under the supervision of Prof. Julius Von Bram in 1927.

On his come back, he founded the Ayurvedic and Unani Tibbi Research Institute at the Tibbia College Delhi, under the guidance of Hakim Ajmal Khan. He was appointed its first Director. Nevertheless, shortly after the demise of Hakim Ajmal Khan, Siddiqui left the post. In 1940, he became member of Indian Council for Scientific and Industrial Research where he worked till 1951 when he migrated to Pakistan on the request of Prime Minister Liaquat Ali Khan.

Siddiqui's first breakthrough in research came when he successfully seperated an anti-arrythmic agent in 1931 from the origins of Rauwolfia serpentina. He named the newly discovered chemical compound as Ajmaline, after his teacher Hakim Ajmal Khan who was one of the illustrious practitioners of Unani system of medicine in South Asia. Later on, Siddiqui also extracted other alkaloids from Rauwolfia serpentina that included Ajmalinine, Ajmalicine ($C_{21}H_{24}N_2O_3$), Isoajmaline, Neoajmaline, Serpentine and Serpentinine. A lot of these are still used all over for cure of mental disorders and cardiovascular diseases, particularly as anti-arrythmic agents in Brugada syndrome.

Siddiqui was the first scientist to bring the anthelmintic, antifungal, antibacterial, and antiviral constituents of the Neem tree to the attention of natural products chemists. In 1942, he extracted three bitter compounds from neem oil, which he named as nimbin, nimbinin, and nimbidin respectively. The action involved extracting the water insoluble components with ether, petrol ether, ethyl acetate and dilute alcohol. The provisional naming was nimbin (sulphur-free crystalline product with melting point at 205°C, empirical composition $C_7H_{10}O_2$), nimbinin (with alike principle, melting at 192°C), and nimbidin (cream-coloured containing amorphous sulphur, melting at 90–100°C). Siddiqui identified nimbidin as the main active anti-bacterial ingredient, and the highest yielding bitter component in the neem oil. These compounds are stable and found in significant quantities in the Neem. They also serve as natural insecticides.

In acknowledgement of these radical discoveries, he was granted the Order of the British Empire in 1946.

In his later career, Siddiqui continued to discover and separate many exceptional antibacterial compounds from various parts (leaves, bark, etc.) of the Neem and other plants. He had more than 50 chemical compounds patented in his name in addition to those discovered as a consequence of his joint research with other colleagues and students. Most of these discoveries still remain vital natural ingredients of various medicines and also biopesticides.

After the emergence of Pakistan in 1947, Siddiqui was entrusted by the Government of Pakistan in 1951 to organize scientific research activities. In 1953, he established the Pakistan Academy of Sciences as a non-political think tank of distinguished scientists in the country. During the same year, he also founded the Pakistan Council of Scientific and Industrial Research (PCSIR) in Karachi.

The aim of PCSIR was to support the industrial base through research and growth. The regional laboratories of the institution were situated in Dhaka, Rajshahi and Chittagong (East Pakistan), and in Lahore and Peshawar (West Pakistan). In appreciation of his scientific leadership, Frankfurt University awarded him the degree of D.Med. Honoris causa in 1958. Also in 1958, the Government of Pakistan granted him with Tamgha-e-Pakistan. In 1960, he became the President of Pan-Indian Ocean Science Association. The following year, in 1961, Siddiqui was made Fellow of the Royal Society, following which he was given the Sitara-e-Imtiaz for distinguished merit in the fields of science and medicine, in 1962. Siddiqui remained the director and chairman of PCSIR till the time of his retirement in 1966. In that year, the President of Pakistan granted him the Pride of Performance Medal for the respectable completion of his service.

In 1967, Siddiqui was invited by University of Karachi to set up a Postgraduate Institute of Chemistry in affiliation with the Department of Chemistry. He was designated as the institute's Founder Director, whereas the additional research staff was provided by PCSIR. In 1976, the institute was offered a generous donation from Hussain Jamal Foundation, as a consequence of which it was renamed as Hussain Ebrahim Jamal Research Institute of Chemistry. In due time, Siddiqui transformed the institute into a distinguished centre of global excellence in the area of chemistry and natural products. In March 1975, he headed the National Commission for Indigenous Medicines his tireless attempts for the advancement of science and technology earned him Hilal-e-Imtiaz by the Government of Pakistan in 1980. In 1983, he played a prominant role in the establishment of the Third World Academy of Sciences and became its Founding Fellow. He remained the director of the Hussain Ebrahim Jamal Research Institute of Chemistry till 1990. Afterward on, he continued research in his personal laboratory.

Siddiqui was a founder-member of the Indian and Pakistan Academies of Sciences, and afterward a founder member of the global body, the Third World Academy of Sciences.

He was awarded many times, most notable being:

- Foundation Fellow, Pakistan Academy of Sciences, 1953
- D. Med. Honoris causa from the Frankfurt University, 1958
- Tamgha-e-Pakistan, 1958
- President, Pan-Indian Ocean Science Association, 1960

- Fellow of the Royal Society, 1961
- Sitara-e-Imtiaz, 1962
- President of Pakistan's Pride of Performance Medal, 1966
- Hilal-e-Imtiaz, 1980

Siddiqui expired on April 14, 1994 due to cardiac arrest in Karachi, Pakistan. He was buried in the Karachi University Graveyard. Despite his demise, the academic and research institutes that he established during more than 65 years of his research career are still contributing to the global level research in natural products chemistry.

REFERENCES

Ansari, Abdul Haq, *Qaumi Yekjuhati Aur Islam*, Delhi: Markazi Maktaba-i Islami, 1996.

Ansari, Muhammad Hasan, *Hazrat Maulana Sayyed Abul Hasan 'Ali Nadwi: Hayat Aur Karnamey Aur Unke Malfuzat-Ek Ajma'ali Khaka*, Lucknow: Maktaba-i Jami'at ulMu'minat, 1999.

Islahi, Sadruddin, *Tehrik-i Islami-i Hind*, Delhi: Markazi Maktaba-i Islami, 1994.

Islahi, Sultan Ahmad, *Maulana Abul Lais Islahi Nadwi: Shaksiyat Ke Chand Numaya Pahlu*, Aligarh: Idara-i Ilm-o-Adab, 1996.

'Islam, Liberalism and Democracy', *Progressive Perspective*, vol. 4, no. 11, November 1995.

Nath, Ram, *Dalit-Muslim Unity: Why? And How?*, Bangalore: Dalit Sahitya Akademy, 1995.

Nazirullah, Abul Sami Muhammad, *Deendar Anjuman Kya Hai*?, Hyderabad: Deendar Anjuman, n.d.

Noor, Farish A., *New Voices of Islam*, Leiden: International Institute for the Study of Islam in the Modern World, 2002.

Vajpeyi, Dhirendra K., 'The Politics of Paradise: Islam, Identity and Politics in India', in Arvind Sharma (ed.), *Hinduism and Secularism: After Ayodhya*, Basingstoke and New York: Palgrave, 2001.

Section: VI

SCHOLARS

1. ABUL KASHEM

Abul Kashem was born on June 28, 1920, at village of Chebandi in Patia Thana of Chittagong district, Bangladesh. Commonly known as Principal Abul Kashem, he was a Bangladeshi author and an eminent educationist. He was also an activist of the Language Movement.

Principal Abul Kashem passed Matriculation Examination from Borma High School in 1939 with first class, and Government district scholarship. He passed I.Sc. from Chittagong government Collage in 1941 with first class. He also obtained Bachelors of Science (honours) and Masters of Science degree in Physics from Dhaka University in 1944 and 1945 respectively with first class.

Principal Abul Kashem was associated with the literary and cultural activities of the country for five decades. He contributed in the movement for recognition of Bengali as one of the state languages of Pakistan soon after the independence of Pakistan in 1947. On September 1, 1947, he founded the Pakistan Tamaddun Majlish as a non-political cultural organization to mobilize students, intellectuals and the people in general for the Bengali language. On September 15, 1947, he published a booklet entitled, Pakistaner Rashtrobasha- Bangla Na Urdu (Pakistan's state language: Bengali or Urdu) demanding introduction of Bengali as one of the state language of whole Pakistan. This booklet also strongly advocated for Bengali as the medium of education, court language and for its use in the offices in East Pakistan.

Also his untiring efforts led to the formation of the first Rashtrabhasa Sangram Parishad (State Language Committee of Action) on October 1, 1947, with Nurul Huq Bhuiyan as the convener and he himself as the treasurer. On December 6, 1947, a meeting was held under the presidentship of Principal Abul Kashem in Dhaka University campus which protested the resolution of the education week held in Karachi suggesting Urdu as the state language and the lingua franca of Pakistan. A protest procession was brought out from the meeting, which met Khawaja Nazimuddin, the provincial Chief Minister, and other ministers. Khawaja Nazimuddin gave a written assurance to the Action Committee that he would do the needful to introduce Bengali as one of the state language of

Pakistan. Principal Abul Kashem actively participated in organizing a countrywide strike on March 11, 1948, to press for the language demand. As the outcome of the strike, on the eve of the impending visit of Muhammad Ali Jinnah (the founder of Pakistan) to Dhaka, the then Provincial Government had no other alternative but to sign an agreement with the action committee on March 15, 1948, for introducing Bengali as one of the state language of Pakistan.

Principal Abul Kashem began his career as a lecturer in the Physics department at the Dhaka University in 1946. As a lecturer, he was the first person who delivered lectures in the Bengali at the Dhaka University. He held his lecturer position until 1953.

Principal Abul Kashem was actively associated with politics. He was one of the founders of the Khilafat-e-Rabbani Party in 1952. He was a member of the provincial assembly as a United Front nominee in 1954 from the Pattia-Boalkhali constituency in Chittagong. While a member of the Legislative Assembly, he moved a resolution for introduction of Bengali as the medium of education at all levels. On September 30, 1956, he proposed Bangla as the state-language and it was approved unanimously and thus, Bengali received constitutional recognition as one of the State language of Pakistan.

He was the founding editor of the weekly Sainik at the 1948, which was the organ of the Tamaddun Majlish and also published the news of the language movement regularly. It was published till 1961. He felt the need of introducing Bangla as medium of higher education in colleges and universities. With his dream, he established the Bangla College at Mirpur, Dhaka in 1962 and served the college as Principal till 1981. He devised a model for the reorientation of spelling of Bengali words and the pattern of Bengali scripts.

A prolific writer, Principal Abul Kashem authored nearly 100 books including textbooks on science for postgraduate student and on education, Islam, culture and politics. These include 40 textbooks on physics and other science subjects for collage and University levels. Some of his well-know books are- Ekush daffer Rupaon, Pakistaner Rashtrobasha Bangla Na Urdu?, Ghosona, Vibartanbad, Dooti Prosno, Sangathan, Islami rushtraneeti, Adhunik Chintadhara, Shristi Tatta O Allahr Astitta, Biggan Samaj O Darmo, Quranic Arthoniti, Biggan Bastubad O Allahr Astitta, Islam Science & Modern Theory, Universal Ideology in the Light of Modern Thought, and Sreni Sangram.

Principal Abul Kashem received a number of national and social awards which includes Independence Day Award in 1993, Ekushey Padak in 1987, Bangla Academy Award (for his book Biggan Somaj O Darmo) in 1982, Islamic foundation Award in 1988, Pakistan Writers guild award in 1964 etc. He was accorded a national reception in Dhaka in 1989 which was attended by eminent scholars and litterateurs of Bangladesh and India.

Abul Kashem died in Dhaka, Bangladesh on March 11, 1991.

2. AZIZUL HAQUE

Azizul Haque was born in 1854, in the state of Khulna, Bangladesh. He was a Kolkata (Calcutta) police officer of British India who worked with Edward Henry to develop the Henry Classification System of fingerprints. Haque, reportedly, provided the mathematical basis for the system. His parents reportedly expired in a boat accident when he was young.

As per family history, Haque left his family home at age 12, as a consequence of "disagreement" with his older brother, and moved to Kolkata, where he befriended a family who became "struck" with his mathematical techniques and arranged for him to get a formal education. As per Dr. Colin Beavan, "Haque studied maths and science at Presidency College in Calcutta. Edward Henry wrote to the college principal asking for the recommendation of a strong statistics student, and the principal nominated Haque."

Henry subsequently recruited Haque as a police sub-inspector to work on the fingerprint project, and thus Haque began his career in Bengal Police Service, and he consequently opted to join the Bihar Police Service, when Bihar was separated from the Bengal Presidency. Upon retirement from service, he settled in Motihari in Bihar state of India, where he expired and was buried there. He had eight surviving children. His wife, and the children and their families migrated to Pakistan during division of India, and presently their descendants are settled in Bangladesh, Pakistan, England, and North America.

Haque was enrolled by Edward Henry to work on the fingerprint project as part of the Calcutta Police service of British India. As per Colin Beavan, "In 1892, Edward Henry wrote to the college principal asking for the recommendation of a strong statistics student, and the principal nominated Haque. Henry recruited Haque as a police sub-inspector, and at first gave him the responsibility for instituting the anthropometric system in Bengal."

Years afterward, when Haque requested attention and compensation from the British government for his contribution to fingerprint classification work, Henry did acknowledge publicly Haque's contribution. He also did the same, when the issue of compensation for Bose came up later on. Recently, Sodhi and Kaur published a wide research paper on the issue of the two Indian police officers' contributions to fingerprint development.

Haque, in his effort to apply the anthropometric system in the first place proposed by Francis Galton, got frustrated in terms of its practical application. He shortly, as per Bevan, "began to work on a classification system of his own borrowing elements of Galton's." He devised a mathematical formula of sorting slips in 1024 pigeonholes in thirty-two columns and thirty-two rows based on fingerprint patterns. "Its use required no maths and no measurements." Beavan further writes, "By 1897, Haque had collected 7000 fingerprint sets in his cabinet. His plain methods of further subclassification, which were easier to study and less prone to mistake than Galton's, meant that even a collection numbering in the hundreds of thousands could be divided into small groups of slips. As he anticipated, his fingerprint sets, equated with anthropometric cards, were far less prone to mistake and could be classified and explored with much bigger confidence.

The registration of a convict or a search for his existing card took an hour under the anthropometric system, but only five minutes employing Haque's classification of fingerprints." Bevan goes on to say, "Haque's boss, Edward Henry, was overjoyed with Haque's results, and Henry saw that they would reflect well on him and career. He asked the colonial government to convene a committee to evaluate the system for widespread use. The committee reported that fingerprints were superior to anthropometry. 1. In simplicity of working; 2. In the cost of apparatus; 3. In the fact that all expert work is transferred to a central or classification office; 4. In the rapidity with which the action can be worked; and 5. In the certainty of results. Fingerprints, in other words, were the new hero in criminal identification."

Upon retirement from service, he settled in Motihari, in Bihar province of India, where he died and was buried there.

3. MAULANA MUHAMMAD ILYAS

Maulana Muhammad Ilyas was born on March 20, 1885, in Kandhla, India. His early days were spent in maternal grandfather's home in Kandhla, and with his father at Nizamuddin. In those days, the Kandhla household was the birthplace of godliness and piousness so much so that reports of the high religiosity, nightly devotions and Zikr and Tilawat of its members, both male and female, would seem notional and fictitious to the fainthearted men of our time.

The ladies used to recite the Quran themselves in the Nafl prayers as well listen to its Tarawih and other Nafl prayers, standing behind the male relatives. The month of Ramadan, in particular, was the springtime for the Quran. It was read for considerable hours, almost in every home. The limit of absorption was that, occasionally, the ladies forgot to pay attention to purdah and would not become aware of the coming of outsiders in the house at a time of urgent requirement.

The Quran with its translation and commentary in Urdu, and Mazaahir-i-Haq Måshariq ul Anwaar and His-i-Haseen formed the limit of the education of the ladies. Deeds and accomplishments of the families of Syed Ahmad Shaheed and Shah Abdul Aziz were the most well liked themes of conversation, and facts concerning these illustrious men of God were on everybody's lips. Instead of the stories of kings and fairies, ladies of the family related these to the children.

The Maulana's maternal grandmother, Amtus Salam, who was the daughter of Maulana Muzaffar Husain and was known in the family as Ammi Bi, was a very devotional lady. About her Salaat, the Maulana, once observed "I saw her likeness of Ammi Bi's Salaat of Maulana Gangohi."

During the last phase of her life, Ammi Bi's state was that she never asked for food and ate only when someone placed before her. It was a large family and there was always so much to do. If the thought of having her meal! didn't occur to her in the midst of domestic chores, she simply went hungry. Once, someone said to her, "You are so old and weak. How do you manage to without food ?" "I draw sustenance from my Tasbihat (remembrance of Allah)" was her reply.

The mother of Maulana Muhammad Ilyas, Bi Safia, had studied the Quran by heart and attained great distinction in it. It was an usual practice with her to recite the entire Quran and additional ten Juze (part) every day during Ramadan. She, thus, finished forty recitals of the Quran in that month and was so fluent in it that her family obligations didn't suffer on account of it.

She, generally, kept herself engaged in some work while doing the recitation. Apart from the month of Ramadan, her daily routine of worship included: Durud Sharif, 5,000 times; Ism-i-Zaat Allah, 5,000 times; Bismillah ar-Rahman ar-Rahim, 1,000 times, Yaa Mughnee-u 1,100 times, La illaaha illallaah, 1,200 times, Yaa-Haiyyu, Ya Qaiyum two hundred times, Hasbiallaah wa ni'mul Vakil, five hundred times; Subhan Allah, two hundred times; Alhamdu lillaah, two hundred times; La ilaaha illallaah, two hundred times; Allah O-Akbar, two hundred times; Istighfar, 500 times; Ofwwizu amree illallaah, hundred times; Hasbunallaah wa ni'mul Vakil, 1000 times; Rabb-i in-ni maghloobun fantasir, 1,000 times: Rabb-i-inni masanni-az-zurru wa anla ar-hamur rahimeen, one hundred times; Laa ilaaha enta subhanaka in-ni kunzu minaz-zalimeen, one hundred times. In addition, she recited a Manzil (1/7) of the Quran everyday.

Like all other children in the family, the Maulana Ilyas began his education in the maktab, and, as per the family custom, studied the Quran by heart. The learning of the Quran was so common in the family, that in the one-and-a-half row of worshippers in the family mosque, there was not a single non Hafiz except the Muezzin. Maulana Muhammad Ilyas was Ammi Bi's favourite child. She used to say to him, "Ilyas, I feel the aroma of the holy Companions in you." Occasionally, placing her hand on his back, she would say, "How is it that I see figures resembling the holy Companions moving together with you?"

From his early days, there was present in Maulana Muhammad Ilyas a touch of the religious ardour and fervent feeling of the blessed Companions which had led Shaikhul Hind Maulana Mahmood Hasan to remark that "when I see Muhammad Ilyas, I am reminded of the holy Companions. Keenness and exuberance for Faith were ingrained in his nature. Even in his early days, he, occasionally, did things which were much above the common level of the children. Riazul Islam Kandhlawi, a class fellow of his Maktab, says that "when we were reading in the Maktab, he, Maulana Muhammad Ilyas, once, came with a stick and said, "Come Riazul Islam, let us do Jihaad against those who do not offer up Salaat."

In 1893, his elder brother, Muhammad Yahya, moved to live at Gangoh with Maulana Rasheed Ahmad Gangohi. Maulana Muhammad Ilyas used to live with his father at Nizamuddin, and, occasionally, with his maternal grand-father's family at Kandhla. At Nizamuddin, his education was being neglected owing to the over- fondness of his father and his own excessive occupation with prayers. Maulana Yahya, thus, requested his father that as the education of Muhammad Ilyas was suffering, he might be permitted to take him to Gangoh. The father agreed - and Maulana Muhammad Ilyas came to Gangoh in 1896 or early 1897 where Muhammad Yahya began to teach him regularly.

Gangoh, in those days, was the seat of Sufi-saints and savants, the benefit of whose company was continuously accessible to Maulana Muhammad Ilyas. A bigger part of his impressionable age was spent there. When he moved to live at Gangoh, he was 10 or 11 years old, and at the time of Maulana Rasheed Ahmed Gangohi demise, in 1905, he was a young man of about 20. Thus, he stayed with Maulana Gangohi for about 9 years.

Maulana Muhammad Yahya was a perfect teacher and benefactor. He wanted his brother to derive the utmost advantage from the society of those illustrious men. Maulana Muhammad Ilyas used to tell that when the Ulema who had been the favourite pupils or disciples of Maulana Gangohi came to Gangoh, his brother would, often, stop the lessons and say that his education, then, lay in sitting with them and listening to their conversation.

Usually, Maulana Gangohi didn't take bait from children and students. It was only when they had finished their education that he permitted them to take the pledge. But owing to the exceptional merit of Maulana Muhammad Ilyas, he, at his request, permitted him to do the bait at his hand.

Maulana Muhammad Ilyas had been born with a loving heart. Such a strong affection did he develop for Maulana Gangohi that he felt no peace without him. He would, often, get up in the night, go and see the Maulana's face, and come back to his bed. Maulana Gangohi, too, had a great affection for him. Once, Maulana Muhammad Ilyas told his brother of severe headache after which he could not bend his head even to the extent of performing the Sajdah on a pillow for months. Maulana Gangohi's son, Hakim Masud Ahmad, who was his physician, had a peculiar method of cure. In certain diseases, he forbade the use of water for a considerable time which was unbearable to most of the patients. But with the strength of mind that was so characteristic of him, Maulana Muhammad Ilyas abided strictly by the advice of his physician and abstained from drinking water for full seven years, and, during the next five years, he drank it only sparingly.

There was little hope that he would be to resume his education after the discontinuation owing to sickness. He was very keen to take it up again, but his well-wishers would not allow. One day, as Maulana Muhammad Yahya said to him what he would, in any case, do by studying, he retorted, "What will I do by living?" Ultimately, he succeeded in resuming his studies.

The demise of Maulana Gangohi happened in 1905. Maulana Muhammad Ilyas who was at his bedside during the dying moments and reciting the Sura of Ya-Sin, was so deeply affected by it that he used, often, to say, "Two shocks have been most painful to me. One was of the demise of my father, and the other, of the demise of Maulana Rasheed Ahmad Gangohi." In 1908, Maulana Muhammad Ilyas moved to Deoband where he studied Tirmizi and Sahih Bukhari under Maulana Mahmood Hasan. The latter suggested to him to approach Maulana Khalil Ahmad Saharanpuri for spiritual guidance and instruction, since his teacher, Maulana Rasheed Ahmad Gangohi, was no more, and, thus, he finished the various stages of Sulook under Maulana Saharanpuri's supervision.

During his stay at Gangoh, after the demise of Maulana Gangohi, Maulana Muhammad Ilyas, generally, remained silent and spent most of his time in meditation. Says Maulana Muhammad Zakaria, "We studies elementary Persian from him those days. His practice, then, was that he sat cross legged, and in utter silence, on a coarse mat behind the tomb of Shah Abdul Quddus. We presented ourselves for the lesson, opened the book, and placed it before him, indicating with the finger where we were to begin from on that day. We would read aloud and translate the Persian verses. When we made an error, he would shut the book with a movement of the finger, and the lesson came to an end. It meant that we were to go back, prepare the lesson thoroughly, and, then, come again. He used to offer Nafl prayers much and often at that time. From Maghrib until a little before Isha, he devoted himself exclusively to Nawafil. His age, then, was between twenty and twenty-five years.

Ardour and keenness, without which no real success is possible in any area, were deeply rooted in him. It was by sheer determination and earnestness that he accomplished what he did in spite of persistent sick-health. One day, during his last sickness, Maulana Muhammad Ilyas related that "once I was so sick and feeling so weak that I could not go down the stairs. All of a sudden, I heard that Maulana Saharanpuri had come to Delhi and I was so excited that I went to Delhi instantly on foot and forgot all about my sickness and exhaustion. It was in the way that I remembered I was sick.

Usual contact with other spiritual teachers and disciples of Maulana Gangohi was maintained during those days. About Shah Abdur Rahim Raipuri and Maulana Ashraf Ali Thanwi, he used to say that they abided in his heart. They, too, had a great regard and affection for him owing to his extraordinary qualities.

Together with Zikr, Saga (spiritual exercises and exertions) Nawafil and Ibadaat, Maulana Muhammad Ilyas was, also, infused with the spirit of Jehad. During his life, he was never without it, and had, as a matter of fact, taken the oath of Jehad at the hand of Maulana Mahmood Hasan for that very reason.

From his early days, he was held in the highest esteem by the elders of the family and also the spiritual leaders of the day. Maulana Muhammad Yahya was like a father to him, yet the former's attitude towards his younger brother was like that of the sacred Prophet towards Hazrat Usman. Indifferent health kept him from taking part in obligations involving physical labour. He concentrated wholly on his studies, and on Zikr, and other forms of worship. Maulana Muhammad Yahya, on the contrary, was a very industrious person. He possessed a bookshop which he managed with great care. It was not only his source of livelihood, but of his brothers as well. One day, the manager of the shop said that Maulana Muhammad Ilyas didn't take any interest in the business which was not good for him to get benefited from it. When Maulana Muhammad Yahya heard of it, he was very annoyed and remarked that "a Tradition has it that the sustenance that reaches you and the assist you get from the Lord is due to the blessedness of the weaker ones amongst you. I believe that I am receiving my sustenance owing to the good fortune of this child. Nothing should be said to him in future. If there is anything to say, it should be said to me."

Occasionally, Maulana Muhammad Ilyas was asked to lead the service in the company of renowned theologians and spiritual leaders. Once Shah Abdur Rahim Raipuri, Maulana Khalil Ahmad Saharanpuri and Maulana Ashraf Ali Thanwi happened to be in Kandhla. When the time for Salaat came and Maulana Muhammad Ilyas was asked to lead it, a senior member of the family, Molvi Badrul Hasan, humorously remarked that "such a small engine has been fastened to several big carriages." "It depends on the power (not the size of the engine", replied one of them.

In 1910, a large number of men, along with most of the senior teachers of the Madrassa of Mazaahirul Uloom, went to the Haj from Saharanpur. It necessitated the recruitment of new teachers for the

Madrassa, Maulana Muhammad Ilyas being one of them. He was given the secondary books to teach. On the come back of the senior teachers from the Pilgrimage, all the new starters were relieved of their obligations, but the services of Maulana Muhammad Ilyas were retained.

At Mazaahirul Uloom, the Maulana had to teach some books which he had not read himself as, in Maulana Muhammad Yahya's scheme of instruction, it was not customary to complete the books, and Maulana Muhammad Ilyas, further, had to miss some secondary books owing to sick-health. During his teaching days, he tried hard to make up for the deficiency and prepared his lectures carefully. For example, for teaching Kinzul Daqa'iq, he studied Bahr-ur-Ra'iq, Shaami and Hadaya, and consulted even Hisami's notes and comments when he taught Nurul Anawaar.

The Maulana married the daughter of his maternal uncle, Maulana Rauful Hasan on Friday, October 17, 1912, and the ceremony was performed by Maulana Muhammad, and Maulana Khalil Ahmad Saharanpuri, Shah Abdur Rahim Raipuri and Maulana Ashraf Ali Thanwi, all the three of them, attended the ceremony. Maulana Thanwi's famous sermon, Fuwayid us Suhbat, which has consequently been published times without number, was delivered on that occasion.

In 1915, Maulana Khalil Ahmad Saharanpuri and Maulana Mahmood Hasan, decided to go on the Haj Pilgrimage. When Maulana Muhammad Ilyas came to know of it, he was deeply seized with the desire to perform the Haj. He felt that it would become dark and gloomy in India with their departure and he would not be able to live in Saharanpur any more. But there was the question of permission. As his sister, the wife of Molvi Ikrarnul Hasan, saw his suffering, she offered her ornaments to meet the expenses of the Pilgrimage. Contrary to expectations, the Maulana's mother gave her consent. After which Maulana Muhammad Yahya, also, agreed. The Maulana, then, wrote to Maulana Khalil Ahmad Saharanpuri asking for his permission, and explained that as far as she wherewithal for the travel was concerned, three courses were open to him. He could take his sister's ornaments or borrow the amount or accept the proposals of money made by certain relations. Maulana Khalil Ahmad Saharanpuri preferred the third course. Maulana Muhammad Ilyas was fortunate enough to travel by the same boat as Maulana Khalil Ahmad Saharanpuri. He sailed in August, 1914, and came back in February, 1915, to resume the teaching at the Madrassa.

The demise of Maulana Muhammad Yahya, on Wednesday, the August 9, 1915, was a tremendously sad and frustrating happening for the Maulana. In addition to being a most affectionate brother, he was, also, his teacher and benefactor. He could not get over the shock until the end of his days. He used to get lost in thought and a peculiar kind of abstraction took possession of him when he talked about his brother.

Two years after the demise of Maulana Muhammad Yahya, the eldest brother of Maulana Muhammad Ilyas, Maulana Muhammad, also, died. He was an individual of angelic disposition and an embodiment of affection, piety and humility. He loved solitude and cared little for worldly comforts. He dwelt in Bangle Wali Masjid, at Nizamuddin, in the place of his late father. There was a Madrassa in the mosque which had been established by Maulana Muhammad Ismail. Only primary education was imparted in it, and, amongst its pupils were mainly the children from Mewat. It had no usual source of income and reliance was placed solely upon God for meeting its requirements.

A lot of people of Delhi and Mewat were devoted to Maulana Muhammad and had benefited from his guidance. His face had the radiance of spirituality. He, often, gave the sermon, but in an informal, conversational way. He remained seated during it, and, generally, read out the Customs on good morals and Zuhd, (Muslim asceticism) and explained their meaning in a plain language.

Once Maulana Muhammad developed a boil under an eye which had to be opened seven times. The doctors insisted on administering the anaesthetic but he refused to take it and lay motionless during the operation. The surgeon, afterwards, said, that he had not seen the like of it in his life.

Maulana Muhammad spent most of his time in prayer and meditation. During the 16 years before his demise, he didn't miss the Tahajjud (before dawn prayer) prayers even once, and breathed his last while performing the Sajda in the Namaz of Witr.

Maulana Muhammad Ilyas had route to Delhi to look after his sick brother and was staying with him in the Nawab Wali Masjid of Qassab Pura. It was there that Maulana Muhammad expired and the burial took place at Nizamuddin. Thousands of men attended the funeral.

After the burial, people urged upon Maulana Muhammad Ilyas to take up residence at Nizamuddin in order to fill the void caused by the demise of his father and brother. They, also, promised monthly donations for the Madrassa to which the Maulana agreed subject to certain circumstances which he observed during his life.

Maulana Muhammad Ilyas had made it clear that he would come to Nizamuddin and take charge of the Madrassa only if Maulana Khaiil Ahmad Saharanpuri approved. Upon it, many persons offered to go to Saharanpur to obtain the permission, but Maulana Muhammad Ilyas checked them saying that it was not the way to do it. He would go himself, unaccompanied by anyone.

The Maulana, thus, moved to Saharanpur and explained the entire thing to Maulana Khalil Ahmad. The latter gave his consent, but added that, in the first instance, only a year's leave be taken from Mazaahirul Uloom and if the stay at Nizamuddin proved useful and it was decided to settle down there permanently, he could resign at any time.

But before Maulana Muhammad Ilyas could move to Nizamuddin, he was all of a sudden taken sick with pleurisy and moved to Kandhla where his circumstance worsened. One night his sickness took such a grave turn that all hope was lost. The pulse sank and the body became cold, but God had to take some work from him. Unexpectedly, he began to improve, and, in a couple of days, was able to leave the bed.

On regaining health, Maulana came to Nizamuddin from Kandhla. In those days, there was no habitation in that part of Nizamuddin, and, adjoining the mosque, there was a thick growth of trees and underbrush. Maulana Ihtishamul Hasan who, in his early days, had come to live, for sometime, with Maulana Muhammad Ilyas tells that "I used to go out and stand in the hope of seeing 'a human face'. When anyone appeared, I felt so happy as if someone had given me a precious gift."

A small pucca (constructed of bricks) mosque, a shed, a living apartment, a small settlement of the attendants of the tomb to the south of it, and a couple of Mewati and non-Mewati students that was all that formed the world of the mosque and the Madrassa.

The resources of the Madrassa were so meagre that, some times, they had to starve, but the Maulana bore it all with a cheerful heart. Sometimes, he would say plainly, that there was nothing to eat. Whoever wanted to stay' might stay and whoever wanted to go might go and make his arrangement elsewhere. The moral and spiritual education the students were receiving, nevertheless, was such that none of them was eager to leave. Often, they would live on wild fruits. The scholars themselves brought wood from the forest to prepare the chappati (flat bread) which they ate with chutney (pickle). The extreme poverty made no impression on the Maulana. What worried him was the prospect of abundance and prosperity which, he was sure, was going to open up, as per the practice of the Lord, after the phase of trial and tribulations.

The outward appearance of the Madrassa held no interest for the Maulana. He was supremely unconcerned with it. Once, during his absence, some residential quarters were made for its staff through the efforts of Haji Abdur Rahman, an old friend of his and an ex-student of the Madrassa, which made the Maulana so angry that he didn't speak to him for a considerable time. The Maulana remarked that the real thing was education, and, referring to a certain Madrassa, said that its building had become pucca, but the standard of education had gone down.

Once an outstanding merchant of Delhi begged the Maulana to supplicate to the Lord for him in a very influential matter, and presented him a purse. The Maulana agreed to pray on his behalf, but refused to accept the money. Haji Abdur Rahman, nevertheless, took it in view of the chronic financial difficulties of the Madrassa, but the Maulana had no peace till he had it returned. He used to impress upon Haji Abdur Rahrnan that the work of faith was not carried out with money, otherwise much wealth would have been awarded to the holy Prophet.

Worshipful Maulana Mohamrnad Ilyas, exclusively, kept himself occupied with prayers and other spiritual exertions in those days. He had inherited the inclination for it from his forefathers which blossomed up during the stay at Nizamuddin. He sought solitude and carried out vigorous exercises for the purification of the soul. As per Haji Abdur Rahman, the Maulana remained in seclusion for considerable hours at the gate of Arab Sara which was the favourite place of worship of Hazrat Nizmuddin Aulia, and was situated to the north of Humayun's tomb. Close to the mausoleum of Abdur Rahim Khan Khana and the grave of Syed Nur Muhammad Badayuni, the spiritual teacher of Mazhar jan-i-Jahan. Usually, his mid-day meal was sent there while the evening meal he took at home. He offered the five daily prayers in congregation. Haji Abdur Rahman and his fellow students used to go to the gate to form the congregation, and for their lessons, they, occasionally, went there, and, some times, the Maulana himself came to Chukkar Wali Masjid.

The Maulana performed the Wuzu (abulation) and offered two Rak'ats of Namaz before commencing the lesson of the Traditions, and remarked that the claim of the Customs was even bigger. He didn't talk to anyone, nevertheless important, while teaching the Customs, nor ever complained if the meal came late from Nizamuddin, nor found fault with food.

The Maulana took keen interest in his pupils and personally taught all the subjects, elementary and also advanced. Occasionally, he had as many as eighty students directly under his instruction, and took the class of Mustadrak-e-Haakim before Fajr.

The main emphasis in his method of teaching was on the application of mind. He wanted the students to come thoroughly prepared. The Maulana didn't follow the general syllabus of the Madrassas in the selection of books and a lot of books that were but prescribed in the other Madrassas were taught at Nizamuddin. He thought of new ways to stimulate the students and develop the faculties of imagination and understanding in them.

The region to the south of Delhi where the Meos have been settled from the olden days is named Mewat. Presently, it includes the Gurgaon district of Haryana, Alwar and Bharatpur and the district of Mathura. Like all other regions, its borders, too, have been changing from time to time and the dimensions of the old Mewat must have been different from what they are now.

The English historians hold that the Meos do not come from the Aryan stock, but are related to the non-Aryan races of ancient India. Their history, thus, dates far back than that of the Rajput families of Aryan blood. As per them, the Khanzadas (lowest order of Mughal nobility) of Mewat, nevertheless, belong to the same ethnic group as the Rajputs, and, in the Persian history books, wherever the word 'Mewati' occurs, it denotes the very Khanzadas. We, further, learn from Ain-i-Akbari that the Jatau Rajputs came to be acknowledged as Mewatis on embracing Islam.

In the annals of Firoz Shahi dynasty, Mewat is mentioned, for the first time, in the memoirs of Shamsuddin Al-timash. The Mewatis had become very troublesome during the early days of the Islamic Kingdom of Delhi. Aided by the considerable range of thick forests that extended up to Delhi, they used to raid it often and had become such a terror that the gates of the capital were shut at sunset. Still, they managed to enter the town in the night in search of plunder. Ghayasuddin Balban, therewith, dispatched a substantial military force against the Mewatis, killing a large number of them. Outposts manned by the Afghan soldiers were set up in Delhi, the surrounding forests were cut down and the land was brought under cultivation. Mewat, after that, remained in oblivion for about a hundred years.

After the considerable lull, the Mewati adventurers, again, became active and began harassing the people of Delhi which forced the authorities to take punitive action against them from time to time. The names of

Bahadur Nahir and his heirs are, especially, cited in the chronicles in this connection. They succeeded in establishing the Kingdom of Mewat which was, afterward, reduced to a Jagir (a feudal estate) by the rulers of Delhi.

Another outstanding Mewatis was Lakhan Pal who brought the entire Mewat and its outlying territory under his domination. He embraced Islam during the reign of Firoz Shah.

Owing to the negligence of the Muslims religious teachers, the moral arid religious circumstance of the Mewatis had sunk so low that there was little to distinguish between their viewpoint and practices and wholesale apostasy. Even non-Islamic historians have commented at length on their estrangement with Islam, as the following extract from the Alwar Gazetteer of 1878, scripted by Major Powlett, will show:

"All the Meos are, now, Muslims, but only in name. Their village deities are the same as those of the Hindu landlords, and they celebrate many Hindu festivals. Holi is a season of distictive rejoicing amongst the Mewatis and they observe it like their own festivals, such as, Moharrum, Id and Shab-e-Barat. The same is the case with Janam Ashtami, Dussehra and Diwali, The Meos engage the services of the Brahmins to fix the dates of marriages. They have Hindu names, with the exception of the word 'Ram', and their last name, often, is 'Singh', although not as often as 'Khan'. Like Ahirs and Gujars, the Mewatis, too, observe Amawas as a holiday on which they abstain from work. When they build a well, they begin with the construction of a parapet in the name of Beeriyi or Hanuman, but when it comes to pillage, they do not show much reverence to the Hindu temples and other places of religious importance. If, on such an occasion, their attention is drawn to the sanctity of these establishments, they, unhesitatingly, says, 'You are "Does" and we are "Meos".' Meos are, largely, ignorant of their faith, i. e., Islam. Very few of them know the Kalima,' and fewer still observe Namaz regularly. About the hours and rules of namaz, their ignorance is complete. This is the state of the Meos of Alwar.

In some parts of Alwar, also, where the mosques have been made, the religious obligations are observed to some extent. A couple of them know the Kalima and offer up namaz and an affection for the Madrassas, also, is found amongst them. As we have seen earlier, the initial rites of marriage are executed by the Brahmins, but the real ceremony (of nikah) is performed by the Qazi. Men wear dhoti and loincloth. The pyjamas are not worn at all. Their dress, thus, is wholly Hinduised. Even ornaments of gold are worn by men."

All the same, the Meos are distinguished for some excellent moral qualities, and their vices and weaknesses are in the nature of the evil ways and practices that become a part of the moral and social pattern of brave and adventurous races as a consequence of want of education, isolation from the civilized world and indifference towards religion. These were rampant even amongst the Arabs during the Age of Ignorance. Natural talents and capabilities had taken a wrong turn owing to the perversity of the atmosphere. Chivalry had degenerated into banditry, man-liness had found expression in mutual warfare and bloodshed, sensation of pride and self-respect, with no better purpose to serve, had sought realization in the defence of imaginary standards of honour and renown, and high mindedness, for its exhibit, had adopted the path of pomp and flourish on petty occasions in the family or clan. In short, God-given gifts of mind and character were being put to unworthy use, otherwise there was no dearth of virtue and merit amongst the Meos.

Rugged simplicity, hardihood and firmness of purpose were the chief characteristics of the Mewatis in which they were far superior to the urban Islamic population. It was on account of these qualities that in spite of having drifted so far away from Islam, the floodtide of Apostasy could not submerge the territory of Mewat even in the darkest period of its history.

For centuries the Maos had been living inside the shell of their ignorance keeping by themselves and seperated from the outside world. A parallel can scarcely be found in the Indian history of a community so large and living in such a close proximity to the key seat of power and yet staying so little-known and seperated. An advantage of it, nevertheless, was that the energies of the Mewatis, on the whole, remained conserved, the soil remained virgin while the deplorable habits and traditions and superstitious belief and practices were, so to speak, like the weeds and scrubs growing on an uncultivated land. The Meos, in the 20th Century, were very much like the Arabs in the Age of Perversion.

Beginning, as we have seen, contact with the Mewatis was founded during the lifetime of Maulana Muhammad Ismail. It was not a chance occurrence, but a deed of destiny that Maulana Muhammad Ismail came to live in Basti Nizamuddin which was the gateway of Mewat, and much before the arrival of Maulana Muhammad Ilyas, seeds of loyalty and devotion of his family had been sown on its soil.

When the adherents of Maulana Muhammad Ismail and Maulana Muhammad came to know that their true heir, the son of Maulana

Muhammad Ismail and the brother of Maulana Muhammad had come to live at Nizamuddin, they, again, started coming to it and requested Maulana Muhammad Ilyas for a visit so that the old suppliants of his family had a chance to renew the ties of fealty and spiritual allegiance.

Maulana Muhammad Ilyas felt that the only Way to the religious reform and correction of the Mewatis was advancement of religious knowledge and familiarization with the rules and ideals of the Shariat.

Maulana Muhammad Ismail, and after him, Maulana Muhammad had adopted the same method. They used to keep the Mewati children with them and educate them in their Madrassa, and, then, send them back to Mewat to carry on the work of reform and guidance, and what little religious awareness was found there was owing to the efforts of these pioneers.

Maulana Muhammad Ilyas went a step ahead and decided to make Maktabs and Madrassas in Mewat itself so that the influence of Faith could spread to a wider region and the pace of change was accelerated.

Stipulation, the Maulana knew, what was, commonly, meant by inviting a spiritual teacher or his heir to their place by his disciples and admirers, and he was not eager to go to Mewat only to fulfil the formalities of attending the dinner given in his honour delivering a couple of sermons and giving good advise. He wanted to make sure before undertaking the trip, that some real advance would be made, as a consequence of his visit, towards bringing the Meos closer to Islam and improving their moral circumstance, arid, during those days, the setting up of Maktabs and Madrassas in Mewat appeared to him to be the most efficient step in that direction. He had, thus, made it clear that he would accept the invitation only on the condition that they promised to make Maktabs in their territory.

For the Mewatis, nevertheless, no undertaking could be harder to give. They considered the establishment of Maktabs next to impossible for the plain reason that no one would be sending his children to them, and, thus, depriving himself of their contribution to the family income as daily wage-earners. The exuberance of those who came to invite quickly subsided as they heard of the stipulation. In desperation, nevertheless, a Mewati, finally, made the promise, leaving the rest to God.

Maulana Muhammad Ilyas, accordingly, moved to Mewat and demanded the realization of the promise. After great persuasion, the starting was made and the first Maktab was founded.

The Maulana used to tell the Mewatis, "Give me the pupils, I will provide the money." The Meos who were, mostly, farmers, could not easily reconcile themselves to the position that their children applied themselves to reading and writing and stopped functioning in the fields or looking after the cattle. It took a plenty of tact and perseverance to bring them round to it.

Ten Maktabs were opened during that visit. Once the ice was broken, the development was easy. Occasionally, many Maktabs were opened in a day until, inside a couple of years, hundreds of such schools were functioning in Mewat. The Maulana had not undertaken the service of Faith as a "national cause", the burden of providing the funds for which fell wholly upon the nation or the community, but as a personal affair and felt no hesitation in spending all he had on it. He believed that a person should perform a religious task as his own and expend his time and money freely in its way.

Once a person presented a purse to him with the request that he used it, exclusively, for his own requirements. The Maulana replied, "If we do not regard Allah's work our own, how can we claim to be His bondmen ?" With a sigh, he added, "Alas! We are not the just appreciators of the sacred Prophet. We do not know his true worth."

This was the Maulana's rule of life. First of all, he spent from his own pocket on the religious endeavour he had started in Mewat, and, then, alone, would accept assistance from others.

Due to Maulana Muhammad Ilyas sincerity and hard work, the work of Tableegh began to spread and Jamaats began to visit all parts of the subcontinent inside his life time. Hazrat Maulana Syed Suleiman Nadwi (RA) remarks, " Hazrat Maulana Muhammad Ilyas (RA) with his simplicity and devotion to the correct ideals of Dawat (invitation) quietly turned the Mewatees into sincere and devotional Muslims over a twenty five years and made them the envy of even the Muslims belonging to conventional religious families.

Maulana Muhammad Ilyas expired in 1944, in Delhi, India.

4. MAULANA TARIQ JAMIL

Maulana Tariq Jamil was born in 1953, in Main Channu, Punjab, Pakistan. He is a famous Muslim scholar of the Hanafi school of though from Pakistan. His father was an agriculturist and was a respected persor in his area and the local region.

Maulana Tariq Jamil was born and raised in Main Channu and is the son of a Feudal agriculturist, also referred to as Lord in Pakistan. In his early days he lived a relatively humble life but religion was not a prominant part of his life and his family in particular. It wasn't till he persuaded his M.B.B.S in Lahore that his focus moved towards Islam. After going through F.Sc. in pre-medical (A-level equivalent) from Government College, University of Lahore, he took admission in King Edward Medical College in Lahore. He intended to do the M.B.B.S degree, but spiritual thought provoked him to gain Muslim education. Then he got his Muslim education from Jamia Arabia, Raiwind (close to Lahore), Pakistan. He studied Quran, Hadith, Sharia, Tasawwuf, logic and Fiqh there.

His leniency towards Islam grew during hostel life in Lahore and can mostly be accredited to the group members of Tablighi Jamaat who he became friends with during his College life. During his stay at the King Edward Medical College in Lahore, he intensively studied Islam and shortly after became a full time student in the studies of Islam. After graduating he devoted his life to the propagation of Islam.

He regularly delivers lectures and speeches encouraging people to follow Muslim values, ideals & practices. He emphasizes non-political, non-violent, non-sectarian Islam. He has travelled extensively for this cause and has delivered thousands of lectures all over the world. In his Hunger for knowledge, he travelled intensively to many Muslim Countries and mastered his capability to fluently speak and understand Arabic. His charming appearance combined with a strong voice and capability to deliver religious lectures shortly saw his rise to fame and inside a matter of years, he became one of the most profound speakers of Islam in Urdu language.

Since early 1990s, he has frequently travelled to countries all around the world and almost every single lecture delivered by him would attract a big number of crowd. As a matter of fact, in February, Maulana Tariq Jamil was a speaker at a happening that took place in Tongi, Bangladesh which attracted an estimate 3,000,000 people and is listed on the, List of largest gatherings in history."

Maulana Tariq Jamil has denounced the killing of harmless civilians and any act of terrorism and has on many occasions demanded, upon all sides, to stop the violence and killing taking place in many Islamic countries. He has been a severe critic of the War on Terrorism and has warned that the consequences of this war have been devastating for average citizens of their respected countries such as Iraq & Afghanistan.

In February 2008, an "Anti-terrorism Conference" organized by the seminary Darul Uloom in Deoband, Uttar Pradesh, denounced all forms of terrorism, saying, "Islam prohibits killing of harmless people," and "Islam sternly condemns all kinds of oppression, violence and terrorism." The conference also denounced widespread attempts to blame religious Muslims for terrorist incidents.

Due to his sermons and plain and humble lifestyle, Maulana Tariq Jamil commands respect from Muslims all over the world. He has a plain, eloquent and a distinctive style of explaining the purpose of human life and its creation and often uses scientific example, to further strengthen his lectures. He has delivered his lectures in all types of the communities of the society with the attendee being doctors, engineers, professors, businessmen, landlords, government officials, TV/film artists, ministers and sports' celebrities. His untiring efforts brought real Muslim values in the lives of some of the biggest Pakistani cricketing legends such as Saeed Anwar, Inzamam-ul-Haq, Muhammad Yousuf, Saqlain Mushtaq, Mushtaq Ahmed, Salim Malik and Hammad Ahmed Abbassi. He has also been the main paradigm for Junaid Jamshed since his reversion towards Islam.

Tariq Jamil is the Khalifah (representative) of the late Mufti Yousuf Ludhianvi, who was martyred in Karachi on Thursday (May 18, 2000) while he was on his way back from the Fajr Salat.

Maulana Tariq Jamil has travelled extensively around the globe for the propagation of Islam. He has been to many Islamic and non-Islamic countries in the past two decades. He First visit the USA took place in the year 1993 and delivered a well-known Lecture named as "Dawt'a Tablig". In 1998, Maulana Tariq Jamil again came to USA and travelled to many states to deliver Sermons and meet with local Muslims. His latest Visit to the USA was in January of 2001. He has also made multiple visits to a lot of Western countries such as United Kingdom, South Africa, Denmark & etc.

5. MUHAMMAD HUSSAIN NAJAFI

Muhammad Hussain was born on April 10, 1932, in district Sargodha Punjab, Pakistan. He belongs to the Dhakku branch of Jat people. He had two paternal uncles, both of whom were Shia ulema: Maulana Imam

Bakhsh was a religious teacher in Jahanian Shah, while Maulana Sohrab Ali Khan was a esteemed alim of Uch Sharif. His father Rana Tajuddin was not an alim, but he had the wish of making his son a great alim. Nevertheless, he expired in 1944 when Muhammad Hussain was 12 years old, after which the family members persuaded the widow that Muhammad Hussain should look after the family lands, but she kept up the wish of her dead husband.

Before going to Najaf for higher religious education, he was married to his maternal cousin in 1952. His mentor Allama Yar Shah had links with ulema of Najaf, and he wanted Muhammad Hussain to get married in a scholarly family of Najaf, but Muhammad Hussain refused this proposal due to cultural differences. In 1954, his only son Muhammad Sibtain was born. At the age of five, he got severely sick and expired, as Muhammad Hussain didn't have enough money for his cure. (Muhammad Hussain used to spend his stipend money on family and buying books.) After Sibtain's demise, Ayatollah Najafi didn't have children for next eleven years. He married the daughter of Haji Muhammad Shafi (Faisalabad) in 1970. He had three daughters from this marriage. His first wife expired in 1996.

After secondary school education, he got admission in Madrasah Muhammadia in Jalalpur Nankiana, Sargodha, where one of his outstanding mentors was Maulana Hussain Bakhsh Jarra. In 1947, he studied the courses of Dars-i-Nizami from Allama Muhammad Baqir Naqvi in Jhang. Allama Baqir had migrated from Iraq to spread Shia formal education in Pakistan. Since Allama Yar Shah, the most outstanding disciple of Allama Muhammad Baqir, had moved from his ancestral city Alipur to Jalalpur, Muhammad Hussain moved to Jalalpur to complete Dars-i-Nizami for the next five years. In 1953, he passed the examination of Molvi Fazil from Punjab University, and moved to Najaf in 1954 for higher education.

After returning to Pakistan in 1960, Pir Fazal Shah (Parhezgar) asked him to become the principal of Dar-ul-Uloom Muhammadia, Sargodha, which he keenly agreed to.

In 1971, due to increased involvement in majalis and Shia political movements it became impossible for him to run the affairs of Dar-ul-Uloom Muhammadia, therefore he stepped down from this post.

In 1963, the principals of Shia madrasaas from all over Pakistan gathered in Karbala Gamey Shah, Lahore, and established Tanzeeme Madarise Arabia Shia Pakistan (Organization of Shia Madrasahs of Pakistan). Ayatollah Najafi was elected its president.

In 1965, a high-level organization of Shia ulema Mautamar Ulemae Shia Pakistan (Conference of Shia Ulema of Pakistan) was formed with Ayatollah Najafi as its president and Mufti Jafar Hussain as its patron. Other members included Allama Gulab Ali Shah, Allama Akhtar Abbas, Allama Hussain Bakhsh Jarra, Hafiz Saifullah Jafari, Allama Safdar Hussain Najafi, Mufti Inayat Ali Shah, Allama Muhib Hussain, Allama Riaz Hussain Najafi and Allama Ghulam Hassan Jarra.

In 1964, Ayatollah Muhammad Hussain Najafi played a crucial role in gathering about 250 Shia ulema and leaders in Imam Bargah Rizvia, Karachi, where "Shia Mutalbat Committee" was formed with Syed Muhammad Dehlavi as its president.

In 1978, after Zia ul Haq's declaration of promulgating Hanafi fiqh, Shia ulema and leaders gathered in Bhakkar and established Tehrik-e-Nifaz-e-Fiqh-e-Jafaria (afterward named Tehrik-e-Jafaria Pakistan) with Mufti Jafar Hussain as its president. Ayatollah Najafi was a part of this organization's supreme council. After Mufti Jafar's demise, it was upon Ayatollah Najafi's recommendation that Allama Arif Hussain Hussaini was elected the new president of the organization.

For past thirty years, he has been addressing majalis in almost all parts of Punjab, Pakistan. For the last five years he has been addressing majalis in Imambargah Shah Gardez, Multan where all the major Shia ulema address majalis before him, including Allama Akhter Abbas, Principal of Madrasah Jamia tus-Saqlain, Multan. Famous Ayatollah Syed Aqeel-ul-Gharavi also addressed majalis at the same place. He has also been addressing majalis in London and Islamabad for many years.

6. MUHAMMAD SHAHIDULLAH

Muhammad Shahidullah popularly known as Dr. Shahidullah was born on July 10, 1885, in the village Peyara, 24 Pargana district of West Bengal in India. He was a famous Bengali educationist, writer and linguist.

Muhammad Shaidullah passed his school finals in 1904 from Howrah Zila School. In 1906, he passed the FA exam (equivalent to HSC) from Presidency College, Kolkata. He received the Bachelor of Arts degree with Honours in Sanskrit in 1910 from City College, Kolkata, and Master of Arts in 1912 in Comparative Philology from the University of Calcutta. He also obtained his law degree two years later in 1914. He also received a PhD from the University of Paris.

Shahidullah's teaching career started in Jessore District School where he taught between 1908 and 1909. He also worked as the headmaster of Sitakunda High School, Chittagong between 1914 and 1915. He practised law for some time and was elected vice-chairman of the Bashirhat municipality. However, he returned to research and worked as Sharatchandra Lahiri Research Fellow (1919-21) under the supervision of Prof. Dinesh Chandra Sen at the University of Calcutta. Subsequently, Shahidullah joined the University of Dhaka as a lecturer of Sanskrit and Bangla languages in 1921. His years at the University of Dhaka constituted the most important period of his life. During his teaching and research career there, he explored the origins of the Bangla language. In 1925, he was able to show that Bangla originated from Gaudi or Magadhan Prakrit (or derivative of Sanskrit).

To pursue his doctoral studies, Muhammad Shahidullah went to France and Germany in 1926. He learnt Vedic Sanskrit, Buddhist Sanskrit, Comparative Philology, and Tibetan and ancient Persian languages at University of Paris, and ancient Khotni, ancient Vedic Sanskrit and Prakrt at Freiburg University in Germany. He received his doctorate from the Sorbonne in Paris in 1928 for his research on the distiches of the Charyapada, the earliest extant specimens of Bangla language.

Dr. Shahidullah was the first Indian Muslim to receive the doctorate degree. He also received a diploma for his fundamental research in phonetics from the University of Paris the same year. After completing his doctorate, he returned home and started teaching. When the Sanskrit and Bangla Department was split into two separate departments, he became head of the Bangla Department in 1937 and retired from this position in 1944.

He became principal of Bogra Azizul Huq College after retirement. He then rejoined the Bangla Department of the University of Dhaka as a supernumerary teacher and taught there for six yeas as departmental head and dean of the Faculty of Arts. Also, he taught part-time at the Law Department (1922-25) and the International Relation Department (as teacher of French language) (1953-55). He also worked as head of the Bangla and Sanskrit Department of the University of Rajshahi from 1955-58.

Muhammad Shahidullah explored deep into the history of old and middle Age Bangla literature. He wrote many books on these subjects, and his research answered many of the interesting questions about specific properties of Bangla language and literature.

He also took active interest in Bangla folk literature. Apart from research, he wrote for children. He also translated and edited a number of books.

Noteworthy among his books are:

- 1922: Sindabad Saodagarer Galpa (The stories of the merchant Sindbad)
- 1931: Bhasa O Sahitya (Language and literatureessays)
- 1936: Bangala Byakaran (Bangla grammar)
- 1938: Diwan-i-Hafiz (Poems of Hafiz, translation)
- 1942: Shikwah O Jawab-i-Shikwah (Questions and their answers translation from Iqbal)
- 1942: Rubaiyat-i-Omar Khaiyam (Quatrains of Omar Khayyam translation)
- 1945: Essays on Islam
- 1949: Amader Samasya (Our problems, essays)
- 1950: Padmavati (Volume I Ed.)
- 1953: Bangla Sahityer Katha (History of Bangla literature, Volume I)
- 1954: Vidyapati Shatak (Collection of Vidyapati's songs text analysis)
- 1957: Bangla Adab Ki Tarikh (History of Bangla literature, Essays in Urdu)
- 1957: Bangla Sahityer Itihas (History of Bangla literature)
- 1959: Bangala Bhasar Itibrtta (History of Bangla language)
- 1963: Quran Sharif (The Quran)
- 1963: Amarkabya (Unforgettable poetical works)
- 1965: Sekaler Rupkatha (Fairy tales of ancient time)
- 1965: Bangla Sahityer Katha (History of Bangla literature, Volume II)

Dr. Shahidullah is also credited with formulating the rules for the reformed Bangla Calendar.

He expired on July 3, 1969, in Dhaka, Bangladesh.

7. MUHAMMAD ZAKARIYA AL-KANDAHLAWI

Muhammad Zakariyya al-Kandhlawi was born on February 3, 1898, in the town of Kandhla, in the district of Muzaffarnagar, India. His lineage stretches back over many centuries to Abu Bakr. Seven days after Hadhrat's birth, his father, Hadhrat Shaykh Maulana Muhammad Yahya Kandhlawi, came to Kandhla. Standing at the door of the house, he expressed his wish to have a look at the newborn baby. The baby was sent to him. He had brought along a barber, who shaved off the baby's hair. After reaching Gangoh, Hadhrat commenced his primary education under a devotional doctor, Hakim Abdur Rahman. Qaidah Baghdadi was studied under him. After that, he commenced Hifz of the Quran under his father. Hadhrat was instructed to recite his daily Hifz lesson hundred times. After finishing Hifz of the Quran, he studied various other kitabs viz. Bahishti Zewar and Persian and Urdu kitabs. Persian kitabs and preliminary Arabic kitabs were taught to him by his paternal uncle, Hadhrat Shaykh Maulana Muhammad Ilyas Kandhlawi. Only the primary textbooks of Nahw (Arabic grammar) were taught to him by his father.

In July of 1940, Hadhrat moved to Saharanpur, where his father had settled. In Saharanpur, he was taught a couple of primary Arabic textbooks by his father and advanced his study of Arabic, studying various classical texts on Arabic morphology, grammar, literature, and logic. His Ustads in the philosophical sciences were Maulana Abdul Lateef and Maulana Abdul Wahid Sambhali. In Saharanpur, hadith became the main focus of Hadhrat's studies.

By 1955, Hadhrat was finishing his final (Daura-e-Hadith) year. In addition to Sunan ibn Maja, he studied all the hadith kitabs under his father. Since Sunan ibn Maja was being taught by Maulana Thabit Ali, Hadhrat studied it under him. Sahih al-Bukhari and Sunan at-Tirmidhi were pursued a second time under Hadhrat Shaykh Maulana Khalil Ahmad Saharanpuri on his come back from Hijaaz. Hadhrat expended great effort and concentration in his study of Hadith. He observed two things rigidly: Never would he miss a lesson and never would he study without wudhu.

When Hadhrat was merely nineteen, his father expired. After finishing his academic studies in 1957, Hadhrat was appointed as a teacher at the primary level in Mazahirul Uloom. His monthly salary was fifteen rupees. Kitabs such as Usulush Shashi and Ilmus Sigha were assigned to him.

These two kitabs were transferred to Hadhrat from senior teachers. In addition to these, he taught another five kitabs: Miat-e-Aamil Manzoom, Sharh-e-Miak, Khulasah Nohmir, Nafhatul Yaman and Munyatul Musalli.

In the following year, he taught the following kitabs: Mirqaat, Quduri, Sharah Tahzib, Kaafiyah, Nurul Idah, Usulush Shashi, Sharah Jami, and Beheth fil Beheth Ism. In the same year, there was further advancement. Higher kitabs such as Maqaamat, Sab'ah Muallaqah, Mir Qutbu, and Kanzud Daqaaiq were assigned to Hadhrat.

In view of the commencement of writing the kitab, Bazlul Majhood, most lessons were taught after hours. Thus, Hamaasah was taught after Isha and some other lessons after Asr.

In Shawwaal, Hadhrat went together with his Shaikh for Hajj. In Madina, he taught Sunan Abi Da'ud at Madrasatul Uloom Shari'ah for a year. While in Madina, he began functioning on Awjaz ul-Masalik ila Mu'atta Imam Malik. He was twenty-nine at the time.

In 1970, the authorities of the Madrasa resolved to assign Sahih al-Bukhari to Hadhrat because the administrative obligations of the Madrasah's Nazim, Maulana Abdul Lateef, had multiplied noticeably. This plan greatly saddened the Nazim because of the loss of his occupation of teaching Hadith. Hadhrat's sensitive and honourable disposition perceived the adverse consequence this plan had on Maulana Abdul Lateef. He therefore submitted an optional plan to the Madrasa authorities. His plan envisaged that the starting of Sahih al-Bukhari should be taught by the Nazim and, after Eid, the first volume of Sahih al-Bukhari should be taught by him (Hadhrat). The second volume should be taught by the Nazim after Maghrib. This plan was gladly agreed to and the Nazim's displeasure dissipated.

In all, Hadhrat taught the first volume of Sahih al-Bukhari twenty-five times, the complete Sahih al-Bukhari sixteen times, and Sunan Abu Da'ud thirty times. He didn't simply teach Hadith as a matter of routine. The work of Hadith became his zeal.

Hadhrat wrote works both in Arabic and Urdu. A number of them treat specialized subjects intended for scholars and the rest have been scripted for the general public. His works demonstrate his deep knowledge and intelligence, his capability to understand the issue at hand, research it thoroughly, and present a complete, clear, and comprehensive discussion, and his moderation, humility, patience, and attention to detail. His respect and awe for his devotional predecessors are apparent in his works, even when he disagrees with their opinions on any particular aspect.

His first scripted work was a three-volume commentary of the Alfiyya Ibn Malik on Arabic grammar, which he wrote as a student when he was only thirteen. His scripted works amount to over one hundred. He didn't hold any rights to his works and made it publicly known that he only published his works for the sake of Allah's pleasure. Whoever wished to publish them was permitted to, on the condition that they were left unaltered and their accuracy maintained.

Hence, his works have acquired overwhelming acceptance all over the world, so much so that his work, Fadha'il-e-Quran has been translated into eleven languages, Fadha'il-e-Ramadan into twelve languages, and Fadha'il-e-Salaah into fifteen languages. He wrote four books on tafsir(Quranic exegesis) and tajwid (proper recitation), forty-four books on Hadith and its related sciences, six books on Fiqh and its related sciences, twenty-four historical and biographical books, four books on Aqida (Muslim creed), twelve books on Zuhd (abstinence) and Riqaq (heart-softening accounts), three books on Arabic grammar and Logic, and six books on modern-day Groups and Movements.

Some of his most renowned works are:

- Awjaz-ul-Masalik ilá' Mu'atta Imam Malik: One of the most comprehensive commentaries on the Mu'atta of Imam Malik in terms of the science of Hadith, Jurisprudence, and Hadith explication. Hadhrat supplies the summaries of a lot of other commentaries in a clear, intellectual, and scholarly way, dealing with the various opinions on each issue, mentioning the differences of opinions amongst the various scholars, and comparing their proofs. This commentary, scripted in Arabic, has won great acclaim from a number of Maliki scholars.
- Fadha'il-e-A'maal
- Lami' al-Dirari ala Jami' al-Bukhari: Scripted in Arabic, a collection of the exceptional remarks and observations on Sahih al-Bukhari presented by Hadhrat Shaykh Maulana Rashid Ahmad Gangohi. These life-long acquired wisdoms were recorded by his student, Hadhrat Shaykh Maulana Muhammad Yahya Kandhlawi (Hadhrat's father) during their lessons. Hadhrat edited, arranged, and commented on his father's compilation, clarifying the text and adding a comprehensive introduction at the starting.
- Al-Abwab wal Tarajim lil Bukhari: An explanation of the chapter headings of Sahih al-Bukhari. Assigning chapter headings in a

Hadith collection is a science in itself, known amongst the scholars as Al-Abwab wal Tarajim (chapters and explanations). In it, the compiler explains the reasons for the chapter heading and the connections between the chapter headings and the Hadiths cited therein. It is famous that the commentators of Sahih al-Bukhari have paid distictive attention to the titles therein, in tune with the Arabic saying: "The fiqh of Sahih al-Bukhari is in the chapter headings" (Fiqh al-Bukhari fi tarajimihi). Hadhrat not only quotes and compiles what has been mentioned by other scholars, but also correlates and clarifies these opinions and presents findings from his own research in a lot of examples.

- Juz Hajjat al-Wida wa Umrat al-Nabi: A comprehensive Arabic commentary on the detailed accounts of the Hajj of Prophet Muhammad. It includes the details of any juridical discussions on the various aspects of pilgrimage, stating the locations, modern-day names, and other details of the places the Messenger of Allah passed by or stayed at.
- Khasa'il Nabawi Sharh Shama'il al-Tirmidhi: Compiled in Urdu, a commentary on Tirmidhi's renowned work, Al-Shama'il al-Muhammadiyya, a collection of ahadeeth detailing the characteristics of the Messenger of Allah. This commentary explains the various aspects related to the various characteristics and practices of Allah's Messenger. It has been translated into English and is broadly accessible.

Muhammad Zakariyya Kandhlawi expired on May 23, 1982, in Saudi Arabia.

8. SYED WAHEED AKHTAR

Syed Waheed Akhtar was born on August 12, 1934, in the city of Aurangabad, India, in a family which migrated from Nasirabad-Jais (Jais-birth place of poet Malik Muhammad Jayasi), boroughs of Sa'adat inhabitants in Raebareily (or Raebareli) district of Uttar Pradesh. His father's name was Syed Nazr-e Abbas, and mother's name was Syeda Aliya Begum. They had seven children. Waheed Akhtar was the second child, amongst six sons and one daughter. After spending his early days in Aurangabad, and finishing high school and intermediate, he moved to Hyderabad, to enroll at Osmania University as a bachelor of art student.

He was in Hyderabad for eight years till he finished his Ph. D. and got appointment as lecturer at Aligarh Muslim University. Years in Hyderabad were crucial for moulding his individuality as a poet and author. Though, after Police Action Hyderabad acceded to the Dominion of India, it was still a very strong feudal society, dominated by rich and elite. At the same time, plenty of muslims who held positions of significance had become defeatist, thinking they had lost their voice and authority in the circumstances prevalent at that time. Hyderabad was still, the only University in subcontinent to teach modern sciences along with medicine and engineering in Urdu, which was the fruit of Allamah Shibli Nomani's hardwork.

Waheed Akhtar was not the one to resign to defeat, nor overwhelmed by the times and existing system. He was a born fighter and he made his ideas and voice heard in his compositions. He was independent minded, freedom loving man who was well aware of political and literary movements of his times around the world. He wrote prolifically in Urdu from very early age. During his initial years, he adopted the pen name "Barq".

He got married to Indo-Iranian lady Syeda Mahliqa Qarai in Hyderabad in the year 1962 and had four sons: Hasan, Husain, Haider (who expired due to polio in the fifth month of his birth) and Mohsin. Mrs. Mahliqa Qarai was killed in the USS Vincennes attack on Iran Air Flight 655 - an Iranian civilian airliner on Sunday, July 3, 1988, in the Persian Gulf during the eight-year Iraq-Iran war. After his wife's demise, he suffered five coronary failures and three cardiac arrests.

His early education took place at Chelipura High School, a government school in Aurangabad. He was educated at Osmania University, Hyderabad, Andhra Pradesh and got his bachelor's degree in arts, and master's and Ph. D degrees in Philosophy. He was appointed Lecturer of philosophy at Aligarh Muslim University and moved on to settle in Aligarh for the rest of his life, where he retired in 1995.

He passed all examinations from Osmania University, Hyderabad in first division with distinction. He finished High School in 1950; B.A. in 1954; M.A. (Philosophy) in 1956; Ph.D. in 1960 in Philosophy, on the dissertation named "Khwaja Mir Dard's Contribution to Sufism."

He was appointed Lecturer in General Education in 1960 at Aligarh Muslim University and Lecturer in Philosophy in 1962; became Reader in Humanities in 1970; Reader in Philosophy in 1975 and became Professor in 1979. He headed the Department of Philosophy at AMU from April

1987-1990 & 1992 until 1995 until his retirement as well as served the University as Dean Faculty of Arts from 1990-92.

He specialized in Sufism, Existentialism, Aesthetics, Literary Criticism and Islamic Philosophy and Shi'ite Thought. More than two hundred articles, besides eight books in Urdu and English published.

His research and originative work has been cited and referred to by a number of scholars in Philosophy, Islamic Studies and Literature, such as Annemarie Schimmel, Dr. Abid Husain, Prof. Aale Ahmad Suroor, Prof. Ehtisham Husain, Prof. Majnoon Gorakhpuri, Ali Sardar Jafari, Prof. Muhi-al-din Qadri Zor, Prof. A.Q. Sarwari, Dr.Wazir Agha, Khalil-al-Rehman Azmi, Prof. Mumtaz Husain, Prof. Qamar Raees, Prof. Mohd. Hasan, Prof. G.C. Narang and a lot of eminent literary critics.

Large number of researchers got Ph.D and M.Phil. degrees under his supervision, in the fields of Islamic Philosophy, Existentialism, Aesthetics and Social Philosophy.

His published collections of poetry comprise mostly ghazals (Ghazal) and nazms (Nazm), but his mastery on other forms of poetry, like Marsia-elegy in the musaddas format; Qasida (Panegyric), Hajv (lampoon), Manqibat, Salaam, Rubai (quatrain)- is exemplary. He was one of the few to tread his own path independent of "Tarraqipas and Tehreek" (Progressive Writers' Movement) and questioned radical principles of the liberal movement, when most of the authors of subcontinent were looking towards communist Soviet Union for motivation and guidance. He argued and predicted that a system which is devoid of personal, political and creative freedom is bound to fail. These ideas were written down in late 1950s in 'Saba'- a literary Urdu journal edited and published by Sulaiman Areeb from Hyderabad. This item evoked a harsh disapproval from none other than founding father of the Progressive Writers' Movement, Sajjad Zaheer. Impact of the item was such that dispute raged for years in the literary journals of the sub-continent.

Some of his memorable awards are:

- 1960: Andhra Pradesh Sahitya Academy Award
- 1967: Ghalib Award of the Uttar Pradesh Urdu Academy – for the best Urdu Book
- 1972: Uttar Pradesh & Andhra Pradesh Urdu Academy Awards on Khwaja Mir Dard's Sufi Doctrines and Poetry.
- 1973: Uttar Pradesh & Andhra Pradesh Urdu Academy Awards, on Philosophy and Literary Criticism

- 1974: Uttar Pradesh & Andhra Pradesh Urdu Academy Awards
- 1983: 'Makhdoom Award'-the Highest National Award in India for Literary Criticism in Urdu by Andhra Pradesh Urdu Academy Hyderabad.

He passed away on December 13, 1996, at All India Institute of Medical Sciences in Delhi, India.

REFERENCES

Azmi, Sheesh Muhammad Ismail, *Ahd-i Saltanat ke Fuqaha, Sufia Aur Danishwaron Ki Nazar Mai Hindu Ki Haisiyat*, New Delhi: Islamic Book Foundation, 1998.

Baghpati, Matin Tariq, *Da'wat-i Haq Aur Ghayr Muslim*, Delhi: Markazi Maktaba-i Islami, 1994.

'Islamic Mission and Inter-Religious Dialogue in a Minority Context: The Jama'at-i Islami of India', *Islam and Christian Muslim Relations*, vol. 13, no. 1, 2002.

Jama'at-i Islami Hind: Policy and Programme (April 1999-March 2003) (henceforth *Policy and Programme*), Delhi: Jama'at-i Islami Hind, 1999.

Omar, Irfan A., 'Islam and the Other: The Ideal Vision of Mawlana Wahiduddin Khan', *in Journal of Ecumenical Studies*, vol. 36, nos. 3-4, summer-fall 1999.

Parekh, Abdul Karim (ed.), *Murshid-i Ruhani Musleh-i Ummat Hazrat Maulana Sayyed Abul Hasan 'Ali Nadwi Urf 'Ali Miyan Sahib Ke Khutut Mufassir-i Quran Hazrat Maulana 'Abdul Karim Parekh Sahib Ke Nam*, Delhi: Farid Book Depot, 1999.

Wright Jr, Theodore P, 'Hindu-Muslim Stereotypes in South Asia', *Journal of Asian and African Affairs*, vol. 3, July 1991.

Section: VII

SOCIAL REFORMERS

1. AKHTAR HAMEED KHAN

Khan was born on July 15, 1914, in city of Agra, India. He was amongst the four sons (Akhtar Hameed, Akhtar Ahmed, Akhtar Mahmud and Akhtar Hamid Khan) and three daughters of Khan Sahib Amir Ahmed Khan and Mehmoodah Begum. His father, a police inspector, was motivated by the reformist thinking of Syed Ahmed Khan. In his early age, Khan's mother introduced him to the poetry of Maulana Hali and Muhammad Iqbal, the sermons of Abul Kalam Azad, and the Sufist philosophy of Rumi. This upbringing inspired his interest in historical and also contemporary social, economic, and political affairs.

Khan married Hameedah Begum (the eldest daughter of Allama Mashriqi) in 1940. Together, they had three daughters (Mariam, Amina, and Rasheeda) and a son (Akbar). After Hameedah Begum's demise in 1966, he married Shafiq Khan and had one daughter, Ayesha.

Khan attended Government High School at Jalam (Uttar Pradesh), and finished his education in 1930 at Agra College where he studied English Literature and Hhistory. He studied English literature, history, and Philosophy for a Bachelor of Arts degree at Meerut College in 1932. At that point, his mother was diagnosed with tuberculosis. She expired in the same year at the age of thirty-six. Khan continued his studies and was granted a Master of Arts in English Literature from Agra University in 1934.

He worked as a Lecturer at Meerut College before joining the Indian Civil Service (ICS) in 1936. As part of the ICS education, he was sent to study Literature and History at Magdalene College, Cambridge, England. During the stay, he developed close friendship with Choudhary Rahmat Ali.

During his ICS career, Khan worked as collector of revenue, a position that brought him into usual contact with living circumstances in rural areas of East Bengal. The Bengal famine of 1943 and subsequent poor handling of the situation by the colonial rulers led him to resign from the Indian Civil Service in 1945. He wrote, "I realized that if I didn't escape while I was young and vigorous, I will forever remain in the trap, and terminate as a bureaucratic big wig." During this period, he was inspired by the philosophy of Nietzche and Mashriqi, and became member of the Khaksar Movement. This affection was short. He quit the movement and turned to Sufism. As per Khan, "I had a profound personal concern; I wanted to live a life free from fear and anxiety, a calm and serene life, without turmoil and conflict, when I followed the advice of old Sufis and sages, and tried to curb my greed, my pride and aggression, fears, anxieties and conflict diminished."

For the following two years, Khan worked in Mamoola hamlet close to Aligarh as a labourer and locksmith, an experience that provided him with firsthand knowledge of the problems and issues of rural communities. In 1947, he took up a teaching position at the Jamia Millia, Delhi, where he worked for three years. In 1950, Khan migrated from India to West Pakistan to teach at Islamia College, Karachi. In the same year, he was invited by the Government of Pakistan to take charge as Principal of Comilla Victoria College in East Pakistan, a position he held till 1958. During this time (1950–58), he also served as President of the East Pakistan Non-Government Teachers' Association.

During his tenure as principal of Comilla Victoria College, Khan developed a distictive interest in grassroots actions. Between 1954 and 1955, he took a break to work as director of the Village Agricultural and Industrial (V-AID) Program. Nevertheless, he was not contented with the development approach adopted in the program that was limited to the education of villagers. In 1958, he attended Michigan State University to acquire education and education in rural growth. Returning in 1959, he founded the Pakistan Academy for Rural Development (PARD) at Comilla on May 27, 1959 and was appointed as its founding director. He also laid foundations for the Comilla Cooperative Pilot Project in 1959. In 1963, he got a Ramon Magsaysay Award from the Government of the Philippines for his services in rural growth. Khan became Vice Chairman of the Board of Governors of PARD in 1964, and in the same year, was granted an honorary Doctorate of Law by Michigan State University. In 1969, he delivered a series of lectures at Woodrow Wilson School, Princeton University, based on his experience with rural cooperatives. During the visit, he founded collaborative links with Arthur Lewis.

On his come back to East Pakistan, Khan remained attached to the Comilla Project till the Division of Pakistan, when East Pakistan became Bangladesh. Finally, Khan moved to West Pakistan. PARD was renamed as Bangladesh Academy for Rural Development (BARD).

Following his move to Pakistan, Khan was asked to implement the Comilla Model in rural settlements of NWFP, Punjab, and Sindh. He refused the proposal on the grounds that the offers were predominantly inspired by political interests rather than the common well-being. Nevertheless, he continued to advise the authorities on various aspects of rural development, such as participatory irrigation management. He worked as a research fellow at the University of Agriculture, Faisalabad from 1971 to 1972, and as Director of Rural Economics Research Project at Karachi University from 1972 to 1973.

Khan attended Michigan State University as a visiting professor in 1973 and remained there till 1979. During this time, he carried on advising the Rural Development Academy at Bogra in northern Bangladesh, and the Pakistan Academy for Rural Development, Peshawar, on the Daudzai Integrated Rural Development Program. He also travelled extensively during this period in the capacities of speaker, advisor, or consultant on rural growth programs across the world. In 1974, he was appointed as a World Bank consultant to study rural growth situations in Java, Indonesia. He also shortly worked as a visiting professor at Lund University, Harvard University, and Oxford University.

In 1980, Khan moved to Karachi and began functioning on the improvement of sanitary circumstances in Karachi suburbs. He laid the foundations of the Orangi Pilot Project for the largest squatter community of Orangi in the city. He remained associated with this project till his demise in 1999. In the meantime, he maintained his support for rural communities around Karachi, as well as assisted to develop the Aga Khan Rural Support program. OPP became a model for participatory bottom-up development initiatives.

The Comilla Model (1959) was Khan's initiative in reaction to the failure of a Village Agricultural and Industrial Development (V-AID) program that was started in 1953 in East and West Pakistan with technical assistance from the US government. V-AID remained a government-level attempt to encourage citizen participation in the sphere of rural growth. Khan started the project in 1959 on his come back from Michigan, and developed a methodology of implementation in the areas of agricultural and rural growth on the principle of grassroots-level participation. At first, the aim was to provide a development model of programs and institutions that could be replicated across the country.

Advisory support in this respect was provided by experts from Harvard and Michigan State Universities, the Ford Foundation, and USAID. Practical assistance was also sought from Japan to improve the local farming skills.

Comilla Model simultaneously addressed the problems that were caused by the inadequacy of both local infrastructure and institutions through a range of integrated programs. The initiatives included the establishment of: an education and development centre; a road-drainage embankment works program; a decentralised, small scale irrigation program; and, a two-tiered cooperative system with primary cooperatives operating in the villages, and federations operating at sub-district level.

After Khan's departure from Comilla, the cooperative's model failed in autonomous Bangladesh because only a couple of occupational groups managed to accomplish the desired success. By 1979, only 61 of the 400 cooperatives were functioning. The model actually fell prey to the inefficient internal and external controls, stagnation, and diversion of funds. This motivated the subsequent scholars and practitioners in microfinance, such as Muhammad Yunus of Grameen Bank and Fazle Hasan Abed of BRAC, to abandon the cooperative approach in favour of more centralised control and service delivery structures. The new strategy targeted the poorest villagers, while excluding the 'less poor'. Nevertheless, Khan's leadership techniques during the course of his association with the project remained a source of motivation for these leaders.

The Orangi poverty alleviation project (acknowledged as the Orangi Pilot Project, or OPP) was initiated by Khan as an NGO in 1980. Orangi is situated on the northwest periphery of Karachi. At that time, it was the largest of the city's approximately 650 low-income squatter settlements (acknowledged as katchi abadi). The locality was first developed in 1963 as a government township of 5 square kilometres (1,236 acres). The influx of migrants after the establishment of Bangladesh, swelled the settlement to about one million people crowded over a region of more than 32 square kilometres (7,907 acres). The working class multi-ethnic population was predominantly composed of day labourers, expert workers, artisans, small shopkeepers, peddlers and low-income white collar workers. The project proved an impetus to the socio-economic growth of the population of the region. As the project director, Khan proved to be a lively and novel leader. The project at first focused on making a system of underground sewers, employing local materials and labour, and succeeded in laying hundreds of kilometres of drainage pipes together with auxiliary facilities. Inside a decade of the initiative, local residents had founded schools, health clinics, women's work centres, cooperative stores and a credit organization to finance enterprise projects. By 1993, OPP had managed to provide low-cost sewers to more than 72,000 houses. The project consequently diversified into a number of programs, along with a people's financed and managed low-cost sanitation program; a housing program; a basic health and family planning program; a program of supervised credit for small family enterprise units; an education program; and a rural development program in the nearby hamlets.

Comparing the OPP with Comilla project, Akhtar Hameed Khan once commented:

The Orangi Pilot Project was very different from the Comilla Academy. OPP was a private body, dependent for its small fixed budget on another NGO. The vast resources and support of the government, Harvard advisors, MSU, and Ford Foundation was missing. OPP possessed no authority, no sanctions. It may observe and investigate but it could only advise, not enforce.

The successful OPP model became a motivation for other municipalities around the country. In 1999, Khan helped to start Lodhran Pilot Project (LPP) to collaborate with Lodhran municipal committee. Learning from past experiences, the project extended its scope to the entire town instead of concentrating on low-income settlements only. The municipal partnership was itself a new initiative that ensured wider civic cooperation.

Akhtar Hameed Khan had been awarded following civil awards:

- 1961: Sitara-e-Pakistan for pioneering work in rural development.
- 1963: Ramon Magsaysay Award for services to rural development.
- 2001: Nishan-e-Imtiaz (Posthumous) for services to the community.
- 2004: Jinnah Award (Posthumous for services to people as founding father of the Orangi Pilot Project.

He died of myocardial infarction on October, 1999, in Indianapolis, U.S.A. at the age of 85.

2. ALLAMA MASHRIQI

Allama Mashriqi was born on August 22,1888, in Amritsar, Punjab, India. He was a Muslim scholar and founding father of the Khaksar movement. Mashriqi was a noted intellectual who became a college Principal at the age of twenty-five, and then became an Under Secretary, at the age of twenty-nine, in the Education Department of the Government of India. He penned an exegesis of the Quran which was nominated for the 1925 Nobel Prize. He was offered an Ambassadorship to Afghanistan at age thirty-two and Knighthood at the age of thirty-three years, but he refused all honours.

He consequently resigned government service and in 1930 established the Khaksar Movement, aiming to advance the circumstance of the masses irrespective of any faith, sect, or religion. As its leader, he was imprisoned many times. Through his thoughtful compositions, he asserted that the Science of Religions was essentially the science of collective evolution of mankind.

Mashriqi was born into an eminent Islamic Rajput family in Amritsar on August 25, 1888. His father, Khan Ata Muhammad Khan, had inherited a large property from his father. His forefathers had held outstanding positions during the Mughal Empire. Khan Ata was also well-connected with the Islamic luminaries of the time such as Sir Syed Ahmed Khan, Jamal Ud Din Afgahani, Shibli Nomani, and Mirza Ghalib.

Khan Ata possessed a bi-weekly publication, Vakil ("Attorney"), published from Amritsar. Vakil talked about political issues with an Islamic focus. Shibli Nomani requested that Khan Ata let Abul Kalam Azad work at Vakil. Azad moved on to work as an editor of Vakil. Mashriqi was thus raised in an intellectual Islamic atmosphere. Khan Ata Muhammad Khan noticed the genius in his son and he guided him accordingly.

Mashriqi had a zeal for mathematics from his early days. He finished his Master's degree in Mathematics from the University of the Punjab at the age of 19 and broke all previous records. In October 1907, he moved to Britain and matriculated at Christ's College, Cambridge, to study for the mathematics tripos. He was granted a college foundation scholarship in May 1908. In June 1909, he was granted first class honours in Mathematics Part I, being placed joint 27th out of 31 on the list of wranglers. For the following two years, he studied for the oriental languages tripos in parallel to the natural sciences tripos, gaining first class honours in the former and third class in the latter.

After three years' residence at Cambridge, he had qualified for his Bachelor of Arts degree, which he took in 1910. In 1912, he finished a fourth tripos in mechanical sciences, and was placed in the second class. He left Cambridge and came back to India in December 1912. During his stay in Cambridge his religious and scientific conviction was motivated by the works and notions of the professor Sir James Jeans.

On his come back to India, Mashriqi was offered the premiership of Alwar, a princely state, by the Raja. He refused owing to his interest in education. At the age of 25, he was appointed Vice Principal of Islamia College, Peshawar, by Chief Commissioner Sir George Roos-Keppel. He was made Principal of the same college in 1917. In October 1917, he was appointed Under Secretary to the Government of India in the Education Department in succession to Sir George Anderson (1876-1943). He became headmaster of the High School, Peshawar on October 21, 1919.

Aged 32, he was offered an ambassadorship to Afghanistan, which he decline. The following year, he was offered a British knighthood, which he also turned down. Mashriqi was amongst the youngest Indians to have been offered such positions.

In 1930, he was passed over for an advancement in the government service, following which he went on medical leave. In 1932, he resigned, taking his pension, and settled down in Ichhra, Lahore.

In 1924, at the age of 36, Mashriqi finished the first volume of his book, Tazkirah. It is a commentary on the Quran in the light of science. It was nominated by the Nobel Prize Committee in 1925, subject to the condition it was translated into one of the European languages. Mashriqi, nevertheless, refused the suggestion of translation.

He delved into the religious scriptures and arrived at the conclusion that all the prophets had brought the same message to man. He analysed the fundamentals of the Message and established that the teachings of all the prophets were closely linked with evolution of mankind as a single and united species in contrast to other ignorant and stagnant species of animals.

It was on this basis that he declared that the Science of Religions was essentially the science of collective evolution of mankind; all prophets came to unite mankind, not to disrupt it; the basic law of all faiths is the law of unification and strengthening of the whole humanity. As per Markus Daeschel, the thoughtful ruminations of Mashriqi offer a chance to re-evaluate the meaning of colonial modernity and notion of post-colonial nation-building in modern times.

After Mashriqi resigned from government service, he laid the foundation of the Khaksar Tehreek (also acknowledged as Khaksar Movement) in 1930. He played a role in directing the Muslims towards the independence of British India. Mashriqi was frequently imprisoned, together with his family, and a large number of Khaksars. Mashriqi was opposed to the division of India which he believed played into the hands of the British.

Mashriqi was first imprisoned in 1939, by the Congress Government of the United Provinces of Agra and Oudh (now Uttar Pradesh) during his efforts in resolving the sectarian conflicts between Sunnis and Shias. In 1940, he was arrested during a clash between the police and the Khaksars. The newspapers reported it as the "battle of spades and guns". He was only freed from solitary confinement in 1942 after he fasted for 80 days.

On July 20, 1943, an assassination attempt was made on Muhammad Ali Jinnah by Rafiq Sabir who was assumed to be a Khaksar worker. The attack was deplored by Mashriqi, who denied any involvement. Afterward, Justice Blagden of Bombay High Court, in his ruling on November 4, 1943, dismissed any association of Khaksars.

In Pakistan, Mashriqi was imprisoned in any case five times: in 1950 prior to election; in 1958 for alleged complicity in the murder of republican leader Khan Abdul Jabbar Khan; and, in 1962 for suspicion on attempt to overthrow President Ayub's government. Nevertheless, none of the charges were proved, and he was acquitted in each case.

In 1957, Mashriqi allegedly led 3,00,000 of his adherents to the borders of Kashmir, intending, it is said, to launch a fight for its liberation. Nevertheless, the Pakistan government persuaded the group to withdraw and the organization was later disbanded.

Mashriqi's important works are:

- Armughan-i-Hakeem, a poetical work
- Dahulbab, a poetical work
- Isha'arat, the "Bible" of the Khaksar movement
- Khitab-e-Misr (The Egypt Address), based on his 1925 speech in Cairo as a delegate to the Motmar-e-Khilafat
- Maulvi Ka Ghalat Mazhab
- Tazkirah Volume I, discussions on conflicts between religions, between religion and science, and the need to resolve these conflicts
- Tazkirah Volume II.
- Tazkirah Volume III.

Mashriqi expired on August 27, 1963, in Lahore, Pakistan.

3. ASMA JILANI JAHANGIR

Asma Jilani Jahangir was born on January 27, 1952, in Lahore, Pakistan. She is an attorney and human rights activist. She has been the United Nations Special Rapporteur on Freedom of Religion or Belief since 2004 (first attached to the former Commission on Human Rights, now to the Human Rights Council). Previously, she served as the UN Special Rapporteur on Extrajudicial, Arbitrary and Summary Executions. Born into a prosperous family with a history of activism (her father, Malik Jilani, was an erstwhile civil servant, got into politics upon retirement and spent time in jail and under house arrest for opposing military dictatorships), Jahangir herself became involved at a young age in protests against the military regime in Pakistan. She finished her law degree in 1978.

She cut her teeth during protests against the Hudood Ordinance put in place as part of Gen. Muhammad Zia-ul-Haq's Islamization program in Pakistan. She is a founding member of the Human Rights Commission of Pakistan, and has served as Secretary-General and later Chair of the organization.

In 1980, Asma Jahangir and her sister, Hina Jilani, got together with few fellow activists and lawyers and formed the first law firm founded by women in Pakistan. They also helped form the Women's Action Forum (WAF) in the same year. The first WAF demonstration was in 1983, when some 25-50 women took to the streets protesting the renowned Safia Bibi case. Safia, a young blind girl, had been raped, yet had ended up in jail on the charge of zina. "We (their law firm) had been given a plenty of cases by the advocate general and the moment this demonstration came to light, the cases were taken away from us." Asma recalls.

In his inaugural address to the nation in 1947, the founding father and first Governor General of Pakistan, Quaid-e-Azam Muhammad Ali Jinnah, suggested to people of the newly established nation, "If you work together in a spirit that everyone of you no matter what is his colour, caste or creed, is first, second and last, a citizen of this state with equal rights, privileges and obligations, there will be no end to the progress you will make."

With the loss of the guiding spirit of Muhammad Ali Jinnah briefly after independence and with passing of time the hope of freedom and chances which gave birth to a new autonomous nation diminished into hopelessness brought on by poverty, rampant corruption, and illiteracy.

It is an atmosphere ripe for fundamentalists who wish to sway the public with emotional religious rhetoric. Under no aiming to subside illiteracy and corruption, most often it is the women and minorities who get subdued and repressed by these religious fundamentalists. In such conditions, human rights activists dedicated to the cause of obtaining equal rights and justice represent hope for those being persecuted. Asma Jahangir is one such human rights activist and attorney.

She has spent most of her career defending the rights of women, religious minorities, and children of Pakistan. Aided in her mission by fellow activists and colleagues from the Human Rights Commission of Pakistan, she has continued her battle for justice amidst constant threats to her safety. Her willingness to relentlessly defend victims of rape, women seeking divorce from abusive husbands, people accused of blasphemy, her work on the issues of child labour, and her continuous disapproval of political parties has made her one of the most debatable figures in Pakistan. She has served as the chairperson of the Pakistan Human Rights Commission. In 1998, she was appointed Special Rapporteur of the UN Commission on Human Rights.

Asma mastered the business of law and politics at an early age. Her father spent much of his life in and out of prison for his political opinions which included open disapproval of actions of Pakistani military in Bangladesh. Asma was eighteen when she filed her first petition to have her father released from jail and began functioning with lawyers on his defence.

Asma has been a staunch critic of the Hudood ordinance and blasphemy laws of Pakistan. These laws were introduced in the Pakistani constitution during the 10-year dictatorship of General Zia-ul-Haq. As per the of the Hudood ordinance, a person accused of adultery or zina can be sentenced to death and as per the blasphemy law, a person accused of speaking or acting against Islam can also be sentenced to death. Whatever the initial intents of these laws might have been, the result has been false detention of hundreds of harmless men and women. Women who defy to report a rape are often accused of zina and locked up in prison while their offenders walk free and are never interrogated or brought to justice. The blasphemy law has also resulted in false detention and even demise of a lot of Pakistani Christians, Hindus, and even some Muslims.

In her article for Dawn, published October 2, 2000, named "Whither are We!" Asma demands that the government of General Musharraf work to improve the record of human rights domestically. Citing examples of human rights abuses, she wrote, "A Hindu income tax inspector gets lynched in the company of the army personnel for allegedly having made a remark on the beard of a trader. Promptly, the unfortunate Hindu government servant is booked for having committed blasphemy, while the traders and the Lashkar-e-Tayaba activists were offered tea over parleys. A seventy-year-old Mukhtaran Bibi and her pregnant daughter Samina are languishing in Sheikhupura jail on trumped-up charges of blasphemy."

In 1999, Asma and her sister, Hina Jilani, a fellow attorney and activist, were again subject to death threats after representing Samia Sawar, a 32 year old women who was seeking divorce from her abusive husband. Samia had turned to her family for assistance but they had refused to assist her attain a divorce. When Samia continued to seek a divorce, Samia's family had her murdered in broad daylight in the very law offices of Asma and Hina. Evidently, the family believed that Samia's actions were dishonourable to the family.

In 1995, Jahangir got the Martin Ennals Award for Human Rights Defenders.

In her ability as a UN official, Jahangir was in Pakistan when a state of emergency was declared by President Pervez Musharraf. On November 5, 2007, UN High Commissioner for Human Rights Louise Arbour indicated that Jahangir was amongst the judicial and political officials detained by the Musharraf government.

On November 5, 2007, The Economist reported that: "Over 500 lawyers, opposition politicians and human rights activists have been arrested. They include Asma Jahangir, boss of the country's human-rights commission and an erstwhile UN special rapporteur. In an e-mail from house arrest, where she has been placed for 90 days, Ms. Jahangir regretted that General Musharraf had "lost his marbles".

4. GHULAM AHMED PERVEZ

Ghulam Ahmed Pervez was born on July 9, 1903, in Batala, District Gurdaspur, Punjab, India. Batala was at that time a very important seat of Muslim learning, philosophy and culture where his grandfather Hakim

Maulvi Raheem Bakhsh enjoyed the status of a famous scholar and eminent Sufi of the Chishtia Nizamia discipline of theology.

As per his own compositions, from a very early age he possessed an inquisitive nature and never let any thought pass unquestioned. As he grew, he often questioned that if the Muslim viewpoint and practices are true and correct, then why do these not produce the results the Quran promises?

He became member of the Central Secretariat of the Government of India in 1927 and worked in the Home Department, Establishment Division. He is also supposed to have come in contact with Allama Muhammad Iqbal whom he became motivated of. In 1938, Parwez began publishing monthly Tolu-e-Islam where he propagated his interpretation of the Quran. After the independence of Pakistan in 1947, he worked the Central Government and was also a counsellor to Muhammad Ali Jinnah. Pervez took premature retirement as assistant secretary in 1955 to focus more on the religious work.

His work and research produced a lot of books on Quranic teachings, the most famous of them being Lughat-ul-Quran in four volumes, Mafhoom-ul-Quran in three volumes, Tabweeb-ul-Quran in three volumes, Nizam-e-Rabubiyyat, Islam A Challenge to Religion, Insaan Ne Kiya Socha (History of Human Thought), Tasawwaf Ki Haqiqat, Saleem Ke Naam in three volumes, Tahira Ke Naam, Qurani Faislay in five volumes and Shahkar-e-Risalat (the biography of the second Caliph Hazrat Omar). He delivered a lot of lectures on Iqbal's viewpoint of implementing the Quranic injunctions, which were afterward compiled and published as a presentation on Iqbal's philosophy under the title "Iqbal aur Quran".

He organized a country-wide network of spreading his ideas of the Quranic teachings named Bazm-e-Tolu-e-Islam. Such organizations have now been formed in a number of foreign countries as well.

He left behind a widow and a brother (both now deceased) and a sister. He had no children. His works are being continued through Idara-Tolu-e-Islam, The Tolu-e-Islam Trust, The Quranic Research Centre, the Quranic Education Society, the Parwez Memorial Library and his audio and video recordings.

Allama Ghulam Ahmed Parwez was one of the most debatable religious figures of the sub-continent in the last century. He together with Sir Syed Ahmad Khan are accused by an overwhelming majority of Muslim scholars for bringing in heterodoxical freethinking into the fold of Islam in the sub-continent. He had a critical opinion of the hadiths and for instance denied the existence of jinns and angels in the conventional context as well as had various opinions on the miracles described in the Quran.

For his openness towards full reinterpretation of all Quranic verses and his controversial ideas, a lot of conservative Islamic ulema declared him a kafir (infidel).

The conventional ulema argue that Islam has always been present in the world in the form of the devotional Muslims and that the Perwezi school of thought borders on the idea that the real spirit of Isalm got vanished and that it was rediscovered by the Allama.

He was very close to President General Ayub Khan, the military ruler of Pakistan and was instrumental in the formulation of the Islamic Family Laws framed during the time.

His major works are:

- Matalibul Furqaan (7 vol)
- Lughat-ul-Quran (4 vols.)
- Mafhoom-ul-Quran (3 vols)
- Tabweeb-ul-Quran (3 vols.)
- Nizam-e-Rabubiyyat
- Islam A Challenge to Religion (English version)
- Insaan Ne Kiya Socha (History of human thought)
- Islam kia he (second part of Insan ne kia socha)
- Tasawwaf Ki Haqiqat
- Saleem Ke Naam (3 vols.)
- Tahira Ke Naam
- Qurani Faislay (5 vols.)
- Meraj-e-Insaaniat (about Muhammad S.A.S)
- Barke toor (about Mosa)
- Joe-noor (about Ibrahim)
- Shola e mastoor (about Esa)
- Shahkar-e-Risalat (about Khalifa Omar)
- Iblis-o-Adam
- Jahane farda
- Mazahebe Alam ke Asmani kitaben

He died on February 25, 1986, in Karachi, Pakistan.

5. MUHAMMAD YUNUS

Muhammad Yunus was born on June 28, 1940, in Chittagong, Bangladesh. His father was Hazi Dula Mia Shoudagar, a jeweller, and his mother was Sofia Khatun. His early childhood years were spent in the hamlet. In 1944, his family moved to the city of Chittagong, and he was moved to Lamabazar Primary School from his hamlet school.

By 1949, his mother was afflicted with psychological sickness. Afterward, he passed the matriculation examination from Chittagong Collegiate School securing the 16th position amongst 39,000 students in East Pakistan. During his school years, he was an active Boy Scout, and travelled to West Pakistan and India in 1952, and to Canada in 1955 to attend Jamborees. Afterward, when Yunus was studying at Chittagong College, he became active in cultural activities and won awards for play acting. In 1957, he enrolled in the department of economics at Dhaka University and finished his BA in 1960 and MA in 1961.

He previously was a professor of economics and is renowned for his successful application of microcredit - the extension of small loans. These loans are given to entrepreneurs too poor to qualify for conventional bank loans. Yunus is also the founding father of Grameen Bank. In 2006, Yunus and the bank were jointly granted the Nobel Peace Prize, "for their efforts to create economic and social development from below."

Yunus himself has got many other national and global honours. He is the writer of Banker to the Poor and a founding board member of Grameen Foundation. In early 2007, Yunus showed interest in launching a political party in Bangladesh named Nagorik Shakti (Citizen Power), but afterward discarded the plan. He is one of the founding members of Global Elders. Yunus also serves on the board of directors of the United Nations Foundation, a public charity established in 1998 with enterpriser and philanthropist Ted Turner's historic $1 billion gift to support UN causes. The UN Foundation builds and implements public-private partnerships to address the world's most pressing problems, and broadens support for the UN.

Following his graduation, Yunus became member of the Bureau of Economics as a research assistant to the economical researches of Professor Nurul Islam and Rehman Sobhan. Afterward, he was appointed as a lecturer in Economics in Chittagong College in 1961. During that time, he also set up a productive packaging factory on the side. He was offered a Fulbright scholarship in 1965 to study in the United States. He received his Ph.D. in Economics from Vanderbilt University in the United States through the graduate program in Economic Development (GPED) in 1971. From 1969 to 1972, Yunus was an assistant professor of Economics at Middle Tennessee State University in Murfreesboro, TN.

During the Liberation War of Bangladesh in 1971, Yunus established a citizen's committee and ran the Bangladesh Information Centre, with other Bangladeshis living in the United States, to raise support for liberation. He also published the Bangladesh Newsletter from his home in Nashville. After the War, Yunus came back to Bangladesh and was appointed to the government's Planning Commission headed by Nurul Islam.

He found the work boring and resigned to join Chittagong University as head of the Economics department. He became involved with poverty reduction after observing the famine of 1974, and founded a rural economic program as a research project. In 1975, he developed a Nabajug (New Era) Tebhaga Khamar (three share farm) which the government adopted as the Packaged Input Program. In order to make the project more efficient, Yunus and his associates proposed the Gram Sarkar (the village government) program. Introduced by then president Ziaur Rahman in late 1970s, the Government formed 40,392 village governments (gram sarkar) as a fourth layer of government in 2003. On August 2, 2005, in reaction to a petition filed by Bangladesh Legal Aids and Services Trust (BLAST) the High Court had declared Gram Sarkar illegal and unconstitutional.

In 1976, during visits to the poorest families in the village of Jobra close to Chittagong University, Yunus discovered that very small loans could make a disproportionate difference to a poor person. Jobra women who made bamboo furniture had to take out usurious loans for buying bamboo, to pay their profits to the moneylenders. His first loan, consisting of USD 27.00 from his own pocket, was made to forty-two women in the village, who made a net profit of BDT 0.50 (USD 0.02) each on the loan. Thus, vastly improving Bangladesh's capability to export and import as it did in the past, ensuing in a bigger form of globalization and economic status.

The notion of providing credit to the poor as an instrument of poverty reduction was not exceptional. Dr. Akhtar Hameed Khan, founding father of Pakistan Academy for Rural Development (now Bangladesh Academy for Rural Development), is accredited for pioneering the idea. From his experience at Jobra, Yunus, an admirer of Dr. Hameed, recognized that the establishment of an institution was required to lend to those who had nothing. While conventional banks were not interested in making tiny loans at reasonable interest rates to the poor due to high repayment risks, Yunus believed that given the chance the poor will repay the borrowed money and hence microcredit could be a viable business model.

Yunus finally succeeded in securing a loan from the government Janata Bank to lend it to the poor in Jobra in December 1976. The organization continued to operate by securing loans from other banks for its projects. By 1982, the bank had 28,000 members. On October 1, 1983, the pilot project began operations as a full-fledged bank and was renamed the Grameen Bank (Village Bank) to make loans to hapless Bangladeshis. Yunus and his colleagues encountered everything from violent radical leftists to the traditional clergy who told women that they would be denied an Islamic burial if they borrowed money from the Grameen Bank.

As of July 2007, Grameen Bank has issued US$ 6.38 billion to 7.4 million borrowers. To ensure repayment, the bank uses a system of "solidarity groups". These small informal groups apply together for loans and its members act as co-guarantors of repayment and support one another's efforts at economic self-advancement.

The Grameen Bank began to diversify in the late 1980s, when it began attending to unutilized or underutilized fishing ponds, and also irrigation pumps like deep tubewells. In 1989, these diversified interests began burgeoning into separate organizations, as the fisheries project became Grameen Motsho (Grameen Fisheries Foundation) and the irrigation project became Grameen Krishi (Grameen Agriculture Foundation). Over the time, the Grameen initiative has grown into a multi-faceted group of profitable and non-profit ventures, along with prominant projects like Grameen Trust and Grameen Fund, which runs equity projects like Grameen Software Limited, Grameen CyberNet Limited, and Grameen Knitwear Limited, and also Grameen Telecom, which has a stake in Grameenphone (GP), biggest private sector phone company in Bangladesh.. The Village Phone (Polli Phone) project of GP has brought cell-phone ownership to 2,60,000 rural hapless in over 50,000 villages since the starting of the project in March 1997.

The success of the Grameen model of microfinancing has motivated alike efforts in a hundred countries all over the developing world and even in industrialized nations, along with the United States. A lot of, but not all, microcredit projects also retain its emphasis on lending explicitly to women. More than 94% of Grameen loans have gone to women, who suffer disproportionately from poverty and who are more likely than men to devote their earnings to their families. For his work with the Grameen Bank, Yunus was named an Ashoka: Innovators for the Public Global Academy Member in 2001.

Muhammad Yunus was granted the 2006 Nobel Peace Prize, together with Grameen Bank, for their efforts to create economic and social growth. In the prize declaration The Norwegian Nobel Committee mentioned:

Muhammad Yunus has shown himself to be a leader who has managed to translate visions into practical action for the benefit of millions of people, not only in Bangladesh, but also in a lot of other countries. Loans to hapless people without any financial security had appeared to be an impossible idea. From humble beginnings three decades ago, Yunus has, first and foremost through Grameen Bank, developed micro-credit into an ever more influential instrument in the fight against poverty.

Muhammad Yunus was the first Bangladeshi and third Bengali to ever get a Nobel Prize. After receiving the news of the important award, Yunus announced that he would use part of his share of the $1.4 million award money to create a company to make low-cost, high-nutrition food for the hapless; while the rest would go toward setting up an eye hospital for the hapless in Bangladesh.

Former United States president Bill Clinton was a vocal advocate for the awarding of the Nobel Prize to Muhammad Yunus. He expressed this in Rolling Stone magazine and also in his autobiography My Life. In a speech given at University of California, Berkeley in 2002, President Clinton described Dr. Yunus as "an individual who long ago should have won the Nobel Prize and I'll keep saying that till they finally give it to him."

Conversely, The Economist stated clearly that Yunus was a bad choice for the award. In their words "...the Nobel committee could have made a braver, more difficult, choice by declaring that there would be no recipient at all."

He has won a number of other awards, along with the Ramon Magsaysay explicitly Award, the World Food Prize, the Sydney Peace Prize, and in December 2007, the Ecuadorian Peace Prize. In addition, Dr. Yunus has been granted 26 honorary doctorate degrees, and 15 special awards. Bangladesh government brought out a commemorative stamp to honour his Nobel Award. In January 2008, Houston, Texas declared January 14 as "Muhammad Yunus Day".

He was invited and gave the MIT commencement address delivered on June 6, 2008.

In early 2006, Yunus, together with other members of the civil society along with Prof Rehman Sobhan, Justice Muhammad Habibur Rahman, Dr Kamal Hossain, Matiur Rahman, Mahfuz Anam and Debapriya Bhattchariya, participated in a movement for honest and clean candidates in national elections. He considered entering politics in the afterward part of that year. On February 11, 2007, Yunus wrote an open letter, published in the Bangladeshi newspaper Daily Star, where he asked citizens for opinions on his plan to float a political party to make political goodwill, proper leadership and good governance. In the letter, he invited everyone to briefly abstract how he should go about the job and how they can contribute to it. Yunus, finally, announced the foundation of a new party tentatively named Citizens' Power (Nagorik Shakti) on 18 February, 2007.

On July 18, 2007, in Johannesburg, South Africa, Nelson Mandela, Graça Machel, and Desmond Tutu convened a group of world leaders to contribute their wisdom, autonomous leadership and integrity together to the world. Nelson Mandela announced the establishment of this new group, The Global Elders, in a speech he delivered on the occasion of his 89th birthday. Archbishop Tutu is to serve as the Chair of The Elders. The founding members of this group include Machel, Yunus, Kofi Annan, Ela Bhatt, Gro Harlem Brundtland, Jimmy Carter, Li Zhaoxing, and Mary Robinson.

The Elders are to be independently funded by a group of Founding fathers, along with Richard Branson, Peter Gabriel, Ray Chambers; Michael Chambers; Bridgeway Foundation; Pam Omidyar, Humanity United; Amy Robbins; Shashi Ruia, Dick Tarlow; and The United Nations Foundation.

Yunus is a member of the Africa Progress Panel (APP), an autonomous authority on Africa started in April 2007 to focus world leaders' attention on delivering their commitments to the continent. The Panel started a prominant report in London on June16, 2008, named Africa's Development: Promises and Prospects.

Some of his famous works are:

- 1974: Three Farmers of Jobra; Department of Economics, Chittagong University
- 1976: Planning in Bangladesh: Format, Technique, and Priority, and Other Essays; Rural Studies Project, Department of Economics, Chittagong University

- 1991: Jorimon and Others: Faces of Poverty
- 1994: Grameen Bank, as I See it
- 2003: Banker to the Poor: Micro-Lending and the Battle Against World Poverty; Public Affairs
- 2008: A World Without Poverty: Social Business and the Future of Capitalism; Public Affairs

REFERENCES

Bahadur, Kalim, *The Jama'at-i Islami of Pakistan: Political Thought and Political Action*, New Delhi: Chetana Publications, 1997.

Bari, Sayyed 'Abdul Bari, *Azad Hindustan Mai Muslim Tanzimey*, New Delhi: Institute of Objective Studies, 2001.

Bedar, 'Abid Reza, 'Post-Independence Indian Islam', in S.T. Lokhandwala (ed.), *India and Contemporary Islam*, Simla: Indian Institute of Advanced Study 1971.

Jones, Kenneth W, 'The Arya Samaj in British India', in Robert D. Baird (ed.), *Religion in Modern India*, New Delhi: Manohar, 1995.

Kashmiri, Ashiq, *Tarikh-i Tehrik-i Islami Jammu Aur Kashmir: 1947 Se 1970 Tak*, Srinagar: Jama'at-i Islami of Jammu and Kashmir, 1984.

Khan, M.A. Saleem, *Early Muslim Perception of India and Hinduism*, New Delhi: South Asian Publishers, 1997.

Qadri, Sayyed Ahmad 'Uruj, *Fasdat Ka Ilaj*, Delhi: Markazi Maktaba-i Islami, 1989.

Quraishi, Muhammad 'Abdur Rahim, 'Muslim Personal Law Tehrik Hazrat Maulana 'Ali Miyan Ke Daur-i Sadarat Mai', in *Rabita*, Delhi, 2000.

Rahmatullah, 'Curse of Allah on Muslim Religious Leaders For Flouting Quran', in V.T. Rajshekar (ed.), *Curse of Allah*, Bangalore: Dalit Sahitya Akademy 1997.

Sikand, Yoginder, 'The *Fitna* of *Irtidad:* Muslim Missionary Responses to the *Shuddhi* Movement of the Arya Samaj in Early Twentieth Century India', *Journal of Muslim Minority Affairs*, vol. 17, no. 1, 1997.

Section: VIII

SPORTS PERSON

1. ALI QAMAR

Muhammad Ali Qamar was born on March 26, 1980, in Kolkata, India. He is a pugilist from Kolkata, India. He was the first Indian to win a gold medal in the field of boxing in the Commonwealth Games at the 2002 Commonwealth Games held in Manchester.

Born into the quarters of Kidderpore in Kolkata, Qamar was initiated into boxing at an early age by his father at the Kidderpore School of Physical Education and was trained by Cheena Bhai. Qamar became the Inter-district winner in the state of West Bengal in 1991. He won the Light Flyweight class at the national sub-junior levels from 1992 to 1996. Qamar had a strong showing in the 1999 World Amateur Boxing Championships in Houston, getting through the quarter finals before losing to Ron Siler of the United States. At the 2002 Commonwealth Games in Manchester, Qamar upset the home favourite Darren Langley 27-25 in the final, outscoring Langley 10-3 and surviving a standing count in the spectacular final round after trailing by five points at the starting of the fourth and last round. Qamar's career was harried by injuries and he didn't win an important contest again, losing in the quarterfinals at the 2002 Asian Games at Pusan.

He is the namesake of boxing celebrity. Muhammad Ali Qamar, who ranks amongst India's best pugilists, is motivating lots of backstreet children in Kolkata to put on the gloves and enter the ring.

Qamar became hooked on boxing when was an eight-year-old kid in downtown Kolkata living in a two-room tenement amid squalor. Ever since his father took Qamar to Cheena Bhai, a boxing coach, at the Kidderpore School of Physical Education fourteen years ago, the youngster has indeed come a considerable way.

Qamar, who was at the National Institute of Sports (NIS) in Patiala for the national camp being held in preparation for the Commonwealth Games, is supposed to be India's most gifted boxer since the likes of Dingko Singh and Gurcharan Singh.

Qamar first made his charisma felt during the 1999 World Championship in Houston. In 2002, he produced history by becoming the first Indian pugilist to win a medal, and that too a gold, at the Manchester Commonwealth Games. There onwards, the spunky Kolkatan has gone from strength to strength.

Harpreet Singh, a senior boxing coach of the Punjab Sports Department, who went together with the team as technical adviser at Houston, thinks that Ali's strong point is his wide- ranging and intelligent combination of punches. "He mixes the right upper cut and the straight right-left hook to devastating consequence. And this lethal combination makes him a difficult pugilist to beat. Look out for him in the Melbourne Commonwealth Games. His aim is to attack and wear out his opponent. With his quick footwork and combination of punches, he may well win the title in the 51 kg class."

At Manchester, in the title match, with just forty-three seconds remaining, Qamar outlasted England's Darren Langley after taking a standing count in the last round to give India its first boxing gold in the Commonwealth Games. By the way, before leaving for Manchester, Qamar had lost in the quarterfinals of the President's Cup to Suban Pannoam, a world-class Thai pugilist and the 1998 Bangkok Asian Games champion. Stirred but not shaken by this defeat, he tasted victory in the Commonwealth Games. In 1991, Qamar was crowned the inter-district winner at Howrah and he followed it up by winning sub-junior titles in the light flyweight class from 1992 to 1996.

With the flamboyant Dingko Singh sliding into oblivion, Muhammad Ali Qamar is India's best bet in boxing at Melbourne. And with a name like that, the sky is the limit.

2. ASLAM SHER KHAN

Aslam Sher Khan was born on July 15, 1953, in city of Bhopal, M.P., India. His father Ahmed Sher Khan has headed India in 1936 at the Berlin Olympics. As he said in his autobiography about his grandfather's saying, "Your father had a streak of madness in him, Like you, he had a great obsession for hockey. He made your mother promise that if they had a son, she would bring him up to be a hockey player." Ahmed Sher Khan was the Hockey coach of Aslam's school but never selected Aslam to play for the school squad. When he asked his father about this thing, he replied back with the words, "you still have a lot to study." Aslam has done his B.Sc. from Saifia College, Bhopal. On October 25, 1981, Aslam married to Smt. Rehana Sher Khan, with whom he has two sons.

Aslam Sher Khan, an erstwhile Indian hockey player, was a member of the Indian squad. In the 1975 World Cup held at Kuala Lumpur, Aslam Sher Khan assisted Indian Hockey Squad to win the gold medal. He as a member of Indian squad also participated in Munich Olympics held in 1972. Aslam Sher Khan has also been a Congress Member of Parliament and a Union Minister as well. In December 1997, Aslam Sher Khan became member of the Bharatiya Janata Party (BJP). He has also authored an autobiography, 'To Hell with Hockey'.

Aslam Sher Khan in the year 1966 was invited for the All India schools hockey camp at Bhopal. But his father fell sick at that time. He didn't want to join the camp but his father moralized him by saying, "The more you play, and the better you play, the more I`ll know you love me." That reverberated like an order to him and he moved to join the camp. He was selected in the All-India schools hockey squad as a forward under the renowned hockey player Roop Singh, who played with his father in the 1936 Olympics in Berlin. Hearing this selection news, his father went on crying. At the age of 13, Ahmed Sher expired. Aslam Sher Khan's ambition was to represent his own country in hockey in the Olympics like his father. Aslam Sher Khan played hockey as a full back. He afterward joined politics and was elected to Lok Sabha.

After the Indian Hockey Federation was suspended in April, 2008, Khan was selected to head a new committee established by the Indian Olympic Association to organize hockey in India. This panel will work in conjunction with the International Field Hockey Federation. The panel also includes Ashok Kumar, Ajit Pal Singh, Zafar Iqbal, and Dhanraj Pillay.

His major achievements are:

Asian Cup record

- 1980: AFC Challenge Cup record
- 2006: Quarter Finals
- 2008: 3rd in Qualifying Stage

South Asian Football Federation Cup record

- 1995: Third Place
- 1999: Runner up

- 2003: Champions
- 2005: Runner Up
- 2008: Group Stage

National Coaches

- Abu Yusuf Muhammad (March 2008-June 2008)
- Shafiqul Islam Manik (August 2008 - Present)

3. HAROON YOUSAF

Haroon Yousaf was born on November 10, 1973, in Mandi Bahauddin, Punjab, Pakistan. He has five brothers and seven Sisters and he is the 2nd oldest of his brothers; one of his brothers, Iqbal Yousaf, plays in Punjab Football as left Defender. His shirt number is fifteen. He was from 1996 until 1999 vice Skipper of Pakistan National Football Squad after Qazi Ashfaq and since twenty-fourth April 1999 (SAFF Cup in Goa) Skipper of Pakistan National Football Squad. He is Skipper of Allied Bank Limited since 1997. He got a proposal to play for Indian side "Mahindra United" but the PFF don't accept this so he can't play for "Mahindra United." He was the erstwhile Pakistan national football squad Skipper and was capped fifty-three times and scored 3 goals in his global career. The versatile footballer played as a defender or midfielder.

Yousaf began his career at Pakistan Railways FC in 1990. He transferred to WAPDA FC the following season and stayed there for five years. In 1995, he moved to ABL FC where he became skipper. He retired in 2003.

He has been a winner of the national football championship 4 times and runner up on 4 occasions. He also won the PFF Cup 4 times and was runner up once. Yousaf also played a short while for Afghan FC where he is still extremely praised as a solid player and leader.

Yousaf is the current skipper of PMC Club Athletico Faisalabad. On 19 March it was announced by the PFF that Haroon Yousuf has been named member of the selection Commitee for the National Football Squad.

His major achievements are:

With WAPDA FC

Pakistan Premier League 1991

With ABL FC

- Pakistan Premier League 1997(1), 1999, 2000
- Pakistan National Football Challenge Cup 1996, 1998, 1999, 2002

4. HASHIM KHAN

Hashim Khan was born in 1916, in Nawakille, a small village close to Peshawar, in Pakistan. He is an erstwhile squash player from Pakistan. He won the British Open seven times between 1951 and 1958. He is broadly believed to be one of the biggest squash players of all time, and was the first great player to emerge from a Pakistani dynasty of squash players which dominated the global game for decades.

Hashim's father, Abdullah Khan, was the Head Steward at club in Peshwar where British army officers stationed in the region played squash. As a youngster, Hashim served as an unpaid ball boy at the club, retrieving balls that were hit out of court by the officers. When the officers had finished playing, Hashim and the other ball boys would take over the courts.

In 1942, Hashim became a squash coach at a British Air Force officers' mess. In 1944, he won the first All-of-India squash finals in Mumbai, and successfully defended this title for the following two years. When Pakistan became an autonomous state, Hashim was appointed a squash professional at the Pakistan Air Force, and won the first Pakistani squash finals in 1949.

In 1950, Abdul Bari, a distant relation of Hashim's who had chosen to remain in Mumbai after the division of India and Pakistan, and who Hashim had crushed in many tournaments in India before division, was sponsored by the Indian Government to play at the British Open where he ended up runner-up to the famous Egyptian player Mahmoud Karim. (The British Open was believed to be the efficient world championship of the sport at the time.) This spurred Hashim to seek backing to compete in the British Open the following year.

In 1951, Hashim visited the United Kingdom to play in the British Open, and won the title beating Karim in the final 9-5, 9-0, 9-0. He again beat Karim in the final in 1952 by 9-5, 9-7, 9-0. He won again for the following four successive years, beating R.B.R. Wilson of England in the 1953 final; his younger brother Azam Khan in two tight five-set finals in

1954 and 1955; and Roshan Khan (another Pakistani who was a distant relative of Hashim and Azam's) in the final of 1956. Hashim was runner-up to Roshan in 1957, and won his seventh and final British Open title in 1958, when he beat Azam in the final.

Hashim also won five British Professional Championship titles, three US Open titles, and three Canadian Open titles.

In his afterward years, Hashim has settled in Denver, Colorado, and has continued to appear in veterans' matches at the British Open.

Hashim had a total of 12 children. His eldest son Sharif Khan became the dominant player on the North American hardball squash circuit in the 1970s, winning a record 12 North American Open titles. Four other sons – Aziz, Gulmast, Liaqat Ali ("Charlie"), and Salim ("Sam") – also became top-level hardball squash players.

Even today with a bad knee that limits his mobility, he plays doubles twice a week with a group of friends.

5. IMRAN KHAN

Imran Khan Niazi was born on November 25, 1952 in Lahore, Pakistan. He is a Pakistani cricketer and politician. Khan played for the Pakistani cricket squad from 1971 to 1992, and led them as skipper to his country's first and only World Cup victory in 1992. With a record of 3807 runs and 362 wickets in Test cricket, Khan is acknowledged as one of the finest all-rounders in the modern history of the game. In April 1996, he established the Pakistan Tehreek-e-Insaf (Movement for Justice), a small and marginal political party, of which he is chairman and also sole ever-elected member of Parliament. He represented Mianwali as a member of the National Assembly from October 2002 to October 2007.

Khan was born to Shaukat Khanum and Ikramullah Khan Niazi, a civil engineer, in Lahore. He grew up as the only son in a family with four sisters. Settled in the state of Punjab, Khan's family descended from the Pashtun, Niazi Shermankhel tribe of Mianwali. His maternal lineage consists of many professional cricketers, along with Javed Burki and Majid Khan, both of whom captained Pakistan's national squad.

Khan began his education at Aitchison College and the Cathedral School in Lahore. After middle school, he left Pakistan to study at the

Royal Grammar School in Worcester, United Kingdom, where he excelled at cricket. He then moved on to study Philosophy, Politics and Economics as an undergraduate at Keble College, Oxford in 1972, graduating with a second-class degree in Politics and a third in Economics.

Khan made a lacklustre first-class cricket entry at the age of sixteen in Lahore. By the start of the 1970s, he was playing for his home teams of Lahore A (1969-70), Lahore B (1969-70), Lahore Greens (1970-71) and, finally, Lahore (1970-71). Khan was part of Oxford's Blues Cricket squad during the 1973-75 seasons, and captained the University XI in 1974. At Worcestershire, where he played county cricket from 1971 to 1976, he was looked upon as only an average medium pace bowler. During this decade, other teams headed by Khan include Dawood Industries (1975-76) and Pakistan International Airlines (1975-76 to 1980-81). From 1983 to 1988, he moved on to play for Sussex.

In 1971, Khan made his Test cricket entry against England at Birmingham. Three years afterward, he debuted in the One Day International (ODI) match, once again playing against England at Nottingham for the Prudential Trophy. After graduating from Oxford and finishing his tenure at Worcestershire, he came back to Pakistan in 1976 and secured a permanent place on his native national squad beginning from the 1976-77 season, during which they faced New Zealand and Australia.

After the Australian series, he toured the West Indies, where he met Tony Greig, who signed him up for Kerry Packer's World Series Cricket. His credentials as one of the fastest bowlers of the world began to establish when he finished third at 139.7 km/h in a fast bowling contest at Perth in 1978, behind Jeff Thomson and Michael Holding, but ahead of Dennis Lillee, Garth Le Roux and Andy Roberts.

Khan attained the all-rounder's triple (securing 3000 runs and 300 wickets) in 75 Tests, the second fastest record behind Ian Botham's 72. He is also founded as having the second highest all-time batting average of 61.86 for a Test batsman playing at position 6 of the batting order. He played his last Test match for Pakistan in January 1992, against Sri Lanka at Faisalabad. His last ODI was the historic 1992 World Cup final against England at Melbourne, Australia, which culminated in the crowning glory of Khan's career.

Khan ended his career with 88 Test matches, 126 innings and scored 3807 runs at an average of 37.69, along with six centuries and 18 fifties. His highest score was 136 runs. As a bowler, he took 362 wickets in

Test cricket, which made him the first Pakistani and world's fourth bowler to do so. In ODIs, he played 175 matches and scored 3709 runs at an average of 33.41. His highest score remains 102 not out. His best ODI bowling is documented at 6 wickets for 14 runs. Khan retired permanently from cricket six months after the 1992 World Cup, in September.

At the height of his career, in 1982, the thirty-year old Khan took over the captainship of the Pakistani cricket squad from Javed Miandad. In the squad's second match under his leadership, Khan led them to their first Test win on English soil for 28 years at Lord's.

Khan's first year as skipper was the peak of his legacy as a fast bowler and also an all-rounder. He recorded the best Test bowling of his career while taking 8 wickets for 58 runs against Sri Lanka at Lahore in 1981-82. He also topped both the bowling and batting averages against England in three Test series in 1982, taking 21 wickets and averaging 56 with the bat. Afterward the same year, he put up a extremely acknowledged presentation in a home series against the formidable Indian squad by taking 40 wickets in six Tests at an average of 13.95. By the end of this series in 1982-83, Khan had taken 88 wickets in 13 Test matches over a period of one year as skipper.

This same Test series against India, nevertheless, also resulted in a stress fracture in his shin that kept him out of cricket for more than two years. An experimental cure funded by the Pakistani government assisted him recover by the end of 1984 and he made a successful reappearance to international cricket in the latter part of the 1984-85 season.

In 1987, Khan led Pakistan to its first Test series win in India, which was followed by Pakistan's first series victory in England the same year. During the 1980s, his squad also recorded three creditable draws against the West Indies. India and Pakistan co-hosted the 1987 World Cup, but neither ventured beyond the semi-finals. Khan retired from international cricket at the end of the World Cup. In 1988, he was asked to return to the captainship by the President Of Pakistan, General Zia-Ul-Haq, and on January 18, he announced his judgement to rejoin the squad.

Shortly after returning to the captainship, Khan led Pakistan to another winning tour in the West Indies, which he has recounted as his proudest moment in cricket. He was declared Man of the Series against West Indies in 1988 when he took 23 wickets in 3 tests. He afterward recalled, "I was 35 and not very fit, we had quite a weak squad and then I got 11 wickets in the first Test. That was the last time I really bowled well." As a skipper, Khan played 48 Test matches, out of which 14 were won by

Pakistan, 8 lost and the rest of 26 were drawn. He also played 139 ODIs, winning 77, losing 57 and ending one in a tie.

Khan's career high as a skipper and cricketer came when he led Pakistan to victory in the 1992 International Cricket Council Cricket World Cup. Playing with a brittle batting line-up, Khan promoted himself as a batsman to provide stability in the top order together with Javed Miandad, but his contribution as a bowler was minimal. In the final match, at the age of 39, Khan scored the highest runs of all the Pakistani batsmen and took the winning last wicket himself.

In 1992, Khan was honoured with Pakistan's most esteemed civil award, the Hilal-i-Imtiaz. Before that, he had got the President's Pride of Performance Award in 1983. Khan is featured in the University of Oxford's Hall of Fame and has been an honorary fellow of Oxford's Keble College. In 1976 and also 1980, Khan was granted The Cricket Society Wetherall Award for being the major all-rounder in English first-class cricket.

Khan has also been named Wisden Cricketer of the Year in 1983, Sussex Cricket Society Player of the Year in 1985, and the Indian Cricket Cricketer of the Year in 1990. On July 8, 2004, Khan was granted the Lifetime Achievement Award at the 2004 Asian Jewel Awards in London, UK. He was acknowledged for continuing "to devote his time between Pakistan and his adopted Britain, acting as a figurehead for a lot of global charities and functioning passionately and extensively in fund-raising activities.

On December 7, 2005, Khan was appointed the fifth Chancellor of the University of Bradford, where he is also a patron of the Born in Bradford research project. On December 13, 2007, Khan got the Humanitarian Award at the Asian Sports Awards in Kuala Lumpur for his efforts in setting up the first cancer hospital in Pakistan.

Khan is placed at Number 8 on the all-time list of the ESPN Legends of Cricket.

6. JAVED MIANDAD

Muhammad Javed Miandad Khan was born on June 12, 1957, in Karachi, Pakistan. He is generally looked upon as Pakistan's greatest ever batsman, and amongst the top tier in cricket history. He also had three successful albeit debatable coaching stints with the Pakistan national squad.

Miandad made his Test entry against New Zealand at Lahore on October 9, 1976. He scored a century in this match, thus becoming the youngest player to do so on entry. In the same series he scored a double century, and on his way broke George Headley's 47 year record, to become the youngest player to accomplish the feat. Miandad made his One Day International entry against the West Indies at Edgbaston, Birmingham in the Cricket World Cup 1975.

Javed Miandad played 124 Tests and appeared in 189 innings. His aggregate of 8,832 Test runs is still a Pakistani record (though Inzamam-ul-Haq came 3 runs shy with 8830), while his 23 centuries and 43 fifties were national records till they were broken by Inzamam-ul-Haq. Javed's Test career batting average of 52.57 puts him amongst the list of greatest batsmen to have played international cricket, and he is one of only two batsmen in cricket history, the other being Herbert Sutcliffe, to maintain an average of above 50 during a career of more than 20 innings. He scored six double centuries which is the most by a Pakistani and 5th overall. He made his highest score of 280 not-out against India.

Javed mastered his craft as a youngster on the tough, blue-collar streets of Karachi, and not amazingly his skill flew in the face of most cricket coaching textbooks. In spite of this, his unorthodox but distinctive square-on batting stance and evenly unusual split-handed grip never hindered him.

Javed sits amongst the elite cricket club of batsmen of his era to maintain an average of above 50. His legacy is shared by the most accomplished batsmen of his era, which is also acknowledged as the era of deadly fast bowling. Batsmen who sit in the club are Vivian Richards, Allan Border, Sunil Gavaskar, and Gary Sobers.

Javed Miandad was instrumental in Pakistan's victory in the 1992 World Cup in Australia. He played his part to perfection and the squad, particularly the batting department lobbied around him. He played with maturity and patience as was required of him. He kept his wicket intact until the last and guided Pakistan to home in the Semi Final against New Zealand, and in the final scored a critical 50 after the openers had fallen cheaply.

One of the highlights of Javed's career came during the Australasia Cup in 1986. The Pakistanis had managed to make it to the final, and were up against India. India batted first and scored 245 runs, leaving Pakistan with a required run rate of 4.92 per over. Miandad came in to bat at number 4, with the score at 39 for 2 wickets, and the required run rate had risen to 7 an over. With four runs required off the last ball, Javed struck a well-known six that sealed the victory for Pakistan.

Viv Richards, was once cited saying, "If there was any batsman whom I could choose to bat for my life, it would be Javed Miandad." Javed, who refused to concede easy victory to India, was complemented by commentator and erstwhile New Zealand skipper John Wright, who noted, "As long as Javed is there, anything can happen". Javed referred to this in his autobiography as one of the best compliments he had got in all his cricketing years.

As a coach, Javed Miandad guided Pakistan to renowned test victories in the Asian Cup and in India during 1998-99 season, when Wasim Akram was skipper. His second coaching duration, when in first year Pakistan has the highest victory ratio in One-Day, slightly above than Australia. Bob Woolmer, who was the coach of South Africa before taking on the work of Pakistan Cricket Coach, once called on Miandad to assist him with coaching batsmen.

Javed Miandad was nicknamed "Prince of Wales" when he played county cricket in England. More so, he was the King of Sharjah. His six in the last ball of a One-Day match changed One day cricket, India - Pakistan competitions and cricket in Sharjah. He maintained close ties with Abdur Rahman Bukhatir, the man who began cricket in Sharjah.

He was also invited to live at the Royal Palace of the King of Brunei for three years in late 1996, who is one of the richest people of the world, the only other cricketer was Viv Richards which also included Jahangir Khan (Squash).

Javed was amongst the three Pakistani players to have his name at the hall of fame at Lords, others included Hanif Muhammnad & Imran Khan. Javed Miandad has some exceptional records in cricket. In the 100th Test match ever to be played, between Pakistan and New Zealand in 1982-83, he scored centuries in both innings. He is the youngest cricketer to make a triple hundred in first class cricket. He scored nine back to back 50s in 1987-88, an ODI world record. He was never dismissed for a duck at home, in both forms of cricket.

Miandad is the only cricketer to appear in six World Cup competitions; the first six. In 1982, Wisden named him as one of the cricketers of the year.

Miandad was the first cricketer to score 1000 runs in World Cup competitions. He attained this feat in the 1992 World Cup final against England.

7. JAHANGIR KHAN

Dr. Muhammad Jahangir Khan was born on February 1, 1910, Jalandhar, Punjab, India. He played cricket for India during British rule and after the division of India served as a cricket administrator in Pakistan afterwards.

Jahangir was a big man who stood six feet and bowled medium pace. He came from a renowned cricketing family that produced Pakistan captains Imran Khan, Javed Burki and Majid Khan, the last being his son. Majid's son Bazid Khan also headed Pakistan for the first time in 2005, making the family the second, after the Headleys, to have three successive generations of test cricketers.

Jahangir scored 108 on his first class entry and took seven wickets in the second innings of the match. He headed India in her first ever Test against England at Lord's in 1932. After the tour, he remained back in England and took a doctor's degree from Cambridge University. He passed the final Bar from Middle Temple. In that time he was Cambridge blue in cricket for four years. He also made two appearances in Gentlemen Players matches. In 1935, playing for Indian Gymkhana, he also scored 138 runs in two months, at an average of seventy.

When India toured England in 1936, he joined the squad and played in all three Tests. His best bowling during his time at Cambridge was a 7 for 58 against the champion county Yorkshire. Back in India, he played in the Bombay Pentangular in 1939. While playing against Marylebone Cricket Club at Lord's in 1936, he bowled a ball to Tom Pearce that hit a sparrow on the way. The sparrow fell dead against the stumps and is preserved in the MCC museum at Lord's.

Jahangir was a selector between 1939-40 and 1941-42. After moving to Pakistan after 1947, he served a selector in Pakistan and managed the squad that toured India in 1960-1961. He was a college principal and then served as the Director of Education in Pakistan before retiring. When Jalandhar hosted its first Test match in 1983, Jahangir was specially invited to attend the match. In his younger days, he was also a champion javelin thrower of India. He headed India in AAA in 1932 and British Empire Games 1934 in London.

Jahangir made 108 runs on his first class entry and took seven wickets in the second innings of the match. His best bowling during his time at Cambridge was a 7 for 58 against the champion county Yorkshire.

He died on July 23, 1988, in Lahore, Pakistan.

8. JEHANGIR KHAN

Jehangir Khan was born on December 10, 1963, in Karachi, Pakistan. He is an erstwhile world number one professional squash player from Pakistan, who is regarded by many to be the biggest player in the history of the game. During his career he won the World Open six times and the British Open a record ten times. Between 1981 and 1986, he was unbeaten in competitive play for five years. During that time he won 555 matches consecutively. This was not only the longest winning streak in squash history, but also one of the longest unbeaten runs by any athlete in top-level professional sports. He retired as a player in 1993, and has served as President of the World Squash Federation since 2002.

Jehangir was trained at first by his father, Roshan Khan, the 1957 British Open champion, and then by his cousin Rehmat Khan, who guided Jehangir through most of his career. Ironically, during his earlier years, Jehangir was a sickly child and physically very weak. Although the doctors had suggested to him not to take part in any sort physical activity, after undergoing a couple of hernia operations his father let him play and try out their family game.

In 1979, the Pakistan selectors decided not to select Jehangir to play in the world championships in Australia, judging him too weak from a current sickness. So Jehangir decided instead to enter himself in the World Amateur Individual Championship and, at the age of 15, became the youngest-ever winner of that happening.

In November 1979, Jehangir's older brother Torsam Khan, who had been one of the major global squash players in the 1970s, expired all of a sudden of a coronary failure during a tournament match in Australia. Torsam's demise affected Jehangir deeply. He considered quitting the game, but decided to pursue a career in the sport as a compliment to his brother.

In 1981, when he was 17, Jehangir became the youngest winner of the World Open, beating Australia's Geoff Hunt (the game's dominant player in the late-1970s) in the final. That tournament marked the start of an unbeaten run which lasted for five years and over 500 matches. The hallmark of his play was his incredible fitness and stamina, which Rehmat Khan assisted him build-up through a punishing education and conditioning regime. Jehangir was quite simply the fittest player in the game, and would wear his opponents down through considerable rallies played at a furious pace.

In 1982, Jehangir astonished everyone by winning the International Squash Players Association Championship without losing a single point.

The unbeaten run finally came to end in the final of the World Open in 1986 in Toulouse, France, when Jehangir lost to New Zealand's Ross Norman. Norman had been in pursuit of Jehangir's unbeaten streak, being crushed time and time again. "One day Jehangir will be slightly off his game and I will get him," he vowed for five years.

Speaking about his unbeaten run, Jehangir said: "It wasn't my plan to create such a record. All I did was put in the effort to win every match I played and it went on for weeks, months and years till my defeat to Ross Norman in Toulouse in 1986."

"The pressure began to mount as I went on winning every time and people were anxious to see if I could be crushed. In that World Open final, Ross got me. It was exactly five years and eight months. I was unbeaten for another nine months after that defeat."

With his dominance over the international squash game in the first half of the eighties secure, Jehangir decided to test his capability on the North American hardball squash circuit in 1983-1986. Jehangir played in thirteen top-level hardball tournaments during this period, winning 12 of them. He faced the major American player on the circuit at the time, Mark Talbott, on eleven occasions (all in tournament finals), and won ten of their encounters. With his domination of both the softball and hardball variations of the game, Jehangir truly cemented his status as the world's best squash player.

His success in North America is regarded by some observers to be amongst the factors which led to burgeoning interest in the international "softball" variation of squash in the continent, and the demise of the hardball game in the late-1980s and 1990s.

Jehangir retired as a player in 1993 after helping Pakistan win the World Team Championship in Karachi. The Government of Pakistan honoured Jehangir with the awards of Pride of Performance and civil award of Hilal-e-Imtiaz for his achievements in squash. They also granted him the title of Sportsman of the Millennium.

In 1990, Jehangir was elected Chairman of the Professional Squash Association, and in 1997, Vice-President of the Pakistan Squash Federation. He was elected as Vice-President of the World Squash Federation in November 1998, and in October 2002 was elected WSF President. In 2004, he was again unanimously re-elected as President of the World Squash Federation at the International Federation's 33rd Annual General Meeting in Casa Noyale, Mauritius.

Jehangir is listed in Guinness Book of World Records as having the most world championship squash titles.

Time Magazine has named Jehangir as one of Asia's Heroes in the last 60 years.

Jehangir Khan was conferred with a Honorary Doctorate of Philosophy by London Metropolitan University for his contributions to the sport.

Due to his immense and absolute dominance in squash, he was nicknamed "The Conqueror" (a loose translation of his first name).

9. MANSOOR ALI KHAN PATAUDI

Mansoor Ali Khan, the ninth Nawab of Pataudi (Jr.) was born on January 5, 1941, in Bhopal, India, He is nicknamed Tiger, and is an erstwhile Indian cricketer and erstwhile skipper of the Indian cricket squad.

Mansoor was born to Iftikhar Ali Khan, eighth Nawab of Pataudi and his wife Sajida Sultan, second daughter of the last ruling nawab of Bhopal. He was educated at Welham Boys' School in Dehra Doon, Lockers Park Prep School in Hertfordshire, Winchester College, and Balliol College, Oxford. His father expired on Mansoor's eleventh birthday in 1952, whereupon Mansoor followed as the ninth Nawab of Pataudi. While the princely state of Pataudi had been merged with India after the end of the British Raj in 1947, Mansoor inherited the titular dignity of Nawab of Pataudi.

On December 27, 1969, Mansoor married the famous film actress Sharmila Tagore, who is a distant relative (not a direct descendant, as often believed) of Rabindranath Tagore, the nobel laureate.

By a turn of fate, Mansoor's mother Sajida sultan came to inherit her father's princely titles and privileges upon his demise, and was acknowledged as "Begum of Bhopal" by the government of India in 1961 From her demise in 1995, Mansoor has been regarded by several as being Nawab of Bhopal and also Nawab of Pataudi. Nevertheless, such "personal unions" are unknown to Indian tradition, and others regard

Mansoor's eldest sister, Begum Saleha Sultan, as being head of the Nawabi family of Bhopal.

Pataudi Jr., as Mansoor came to be known in the cricket world, was a right-hand batsman and a right-arm medium pace bowler. He played in 46 Test matches for India between 1961 and 1975.

In March 1962, at the relatively young age of 21, Pataudi Jr. was elevated to the captainship of the Indian cricket squad. This was a couple of months after a car accident permanently damaged vision in his right eye. He also captained Sussex in 1966.

Pataudi Jr. was skipper of the Indian cricket squad in 40 matches, only 9 of which resulted in victory for his squad. He was, nevertheless, skipper when the Indian squad recorded its first ever overseas Test victory, against New Zealand in 1967. He contested in 1971 elections to the Lok Sabha to protest the abolition of Privy Purse in India. He contested from Gurgaon as a candidate of the Vishal Haryana Party.

10. MUHAMMAD AZHARUDDIN

Muhammad Azharuddin was born on February 8, 1963, in Hyderabad, Andhra Pradesh, India, He is an erstwhile skipper of the Indian cricket squad. He was an elegant right-handed batsman and usually batted at five in Test cricket.

In his prime, he had a graceful, fluid batting style, comparable to that of his English contemporary, David Gower. The wrist flick was his most characteristic shot and he fared best against spinners. The grace and fluidity of his wrist once motivated John Woodcock, a famous cricket author, to say, "It's no use asking an Englishman to bat like Muhammad Azharuddin. For, it would be like expecting a greyhound to win the London Derby!"

Azhar, as he is commonly known, grew up in Hyderabad and attended a catholic convent boys school All Saints High School. By the way, a plenty of other cricketers from Hyderabad - Venkatpathy Raju, Noel David - also attended the same school.

Azhar scored a total of 22 centuries in Test cricket at an average of 45, and 7 in ODIs at an average of 37. He scored a century in each of his first three Tests which is a record. An excellent fielder, he took a world record of 156 catches in ODI cricket.

He was given LBW out for 199 in a test match against Sri Lanka and it was his highest Test Score.

In 1991, he was named Wisden Cricketer of the Year and was for a lot of years a motivational figure in the Indian squad with his athletic fielding and leadership.

Azhar was skipper of the Indian squad for most of the 1990s. Statistically, he is one of India's most successful captains. He won a record of 103 ODI matches as the skipper of the Indian squad. His 14 Test Match wins as skipper, was a record till it was bettered by Sourav Ganguly.

Towards the end of his career Azharuddin was accused of match-fixing ; South African skipper Hansie Cronje in his confession for match-fixing had indicated that Azharuddin was the one to introduce him to the bookies. This led the BCCI to ban him from the game of cricket for life in 2000.

The BCCI lifted the ban on Azharuddin in 2006 and even honoured him together with other Indian Test captains in a ceremony in Mumbai during the 2006 ICC Champions Trophy. The ICC, nevertheless, claimed that it alone had the right to revoke the ban despite playing no role in handing out the original ban.

In one of his interviews, he claimed that he was being targeted because he was from a minority community. Nevertheless, this statement backfired badly and invited severe disapproval from all parts of the country and even from important minority community organizations in India. Ultimately, Azharuddin had to apologize publicly and retract his statements. The ban cost him a chance of joining the 100 Test club, in the end finishing stranded on 99 Test matches. Since 2004, Azhar has run a Physical Education Centre in Hyderabad. He is married to Sangeeta Bijlani, a Bollywood actress after divorcing his previous wife.

His record with different teams is:

Australia

- 780 runs at 39.00 with 2 hundreds

England

- 1278 runs at 58.09 with 6 hundreds

New Zealand

- 796 runs at 61.23 with 2 hundreds

Pakistan

- 769 runs at 40.47 with 3 hundreds

South Africa

- 779 runs at 41.00 with 4 hundreds

Sri Lanka

- 1215 runs at 55.23 with 5 hundreds

West Indies

- 539 runs at 28.37 with 0 hundreds

Zimbabwe

- 59 runs at 14.75 with 0 hundreds

Total

- 6215 runs at 45.04 with 22 hundreds

11. MUHAMMAD ESSA

Muhammad Essa was born on November 20, 1983, in Pakistan. He is a Pakistani footballer playing presently for KRL FC. The striker is also the skipper of Pakistan national football squad and is one of the most gifted football players Pakistan has seen in present times. He can be used as a playmaker especially in support of a striker, or a real centre forward because of his ball holding and passing techniques. He is also a left-footed free-kick specialist. Essa has become one the most famous faces in Pakistani football, due to his usual goal scoring at global level.

Born in the city of Chaman in Pakistan's Balochistan state, he took up the sport with great interest and zeal. He played in the Afghan Club Chaman youth squad before signing for PTCL FC.

He was discovered by then Pakistan youth squad and Under 23 manager John Layton back in early 1999 and found his way into the Pakistan national football squad shortly enough, receiving his first cap in 2000.

He won the old 2003 PFF President's Cup with PTCL FC. In 2004, Essa was called up to the Pakistan U23 team for the SAF Games. He ended the tournament as top scorer and was player of the tournament, and assisted Pakistan win Gold.

Essa most renowned moment came when he scored from a free-kick against India in the first match of the 2005 Pakistan-India friendly series, at the Ayub National Stadium, Quetta to tie the game 1-1 with minutes to go before the final whistle. With a 3-0 victory in the final game in which Essa scored, he was offered a playing agreement from prominant Indian football squad East Bengal Club, but the PFF seemingly turned it down to the disappointment of a lot of Pakistani football fans.

In the inaugural 2004 PPL season he came back to his home town club Afghan Club Chaman with his goals helping them to survive relegation. The following season, the striker transferring to WAPDA FC but couldn't help them retain their PPL title; finishing second to Pakistan Army FC. In 2006, he captained Pakistan to another SAF Games gold medal. Returning from the Games, he moved to KRL and helping them finish 3rd in the 2006-07 season.

There had been talk of a couple of Iranian clubs, notably Foolad F.C. and also Homa F.C. inviting Essa over for a trial during the previous season but it couldn't be finalised due to Essa's commitments with KRL. A proposed move to important Bangladesh Pro League side Muhammadan Sporting Club also failed to materialise.

Essa played in the Geo Super Football League for Quetta Zorawar as skipper with the club coming second in the league round and losing semi-finalists in the knock-out round of the tournament, though he was granted the SFL 2007 Player of the Tournament trophy. The striker was granted the 'Salaam Pakistan Award' together with tennis star Aisam-ul-Haq Qureshi and female squash player Maria Toor Pakay for their contributions to sport by the President of Pakistan, Pervez Musharraf on August 13, 2007. He captained Pakistan to a surprise nil-nil draw against Iraq in Syria in the second leg of the World Cup 2010 qualifiers, but were knocked out due to a 7-0 aggregate loss.

In the 2007/08 season of the PPL, Essa fought to score goals, only scoring 9 goals in 21 appearances. He held his Captainship for the 2008 AFC Challenge Cup qualifying movement. Despite a 2-0 win against Chinese Taipei in the first match, they lost 7-1 to Sri Lanka which made Pakistan's 9-2 demolition of Guam meaningless as they finished behind on points to Sri Lanka, thus failing to qualify for the main round. Because of injuries, Essa had to miss the SAFF Cup 2008.

Muhammad Essa can be described as a very capable player whose presentations for Quetta Zorawar in Geo Super Football League were very delightful to watch.

12. QAMAR ZAMAN

Qamar Zaman was born in 1952, in Quetta, Pakistan. After Roshan and the Egyptian Muhammad Dardir, experts opine that Qamar was the most brilliant stroke player of the squash ever. Like any brilliant player he was prone to mistake. Qamar was plucked out of obscurity by Mr. Muneer Ahmed in 1968 and brought to Lahore from Quetta. The encouragement he got resulted in his making an immediate impression and he quickly won the Pakistan junior championship the same year. He was afterward initiated into PIA and moved to Peshawar where he together with Mohibullah were placed under the tutelage of Omar Daraz but under the management of Aftab Javed (His paternal uncle).

On his very first trip to England he reached the semi finals of the British Amateur in 1973. The following year Qamar reached the semi-finals of the British open, won the Australian Amateur and from then on there was no looking back for him.

In the Britain Open of 1974-75, Qamar stunned Geoff Hunt in the Quarter finals and moved on to win the championship beating Gogi Alauddin. Consequently, Qamar stayed at the top of his sport until 1983 and never slipped below No. two in the world rankings.

Qamar was an adornment for his sport. His stroke making was breath taking. Winners, drop shots played from the back of the court, delectable boasts used to flow from the racket which he used like a magic wand mesmerising his opponents. If Qamar had a flaw it was lack of resolve. Despite major successes against Geoff Hunt at first, Qamar yielded to Hunt's relentless pursuit and the margins of victories for Hunt became greater and greater. This was because Qamar was not prepared to go through the labour and was satisfied to play second fiddle to Geoff Hunt. On Geoff's retirement and Jahangir's advent, Qamar acquiesced to the same situation i.e. No. 2. In his heart Qamar knew he could have crushed them both. He simply was not mentally prepared to endure the torture.

Qamar won the Pakistan junior squash championship in 1968. On his first trip to the United Kingdom in 1973, he reached the semi-finals of the British Amateur championship. In 1974, he reached the semi-finals of the British Open and won the Australian Amateur championship.

In the 1975 British Open, Qamar beat the defending-champion Geoff Hunt of Australia in the quarter-finals, and moved on to win the title beating his fellow Pakistani player Gogi Alauddin in the final by 9-7, 9-6, 9-1.

Consequently, Qamar reached the British Open final on four further occasions. He was runner-up to Hunt in 1978, 1979 and 1980, and to Jahangir Khan in 1984. He was also runner-up at the World Open four times, losing to Hunt in the finals of 1976, 1979 and 1980, and to Jahangir in 1984.

13. SAEED ANWAR

Saeed Anwar was born on September 6, 1968, in Karachi, Pakistan. He is an erstwhile Pakistani opening batsman. A stylish left-hander, Anwar is most notable for scoring 194 runs against India in Chennai, the highest personal score in a One Day International. Anwar graduated from NED University, Karachi in 1990 and is an engineer by profession. He was planning to go to the United States for his master's studies before becoming a professional test cricketer.

An opening batsman capable of dismantling even the best bowling attacks, Anwar was an attacking batsman in one-day matches and once settled in Test matches, scored quickly and all over the area. His success came from good timing and wristy flicks instead of physical power, being renowned for his trademark flick, and he could lift a ball that had pitched outside off stump for six over mid-wicket. His timing and capability to score quick runs made him a crowd favourite. He was named as a Wisden Cricketer of the Year in 1997.

He was the first Pakistani batsman to score a century against India on Indian soil in a One-day match. He has the highest Test batting average (59.06) of any Pakistani against Australia, and once scored three successive centuries against them. He scored a classic century against South Africa in Durban, which permitted Pakistan to win a Test match for the first time in South Africa.

On May 21, 1997, in Chennai, he scored 194 against India in an ODI match. This is the highest personal score by any batsman in the world and his record stands, almost a decade after he attained it, though batsmen have come close to his score in present years (lately, Matthew Hayden of Australia made 181 not-out against New Zealand).

He is a member of the exclusive club of batsmen who have scored three successive hundreds in ODIs, with hundreds against Sri Lanka, West Indies and Sri Lanka during the 1993–94 Champions Trophy in

Sharjah. He scored 2 consecutive hundreds on three other occasions in his career, and was the first batsman to complete this feat in ODIs.

- The highest personal score in an ODI match (194).
- He scored 2 or more consecutive hundreds on four occasions.
- He holds the highest Test batting average (59.06) of any Pakistani against Australia in Test matches.
- 20 hundreds in one day internationals.

Anwar's loss of form coincided with a great personal tragedy in 2001, when his three year-old daughter expired. After this, Anwar became a born-again Islamic. He made his come back to cricket after a considerable hiatus and was one of the most reliable Pakistani batsmen in the 2003 World Cup, with a century against India in his penultimate inning and an unbeaten 40 in his last inning, against Zimbabwe. The PCB axed most of the senior players in light of Pakistan's inability to make the second round of the 2003 CWC and Anwar was not selected again.

14. SANIA MIRZA

Sania Mirza was born on November 15, 1986, in Mumbai, India. Trained by her father, Imran Mirza, (and also her other family members), she began playing tennis at the age of six, turning professional in 2003. She is the highest ranked female tennis player ever from India, with a career high ranking of 27 in singles and 18 in doubles. She was ranked 91st in the singles class and 44th in the doubles class in the WTA rankings of September 8, 2008.

Sania Mirza holds the distinction of being the first Indian woman to be seeded in a Grand Slam tennis tournament when she was seeded 26th in the 2007 United States Open. Earlier in 2005, she had become the first Indian woman to reach the fourth round of a Grand Slam tournament at the 2005 United States Open, defeating Mashona Washington, Maria Elena Camerin and Marion Bartoli. In 2004, she finished runner up at the Asian Tennis Championship. In 2005, Mirza reached the third round of the Australian Open, losing to eventual champion Serena Williams. On February 12, 2005, she became the first Indian woman to win a WTA singles title, defeating Alyona Bondarenko of Ukraine in the Hyderabad Open Finals.

Mirza won the 2003 Wimbledon Championships Girls' Doubles title, teaming up with Alisa Kleybanova of Russia. Mirza does not enjoy playing on clay. Her best presentation in French Open singles was a second round appearance in 2007.

As of September 2006, Mirza has notched up three top 10 wins against Svetlana Kuznetsova, Nadia Petrova and Martina Hingis.

At the 2006 Doha Asian Games, Mirza won the silver in the women's singles class and the gold in the mixed doubles partnering Leander Paes. She was also part of the Indian women's squad that won the silver in the team event.

Mirza had the best results of her career during the 2007 summer hardcourt season, finishing eighth in the 2007 United States Open Series standings. She reached the final of the Bank of the West Classic and won the doubles event with Shahar Pe'er, and reached the quarterfinals of the Tier 1 Acura Classic.

At the 2007 United States Open, she reached the third round before losing to Anna Chakvetadze for the third time in current weeks. She fared much better in the doubles, getting through the quarterfinals in mixed with her partner Mahesh Bhupathi and the quarterfinals in the women's doubles with Bethanie Mattek, along with an impressive win over number two seeds Lisa Raymond and Samantha Stosur.

She headed India at the 2008 Summer Olympics in Beijing, in the women's singles and doubles events. In singles, she retired in the round of 64, while she was trailing 1-6, 1-2 against Iveta Benesova of Czech Republic. She teamed up with Sunitha Rao for the doubles event. They got a walk-over in the round of 32, but lost to Russia's Svetlana Kuznetsova and Dinara Safina by 4-6, 4-6, in the round of 16.

She has stated that two of her best friends are fellow WTA tour players, Anna Chakvetadze and Bethanie Mattek.

Her main achievements are:

- 2003: Afro-Asian Games: won four gold medals - Women's singles, Mixed doubles (with Mahesh Bhupathi), Women's doubles and Women's team events (the last two golds in partnership with Rushmi Chakravarthy).
- 2003: Wimbledon Championships Juniors doubles: Won the tournament (partnering with Alisa Kleybanova) to become the youngest Indian and the first Indian woman to win a junior Grand Slam title.

- 2004: Hyderabad Open doubles: Won the tournament (partnering with Liezel Huber) to become the youngest Indian to win a WTA or ATP tour title and the first Indian woman to capture a WTA tour title. got into the singles as wild card but lost in the first round to the eventual winner Nicole Pratt.
- 2005: Acura Classic: upsets Nadia Petrova in 2nd round but loses in the third round to Akiko Morigami of Japan (2–6,6–4,4–6). By beating the 8th-ranked Petrova, she breaks into top 50 in world rankings for the first time ever.
- 2005: Australian Open singles: 3rd round: Became first Indian woman to reach the 3rd round of a Grand Slam tournament.
- 2005: Dubai Tennis Championships: Upset ruling US Open Champion Svetlana Kuznetsova 6–4, 6–2 in 2nd round to reach the quarter-finals.
- 2005: Forest Hills Tennis Classic, New York: reaches her second WTA final but fails to win.
- 2005: Hyderabad Open singles: Won the tournament defeating Alyona Bondarenko of Ukraine 6–4, 5–7, 6–3 in the final and became the first Indian woman to capture a WTA singles title.
- 2005: Japan Open: reaches the semi-finals of women's singles and doubles (partnering Shahar Peer of Israel); reaches her highest doubles ranking of 114.
- 2005: United States Open: reaches 4th round by defeating Marion Bartoli of France in straight sets (7–6(4), 6–4) before losing to top seed Maria Sharapova 6–2, 6–1. Voted Best Player of the day on the 3rd day for winning her 2nd round match despite bleeding toes.
- 2006: 15th Asian games, Doha, Qatar: Mixed doubles - won gold medal for India partnering Leander Paes. They beat Japan's Satoshi Iwabuchi and Akiko Morigami 7–5, 5–7, 6–2.
- 2006: 15th Asian games, Doha, Qatar: Singles - won silver medal losing to China's Jie Zheng 4–6, 6–1, 1–6.
- 2006: 15th Asian games, Doha, Qatar: Team Tennis - won Silver medal for India pairing Shikha Uberoi. They lost to Chinese Taipei team.
- 2006: Bangalore Open (Hyderabad Open in the previous years) doubles: Won the tournament (partnering with Liezel Huber).

- 2006: Sunfeast Kolkata Open singles: reached semi-finals, losing to eventual champion, Martina Hingis 6–1 6–0.
- 2006: Sunfeast Kolkata Open doubles: Won the tournament partnering Liezel Huber. They beat Yulia Fedak and Yuliana Beygelzeimer 6–4 6–0.
- 2006: Won Silver medal in Qatar Asian Games 2006 Women's singles final and Gold medal in mixed doubles (partnering with Leander Paes).
- 2007: Acura Classic, reaches quarter-finals after defeating two Top 20 players Shahar Pe'er and Dinara Safina. Nevertheless, she lost to top-seed Maria Sharapova 6–2, 6–1.
- 2007: Bank of the West Classic, reached third career final after defeating Akiko Morigami, Tatiana Golovin, Patty Schnyder and Sybille Bammer, but lost to Anna Chakvetadze 6–2 6–3. Claimed the Doubles title with partner Shahar Pe'er, beating Anna Chakvetadze and Victoria Azarenka 6–4, 7–6.
- 2007: East West Bank Classic, beats Martina Hingis for the second time in a row in the second round 6–2, 2–6, 6–4.
- 2007: Pilot Pen Tennis tournament, won the doubles title partnering Italian Mara Santangelo, beating the top seeds Liezel Huber and Cara Black 6–1, 6–2.
- 2007: United States Open, seeded 26th in the tournament, reaches the third round defeating US veteran Laura Granville 6–3, 7–5, before losing to Anna Chakvetadze 2–6, 3–6.
- 2007: Western & Southern Financial Group Women's Open, reached the semifinals as the 3rd seed, finally losing to 1st seeded, and eventual champion, Anna Chakvetadze 2–6, 7–5, 3–6.
- 2007: Western & Southern Financial Group Women's Open, won the doubles title with Bethanie Mattek as the 1st seeds. In the final they defeated Alina Jidkova and Tatiana Poutchek 7–6 7–5.
- 2008: Australian Open, lost in the final of Australian Open mixed doubles with partner Mahesh Bhupati.
- 2008: Australian Open, seeded 31st in the tournament, loses to Venus Williams in the third round 7–6(0), 6–4. Reached Finals of mixed doubles with Mahesh Bhupati.

15. SOHAIL ABBAS

Sohail Abbas was born on June 9, 1977, in Karachi, Pakistan. He is a field hockey defender and penalty corner specialist from Pakistan. He is the holder of the world record for the most goals scored in global competition.

Born at Karachi's Holy Family Hospital, Soldier Bazaar on June 9, 1977, Sohail is an erstwhile pupil of Karachi's Habib Public School, the school of a lot of other hockey stars. As a matter of fact, it has been rightly remarked that hockey is taught as a subject in this school.

Educated at Nazimabad No.1 (Liaquatabad Town), he came from a sporting family; his father, Syed Iftikhar Hussain, was an erstwhile first-class cricketer. He headed Karachi and also Pak Crescent Club, renowned for producing Zaheer Abbas. Sohail is eldest of three brothers. Raheel Abbas his younger one is a Professional First Class Cricketer and involve in Media Doings as Well. Sohail has often said that his motivation came from his uncle, Safdar Abbasa left-winger who scored against Argentina during the 1973 World Cup as sixteen-year-old boy. Sohail is keen to stress the part played by Safdar, who, Sohail says, motivated him as a youngster.

As a young hockey player, his talent was not recognized for some time. He had trouble making an impact on the professional hockey leagues 1995-98. Like a lot of Pakistani hockey players, he is a passout of the Pakistan Junior Team. An impressive presentation in the eighteenth Junior National Hockey U18 Championship at Quetta 1995 acquired him a place in Pakistan Junior team which drew their home series 2-2 against Germany Juniors. He was not selected for the tour of Netherlands, Germany and Poland, playing next for Pakistan in the third Junior Asia Cup at Singapore in 1996. He staged a reappearance in the Pakistan Junior side in 1997, a side which crushed Germany Junior in four successive test matches.

Four months afterward, he was dropped from the Pakistan Junior team. Pakistan Junior squad manager Samiullah Khan, now the manager of the national squad, and coach Ayaz Mahmood were not confident to include him for the 1997 World Cup staged in Milton Keynes - an underwhelming team that failed to making it to the Junior World Cup semi-finals for the first time in the cup's 25-year history. Finally, he made his entry the following year on the national squad and has since become arguably hockey's most productive goalscorer of all time.

Sohail, who struck twenty goals in 1998, was in terrific form in 1999 when Pakistan won the Azlan Shah Cup for the first time and got silver in Asia Cup. He was major scorer in 8th Pakistan-India Series (10 goals), 9th Azlan Shah Cup (twelve goals) and 5th Asia Cup (16 goals). Of sixteen Asia Cup's goals, seven were against Sri Lanka which permitted him a place in a select band of nine players who registered double hat-tricks in global circuits for Pakistan. His sixty goals in 1999 beat the world record of Litjens (fifty-eight goals) and national record of Sardar (fifty goals) in one calendar year.

When he made his international entry during the seventh Pak-India series 1998, his function was only to come from the bench for penalty corner drills. His entry was at Peshawar's Lala S.M. Ayub Hockey Stadium on Saturday, 28 February, 1998. Pakistan manager Islahuddin Siddiqui effected a substitution midway through the tie, but failed to make an impact. He failed to score in three penalty corners as Pakistan won by 4-1. The following day, on March 1, 1998, in the second test at Rawalpindi's Army Hockey Stadium, Abbas announced his arrival on the global scene in dramatic fashion, scoring a drag flick from a penalty corner which proved to be the match-winner in Pakistan's 2-1 victory.

When the rule was altered after the 1998 World Cup, he was not considered for the 16th Commonwealth Games by trainer Shahnaz Sheikh. But he staged a reappearance to win silver in Lahore's 20th CT and bronze in Bangkok's 13th Asian Games in the same year.

Abbas has scored 274 international goals, surpassing the 22-year-old record of Dutch penalty corner specialist Paul Litjens. He retired in December 2004, just after the Champions Trophy in Lahore together with another Pakistani famous Waseem Ahmad, when he was only 27 years of age but on July 04, 2006, he has decided to come back to the international hockey. Since the summer of 2005, he and Waseem have both played for Dutch club Rotterdam. He struck his 33rd goal to break Mark Hager's 9-year old record. His 33rd goal emerged from penalty-mark when he converted 66th minute penalty-stroke against India in Pakistan's 2-1 win on fourth day of 26th Champions Trophy. The Australian striker had registered 32 goals from 1985 to 1995. He took 11 editions for his 32 goals while Sohail did the needful in his 6th CT and added another on December 12 tie to make his final Champions' Trophy total 34.

Sohail was also major scorer at the 2000 Olympic Games, Athens, with 11 goals, and of the 9th Indo-Pakistan series, with seven goals.

Mixing his impressive hitting abilities with drag-flicks, Abbas has proved himself to be the world's most reliable drag-flick converter, his success rate over 65% mark. Sohail was the key figure when Pakistan won a place at the Athens Olympic Hockey Tournament by finishing third at Madrid's Olympic Qualifier on 13 March 2004. Three times Olympic Champion Pakistan also qualified for Sydney Olympics four years ago by taking part in Osaka's Olympic Qualifier in March 2000. Pakistan finished second on the Japanese soil, with Sohail scoring 13 goals to finish as major marksman. Sohail was also major marksman at Madrid with nine goals. Four of these nine goals were against India in league encounter when he converted four out of four penalty corners. At Athens, he became the record Pakistani goalscorer in a single Olympiad, beating the 10-goal record of centre-forward Hassan Sardar, established at the Los Angeles Olympiad twenty years beforehand. Only Sohail, Sardar and Abdul Rashid Jr. have topped the goal scoring-chart in Olympics hockey. Rashid did it in 1968, when he was joint leader with Brian Glencross (Australia) and Prithipal Singh (India).

Sohail matched the world record on October 4, 2000, during the fifth test of the current series at the stadium named after Hockey Wizard Dhyan Chand ; part of three gold medal-winning Indian teams in the Olympics - Amsterdam 1928, Los Angeles 1932 and Berlin 1936, where he was the skipper. Sohail scored his 267th international goal at this historic venue from the 65th minute penalty-stroke. Sohail was already the owner of three world records in his six-year international career, before Amritsar's landmark. He is the scorer of the highest number of goals (60) in a calendar year and also the owner of the title of fastest century and double century of goals in international hockey. He reached double century of goals on August 17, 2003, at Wagener stadium when he struck twice in 6-5 thrilling win over Argentina during 25th CT.

Sohail is amongst the seven Pakistanis who finished 200-plus caps in the global hockey circuit. Others are Shahbaz Ahmed, Tahir Zaman, Mansoor Ahmed, Muhammad Usman, Wasim Ahmed and Muhammad Nadeem. He played his 200th international hockey match on July 1, 2004, when Pakistan clashed with the Netherlands in 4-Nation Rabobank Trophy 2004, at Amstelveen's Wagener Stadium.

It was fifth CT for Sohail, and, in the action, he became the all-time major scorer of Pakistan in this esteemed annual event, topping Hanif Khan's 21-goal record by converting the PC against Argentina in the 7th minute. It was his 22nd goal of CT history.

Sohail can easily be looked upon as the best short corner expert in world hockey. Argentina's Jorge Lombi and Netherlands's Taeke Taekema are second in line. He is a natural short corner expert with a very strong wrist, a powerful drag flick and a perfected dummy "body dodge" action. He was Pakistani candidate for the FIH Player of the Year award in 1999, 2000, 2001, 2003 and 2004, but failed to outpoint Jay Stacy (Australia), Stephan Veen (Netherlands), Florian Kunz (Germany), Teun de Nooijer (Netherlands) and Jamie Dwyer (Australia) respectively.

Sohail, who struck 20 goals in 1998, was in terrific form in 1999, when Pakistan won the Azlan Shah Cup for the first time and got silver in Asia Cup. He was major scorer in 8th Pakistan-India Series (10 goals), 9th Azlan Shah Cup (12 goals) and 5th Asia Cup (16 goals). Of 16 Asia Cup's goals, seven were against Sri Lanka which granted him a spot in a select band of nine players who registered double hat-trick in international circus for Pakistan. His 60 goals in 1999 shattered the world record of Litjens (58 goals) and national record of Sardar (50 goals) in one calendar year.

Sohail's extraordinary ability and goal scoring prowess mean that he is a target of hockey clubs all over the world. He gets proposals from clubs of many countries and headed Dutch club Amsterdam in 1999. In Netherlands, the hockey league, like soccer, runs for as long as six months with a winter break in between. Due to his commitments with the Pakistan squad, Sohail only played for nine weeks and that too in two spells. He was provided with free lodging and boarding, offered a car and paid as much as 700 dollars per match.

Time spent in Netherlands did tone his techniques and he pays warm compliment to the club boss Jons Hanset, who helped make his stay enjoyable. Twelve goals in 5 matches and assisted his squad qualify for the play-offs was no mean feat and he has no hesitation in stating that Netherlands remains his favourite country to visit. Close to his mother, he describes her as "my biggest follower. I credit her with all I have attained." His heroes of various sports are Shahbaz Ahmed Sr (hockey), Diego Maradona (soccer) and Andre Agasssi (tennis).

Sohail is quickest to complete the century of goals, reaching the three figures, when Pakistan thrashed Britain by 8-1 in Sydney Olympics on September 18, 2000 (His 50th goal was recorded on August 12, 1999 when he got hat-trick against Spain during Rabobank Challenge at Amstelveen). Thus he finished his century in world record timing of two years, six months and 18 days. He was the sixth Pakistani to reach three figures in global field after Hassan Sardar (150 goals), Tahir Zaman (134 goals), Kamran Ashraf (129 goals), Hanif Khan (127 goals) and Manzoorul Hassan Sr (101 goals).

He got eight goals at Sydney after handsome exhibit at Osaka's Olympic qualifiers. His achievement at Japan was all the more remarkable considering he had only just came back to the fray after spending four months on the sidelines with a groin injuries. His total goals in 2000 were 26, followed by 37 in 2001.

Sohail attracted worldwide attention in 2002, when he emerged as the joint highest scorer together with Argentina's Jorge Lombi in the 10th World Cup at Kuala Lumpur. And all 10 goals that Sohail scored at the Bukit Jalil Stadium in the Malaysian capital were off PCs.

He managed 44 goals in 2002 and added yet another feather to his cap in that year. Hasan Sardar was Pakistan's top scorer with 150 goals before Abbas unveiled his goal-scoring prowess. During the Six-Nation Invitational tournament at Kuala Lumpur, a month before World Cup 2002, Sohail scored his 151st international goal, becoming Pakistan's all-time highest scorer in international hockey. He struck nine goals as Pakistan managed bronze medals in 17th Commonwealth Games hockey tournament at Belle Vue Regional Hockey Centre at Manchester. He struck hat-trick when Pakistan routed South Africa by 10-2 in bronze-decider on August 4, 2002. Afterward, in the 24th CT in Cologne, Germany, Sohail played a prominant function and Pakistan finished third ahead of India.

The full-back, who joined Sui Southern Gas Company (SSGC) on July 27, 2004, had scored 274 goals in 224 matches.

He was back bone of his previous organization Pakistan WAPDA in domestic hockey. WAPDA is presently national champion of Pakistan and their back-to-back triumphs, thanks to Sohail, recorded during 50th and 51st National Championship at Karachi 2003 and Peshawar 2004 respectively. Sohail also assisted his previous domestic squad HBL to reach the final of the National Championship in 2001.

Sohail managed 28 goals in 2003 and for the sixth time running, he finished as annual major scorer for Pakistan. He struck five goals as Pakistan met success in Ipoh's 12th Azlan Shah Cup in March 2003, but afterward on Pakistan moved to Australia without him, Nadeem Ahmed and Wasim Ahmed as the trio had defied the PHF by skipping the national training camp to play professional league in Germany. Sohail and Wasim headed German club Harvestehuder THC of Hamburg while Nadeem played for Gladbacher HTC. It was Sohail's third spell as pro hockey player after Dutch league 1999 and Malaysian League 2002 (he headed Bank Simpanan Nasional BSN together with Kashif Jawwad).

Nadeem did come back in time for the trials for the Australia-bound team, but he was not considered for selection and Pakistan suffered embarrassment, finishing last in both twin 4-Nation tournaments at Perth and Sydney.

Nadeem, afterward on, was rebuked for his act while Sohail and Wasim were not permitted to appear in Pakistan-China series in July. They faced an interrogation committee on July 14, 2003, during which they regretted the error.

Both were permitted to join the camp and seven days afterward were included in the squad for the 25th CT. But their inclusion only came after hefty fines of Rs. 1,00,000 each on the players. PHF interrogation committee had also advocated a one-year ban on the duo. But PHF President Gen. Muhammad Aziz Khan brought an amicable end to the dispute when he said that the under-fire players will compete in the CT in better national interest.

Sohail also began 2004 in whirlwind fashion and won the top scorer award in 13th Azlan Shah Cup at Bukit Jalil Complex. He struck ten goals with the help of two hat-tricks against India and Germany. He managed one double hat trick and 21 hat-tricks in international hockey so far: a record unmatched in international field hockey. Sohail recorded 59 goals in 2004 and was well poised to break his own world record of most goals in calendar year (60 in 1999) before retirement.

Sohail won bronze in Amstelveen's CT, followed by silver in KL's 6th Asia Cup. The PHF sent under-strength squad at the First Afro Asian Games hockey event at Hyderabad Deccan 2003 by resting Sohail saying he required rest after the CT and Asia Cup.

Despite such tremendous show, Sohail failed to win gold in a prominant event. He headed Pakistan in Olympics 2000, 2004 and World Cup 1998 and 2002, but Pakistan failed to win any medal. He was silver medalist in CT of 1998 and bronze medalist in CT 2002, 2003 and 2004. He also played in CT of 1999 and 2001.

16. SYED KIRMANI

Syed Mujtaba Hussain Kirmani was born on December 29, 1949, in Chennai, India. He played cricket for the India and Karnataka as a wicket-keeper.

Commonly acknowledged as 'Kiri', Syed Kirmani is generally looked upon as the finest wicket keeper to play for India. He began as an understudy to Farokh Engineer in the tours of England in 1971 and 1974 and to the 1975 Cricket World Cup.

Kirmani made his entry against New Zealand and in his second Test, equalled the world record of six victims in an innings. He followed this with an atrocious series in West Indies where he missed many chances and noticeably contributed to Vivian Richards scoring hundreds in three successive Tests.

When New Zealand toured India the following year, he topped the batting averages with 65.33, and scored 305 runs in the tour of Australia. He didn't have a very good time behind the stumps against Pakistan and West Indies in 1978–79. He was dropped in favour of Bharath Reddy, who was considered an inferior 'keeper, for the 1979 Cricket World Cup and the tour of England that followed. Sunil Gavaskar was also sacked as the skipper. Although Kirmani was dropped seemingly for presentation, there was a rumour that the real reason was that both he and Gavaskar had been approached by the organizers of the Kerry Packer's World Series Cricket.

Back in the squad for the series against Australia in 1979–80, he scored a hundred as a nightwatchman in Mumbai. His innings of 101* in five hours almost lasted out the day. He had 17 catches and two stumpings against Pakistan in the same season and it equalled Naren Tamhane's Indian record for a single series. Against England in 1981–82, he didn't concede a single byc in three successive Tests while 1964 runs were scored.

In the Madras Test in the same series, he missed some crucial catches which contributed to an Indian defeat. He was dropped at the end of that series in favour of Sadanand Viswanath.

Kirmani made a reappearance in the Australian tour of 1985–86, where he fared reasonably well. He had just taken an outstanding catch to dismiss Allan Border in a World Series Cup match, when he hurt his leg badly. He was forced to sit out of the rest of the matches of the tournament and that effectively ended his international career. India went for younger keepers like Kiran More and Chandrakant Pandit and despite trying hard; Kirmani was never able to regain his place. Afterward in his career, he played for Railways in domestic cricket for a season, after which he returned to his former squad, Karnataka.

Kirmani played the role of an underworld character in the movie Kabhi Ajnabhi The, which also featured two other cricketers, one was Sandip Patil. One of his distinguishing characteristics was his clean shaven head. He served as the chairman of the selection committee for India in the early 2000s.

Kirmani won the award for the best wicket keeper in the 1983 Cricket World Cup, his highlight of which was the catch of Faoud Bacchus that he took in the final against the West Indies. In the first round match against Zimbabwe, he equalled the then record by effecting three catches and two stumpings. Against West Indies at home, he partnered Sunil Gavaskar - who scored 236 (not out) in a record stand of 143(not out) for the ninth wicket in the Madras Test.

At Mumbai the following year, he scored his second hundred in Tests making 102 and adding 235 with Ravi Shastri, still an Indian record for the seventh wicket.

17. WASEEM AHMAD

Waseem Ahmad was born on April 10, 1977, in Vehari, Pakistan. He is field hockey player and ex- skipper of Pakistan hockey squad. He is looked upon as one of the best left halfs in the world, and became the most capped midfielder and most capped player for Pakistan. After announcing his retirement from International hockey during Press Conference held after Pakistan-India third-place match of 26th Champions Trophy in Lahore, former Pakistan skipper Waseem Ahmed afterward staged a reappearance to international hockey in 2006 for World Cup.

Pakistan's most-capped player and midfielder became the 34th National hockey Skipper of Pakistan when Pakistan clashed with India in the opener of 9th Indo-Pak Series (Friday, 24 September) at Karachi's HCP. He was the 17th skipper to lead Pakistan in Champions Trophy. Apart from Shahbaz Ahmed, who captained Pakistan 6 times (1990-95) in Champion Trophys, only three players have captained Pakistan on two occasions. They are Hanif Khan (1983, 1985), Mansoor Ahmed (1996, 1997) and Muhammad Sarwar (2001-02). Islahuddin, Munawwaruz Zaman, Akhtar Rasool, Samiullah Khan, Manzoor Hussain Jr., Hassan Sardar, Rashidul Hassan, Nasir Ali, Qazi Mohib, Muhammad Usman, Atif Bashir and Muhammad Nadeem ND captained once only.

The important left-half is first in the list of most-capped Pakistanis. Shahbaz Ahmed Sr. (303 caps) is the second one. Third-placed Tahir Zaman earned 252 caps in a career spanning from 1987 to 1998. Other Pakistanis with 200+ caps in international hockey circuit are Mansoor Ahmed, Muhammad Usman, Muhammad Nadeem and Sohail Abbas.

Waseem Ahmad was the seventh midfielder to lead Pakistan. Hamidullah Burki was the first one when he led Pakistan in 1950 World Championship at Barcelona. Burki was followed by midfielders Ghulam Rasool, Anwar Ahmed Khan, Akhtar Rasool, Rashidul Hassan and Muhammad Usman. He replaced former skipper Muhammad Nadeem alias ND, who quit international hockey after Pakistan finished 5th at the 28th Olympic Games.

The little fellow, with a perpetual grin on his face, is one of the few universally acclaimed stars of modern era Pakistan hockey. The position of left-half is generally looked upon as a defensive one in Asian style hockey but, like Fazalur Rahman (1965-72) and Naeem Akhtar (1982-88), Waseem proved this percept wrong. He is not only a dynamo in protection but also in attack. He exhibits a tremendously high work-rate. Waseem, also acknowledged as Muhammad Waseem in media, struck 6 goals in 303 international outings. He is an ex-student of Government College, Lahore, now acknowledged as GC University (Ravian) which in itself is a rare distinction for a hockey player.

Born in Vehari, situated close to Multan, a district of Punjab State, on April 10, 1977, Waseem made his international entry during 16th Champions Trophy 1996 at Chennai (formerly Madras), India. He possesses excellent tackling and positioning sense in protection. Similarly, he has great ball-control to move up-front, making gaps in the opponents' defence and supplying superb passes to the strikers.

Waseem played his 200th international hockey match on September 24, 2003, when Pakistan inflicted a 4-2 win over India in the Group-B encounter of 6th Asia Cup Hockey Championship at National Hockey Stadium of Bukit Jalil Sports Complex at Kuala Lumpur, Malaysia.

Waseem also struck a precious goal in that match when he converted Pakistan's first penalty corner by beating Indian keeper Devesh Chauhan. He scored that crucial goal when the match was evenly poised at 2-2.

Being skipper of Pakistan Hockey squad for the 1st time, squad won the 9th Indo-Pak Test Hockey Series and came back back to Pakistan with a victory under his captainship.

Waseem won silver medals in Champions Trophy at Chennai 1996 and Lahore 1998 in addition to bronze medals in 2002,2003 and 2004 editions. He also played in CTs of 1997, 1999, and 2001. Waseem also headed Pakistan in Olympics 2000, 2004, World Cup 1998, 2002 and Junior World Cup 1997. He has also won silver medal in 5th and 6th Asia Cup at Kuala Lumpur 1999 and 2003 respectively, and bronze medal in thirteenth Asian Games at Bangkok 1998. Pakistani squad won Sultan Azlan Shah Cup three times and Waseem Ahmad was in the side everytime.

Together with Sohail Abbas, he was the only Pakistani to be included in the World XI which played against the Netherlands in Alexandria on October 27, 1999, as part of FIH's 75th Anniversary Celebrations. Waseem used to play for current national champions of Pakistan, WAPDA and he was the vice-skipper of Pakistani squad that won the third Junior Asia Cup at Singapore 1996.

He also won the gold medal in FIH World Youth U18 Festival at Rawalpindi/Wah 1995-96. He captained Pakistani squad in two events before he announced his retirement. First was India-Pak Hockey Test Series 2004 which Pakistan won easily. Second was Champions Trophy in December at Lahore in which Pakistani squad got bronze medal under his captainship.

He became Pakistan's second most-capped player when he earned his 253rd cap on December 4, 2004, in a match against Germany and he became Pakistan's most-capped (304) December 12, 2004 in his last match before retirement against India which was for Bronze medal and Pakistan won it. He was declared man of the match in this match for his excellent captainship and midfield work.

He also became the most-capped midfielder of Pakistan's hockey history by edging out Muhammad Usman's record of 210 caps. Former national skipper Usman played as a right-half from 1994 to 2002. He came back in the side for playing Champion's Trophy and World Cup in 2006 for Pakistan Hockey Squad after taking his retirement back.

18. WASIM AKRAM

Wasim Akram was born on June 3, 1966, in Lahore, Punjab, Pakistan. He is an erstwhile Pakistani cricketer. He was a left-arm fast bowler and left-handed batsman, who headed the Pakistani cricket squad in Tests and One Day Internationals. Broadly looked upon as one of the finest fast bowlers ever, Akram holds world records for the most wickets taken in both ODIs (502) and List A cricket (881), and was one of the pioneers of reverse swing bowling. The radical nature of reverse swing at first resulted in accusations of ball tampering, though reverse swing has now been accepted as a legitimate feature of the sport. Akram's afterward career was also tarnished with accusations of match fixing, though these remain unproven.

Wasim signed for Lancashire in 1988 and moved on to become one of their most successful overseas players. From 1988 to 1998, he spearheaded their attack in their NatWest Trophy, Benson & Hedges Cup and Sunday League winning sides. He was a favourite of the local fans who used to sing a song named "Wasim for England" at Lancashire's matches.

Wasim made his Test entry for Pakistani cricket squad against New Zealand in early 1985 and in only his second Test he made his charisma felt with a ten-wicket haul. Like a couple of other Pakistani cricketers of his time, he was identified at club level and bypassed first-class domestic competition, entering international cricket directly. A couple of weeks prior to his selection into the Pakistani squad, he was an unknown club cricketer who had failed to even make it to his college squad. He was found by Javed Miandad, and as a consequence of his insisting was it that Wasim was given an chance to play for Pakistan. Later that season he paired with Imran, who became his teacher, at the World Championship of Cricket in Australia.

Wasim's rise in international cricket was rapid during the initial years. When Pakistan toured the West Indies in 1988, he looked to be the quickest bowler between the two sides. Nevertheless, serious groin injuries impeded his career in the late 1980s. Following two surgeries, he re-emerged in 1990 as a bowler who focused more on swing and control than speed.

Wasim was instrumental in Pakistan's renowned World Cup victory in 1992, in Australia. In the final against England his late flurry of an innings, 33 off 19 balls, pushed Pakistan to a respectable 249 for 6.

Wasim then took the all-important wicket of Ian Botham early on, and when brought back into the attack later on, with the ball reverse swinging, he produced a devastating spell which led to Allan Lamb and Chris Lewis being clean-bowled in consecutive deliveries. His excellent presentations earned him the Man of the Match award for the final.

He also captained Pakistan with some success. The high points of his captainship were the 1996-97 victory in the World Series in Australia, two Test match wins in India in 1998-99 and in 1999, when Pakistan reached the World Cup final for the second time. The low point was the 1996 World Cup in Pakistan and India, when he had to pull out of the crucial quarter final match against India. After Pakistan's defeat, there were angry protests outside his homes, and a government interrogation was started into the failure.

In 1999, he led Pakistan to the brink of victory in the World Cup before they rolled over and gave the final to Australia. This was the start of the match-fixing controversies, as people believed Wasim had set up the match for Australia. He was pardoned by Justice Qayyum.

He was Pakistan's top bowler in the 2003 World Cup taking 19 wickets in 7 matches. Nevertheless, Pakistan failed to reach the "Super Six" phase of the tournament, and Wasim was one of the eight players to be sacked by the Pakistan Cricket Board as a result.

Wasim was diagnosed with diabetes at the peak of his career, but despite the initial psychological blow, he managed to regain his form and moved on to produce fine cricketing exhibits. There onwards, he has actively sought to be involved in various awareness-raising movements for diabetes.

His main Achievements are:

- In his Test career, Wasim took 414 wickets in 104 matches, a Pakistani record, at an average of 23.62, and scored 2,898 runs, at an average of 22.64.
- In One Day Internationals, Wasim took a world record 502 wickets in 356 appearances, at an average of 23.52, and scored 3,717 runs, at an average of 16.52.
- Wasim was the first bowler in international cricket to take more than 400 wickets in both forms of the sport, and only Muttiah Muralitharan has since attained this.
- Wasim also held the record for the most wickets in Cricket World Cups — a total of 55 in 38 matches. Australia's Glenn

McGrath broke the record during the 2007 World Cup, ending with a final tally of 71 from 39 matches. On passing Wasim's record, McGrath said, "Wasim Akram, to me, is one of the best bowlers of all time. Left-armer, swung it both ways with the new ball and he was so dangerous with the old ball. To go past him is something I will always remember. Probably the other side of the coin is that if you play long enough, you're going to break records here and there."

- Exceptionally, Wasim took four hat-tricks in international cricket, two each in Tests and ODIs. He is one of only three bowlers to have taken two Test hat-tricks (the others being Hugh Trumble and Jimmy Matthews), as well as one of only three bowlers to have taken two ODI hat-tricks (the others being fellow Pakistani Saqlain Mushtaq and Chaminda Vaas of Sri Lanka). Wasim's Test hat-tricks are exceptional, since they were taken in successive Test matches in the same series, both against Sri Lanka in the 1998-99 Asian Test Championship. Wasim is also one of only two bowlers to have taken both a Test and ODI hat-trick (the other being fellow Pakistani Muhammad Sami).
- Playing in a Test against the West Indies at Lahore in 1990-91, he became one of only six players to have taken four wickets in an over during a Test match. In Wasim's case, the feat was not part of a hat-trick, the third ball of the series being a dropped catch, which granted a single.
- Wasim has also attained the highest score by a number eight batsman in Test cricket — 257 not out from 363 balls against Zimbabwe at Sheikhupura. The innings contained 12 sixes which is also a world record for Test cricket.
- He also has the third highest number of Man of the Match awards in Test cricket, seventeen.

Wasim retired in 2003, after a short spell with Hampshire in England. There onwards, Wasim has taken up commentary and can presently be seen as a sportscaster for the ESPN Star network, and is also running appearances on ARY Digital. He is married to Huma Mufti, daughter of Mr. Humayaun Mufti. Wasim and Huma have two sons from their marriage of fourteen years.

19. ZAFAR IQBAL

Zafar Iqbal was born on June 20, 1956, in the state of Uttar Pradesh, India. He finished his study with a degree in civil engineering from the noted Aligarh Muslim University. Zafar Iqbal, a far famed Indian field hockey player, with Indian blue jersey number 11, played Left Out. This promising filed hockey player Iqbal hails from an erudite family. His father by profession was a learned Professor and served as the Head of the Department of Chemistry at Aligarh Muslim University. His elder brother is an established researcher at this time functioning at King saud University, Riyadh, Saudi Arabia. His sister is an accomplished Doctor, a gynaecologist to an exceptional degree, good academic record at AMU, bestowed eleven gold medals and got the award from the President of India for being the best woman medical graduate for the year of 1987.

Zafar Iqbal's valuable contribution as a skipper of Indian national squad benefited for India and in Moscow Olympics, the squad won the last Olympic Gold Medal. In various International events, he has headed Indian squad and glorified amongst them being Asian Games, in 1982 and 1983 Champions Trophy and 1984 Los Angeles Olympic Games. At the youth festival held in Moscow, Zafar Iqbal was also chosen to carry flag of Indian Team later on and later in the opening ceremony of the 1984 LA Olympics, the tricolour.

In early 80's, Zafar Iqbal and Muhammad Shahid, who played for India, enriched Indian hockey. The last glimpse of hockey India experienced with these great players as a world force. They formed a deadly accumulation who could shatter any defence in the world. In a deplorable manner, Zafar is also recollected for the miss in front of an open West German goal. It was a crucial match, which resulted in a draw and cost India the semifinal spot in the 1984 LA Olympics.

The highest award given in sports by India, the Arjuna Award was coferred to him for his outstanding contribution to the Indian hockey. For Indian hockey, he has also served in the capacity of Chief National Coach. Under his Coaching, India played for the Asian Games, which was held in Korea and India won silver in that tournament. He was the hockey coach of Indian squad from early 1993 to October 1994. After that he became member of Indian Airlines as Manager (Civil).

This former Olympic hockey skipper Zafar Iqbal has also showed his interest even after his retirement from the sports. He has defended

Indian Hockey Federation president Kanwar Pal Singh Gill's disputation concerning the issue of hiring foreign coaches to be restored to awareness about the game hockey in the country. While giving an interview, he said, "The time has come, when Indian hockey should have not only foreign coaches to brush up our hockey-playing skills, but also a foreign trainer who would keep an eye on the fitness level of the Indian players. If you want to be a power in hockey, then you have got to spend money."

He made valuable contribution for winning the last Olympic Gold Medal for India in Moscow Olympics. He has captained Indian team in various International events important amongst them being Asian Games, in 1982 and 1983 Champions Trophy and 1984 Los Angeles Olympic Games.

Zafar is remembered for his powerful attack. Unfortunately, he is also well remembered for missing a goal, in front of an open goal against West Germany, that would have secured India a semifinal spot in the 1984 LA Olympics.

He was granted the Arjuna Award, the highest award given in sports by India. He has served as Chief National Coach for Indian hockey from early 1993 to October 1994. Zafar presently works as manager for Indian Airlines.

20. ZESHAN REHMAN

Zeshan "Zesh" Rehman was born on October 14, 1983, in Birmingham, England. He is a British Pakistani football defender presently playing for Blackpool on loan from Queens Park Rangers. He also plays for the Pakistan national football squad. He is the first Pakistani international footballer to play professional football in England.

A passout of the FA Youth setup and Fulham Academy, Rehman was also an England youth international at Under-seventeen and Under-20 levels. He was with Fulham Academy when he was twenty years old and the Premier League club from London was able to earn some media attention from British Asian groups by being possibly the first Asian player to ply his trade in the top division of English football. Though a centre-back by trade, Rehman had been used as a holding midfielder and also right-back in his career there, which also involved a short loan stint at Brighton & Hove Albion where he impressed with his devotion towards the sport and also good strong character at such a young age.

Having made thirty appearances in all contests for Fulham, twenty-six from the beginning line up and four as a replacement, Rehman had to consider his alternatives if he was to get usual football. Though he had two years remaining on his Fulham agreement his hunger for usual first squad football was too strong and he decided to spend the following two seasons getting as much skill as possible.

Rehman was lent out to Championship club Norwich City for the rest of the season, as a defensive cover to the injuries-hit Canaries. He made five starts for the Canaries. Before the 2006-07 season, Rehman finished a shift to Queens Park Rangers from Fulham on a three-year agreement for an unrevealed amount in August 2006. Rehman was cited as saying, "All I want to do is play; the money doesn't interest me anymore". He further added, "I could have sat at Fulham and just been happy to pick up my wages but that's not what I am all about".

In his first season at QPR Rehman made twenty-seven appearances (25 from the start and two as a replacement). It was not easy joining a squad that had just avoided relegation the previous season, had very little budget and had an raw manager in charge. Rehman struggled, but acquired valuable skill of how tough life can be at other clubs. Towards the end of the season he agreed to a loan proposal to former club Brighton for a month and acquired some more first squad football skill.

This was his second loan stint with the club after a former loan deal during the 2003-04 season while at Fulham. He made his come back to Brighton & Hove Albion on 24 March 2007 in a 0-0 draw against visitors Huddersfield Town. In an interview, Rehman suggested to fellow British Asian football players to "stick with their roots" as he feels, given his own skill, that Asians will not get chances to represent England if they're not good enough, and should instead in any case make their mark at the global stage by playing for their countries of origin. Rehman ended his loan stint by playing the full 90 minutes and earning a yellow card in the action for the final game of the Football League One season in a 1-1 draw for Brighton & Hove at Cheltenham Town on May 5, 2007, claiming an assist for the opening goal. He featured in eight full games during his loan stint. The final game was his 35th appearance of the season. (33 from the start and two as a replacement).

Returning to QPR at the start of the new season, chances were limited. Nevertheless, hard work, good attitude plus njuries and suspension problems in the team permitted him to get his chance in the club during the packed Christmas period of the season which assisted him gain the confidence of the fans and the manager with some solid and reliable exhibits with QPR who picked up four wins and two draws out of eight games when he got back into the squad. He helped to lift the squad off the foot of the table and into a more respectable league position. The 3-1 win over Leicester City on New Years Day 2008 was Rehman's 50th game in all competitions since leaving Fulham in 2006.

Rehman finished the 2007-08 season in the beginning line for QPR against the Championship champions West Bromwich Albion. During this season he reached another milestone - playing over 100 professional games both in league and cup competitions.

Rehman became member of Blackpool in a six-month loan deal together with Daniel Nardiello who joined the club on a permanent basis, with Blackpool defender Kaspars Gorkss moving to QPR. Rehman made his entry for Blackpool as a second half replacement in a shock 2-0 defeat at Football League Two club Macclesfield Town in the first round of the Football League Cup 2008-09 on August 12, 2008. He was although used as a striker due to injuries to three of the clubs strikers. Rehman made his league entry the following Saturday, August 16, in a 1-1 draw at Norwich City, coming on early in the second half to replace defender Danny Coid.

Rehman always wanted to represent England, but becoming the first British Asian to don an England senior football shirt seemed too far away, due to lack of first squad chances at Fulham. Because of his Pakistani parentage and possessing double Pakistani and British nationality, he also qualified to represent Pakistan. At first he was reluctant to become a Pakistani international, but finally opted for the Asian country, though a plenty of British Asian groups were against this and wanted him to fight for an England place more to set a standard for British Asian youth. It was, nevertheless, an unrealistic aspiration. With that in mind, and with the blessings of his father, Rehman made his global entry for Pakistan, on December 7, 2005 at Karachi against Sri Lanka in the 2005 SAFF Cup, receiving decent attention from the Pakistani media circles and fans. Pakistan ultimately reached the semi-finals before losing out to Bangladesh 1-0.

In that brief space of time Rehman helped to raise the profile of the game in Pakistan, encouraging youngsters to play the game as well as help to raise the profile of Pakistan in the United Kingdom and on a global stage. There onwards, worries of little first squad action for club have made him ignore the AFC Challenge Cup 2006 and the AFC Asian Cup 2007 qualifiers for Pakistan, and consider his next move very carefully recognising that club football is the bread and butter but global football is also important.

Rehman was named in the Pakistan team for the World Cup 2010 qualifiers against Iraq in October 2007, and played the match in Lahore but couldn't help contain the current Asian champions Iraq from winning 7-0. In the second leg, he put in a commanding exhibit in the reverted 4-4-2 formation, leading Pakistan to a very credible 0-0 draw.

Due to club commitments and injuries he had to miss out on the 2008 AFC Challenge Cup qualifiers for Pakistan, a situation that proved costly for the national squad as defensive blunders cost them the chance of qualifying despite a promising start to the movement. He also had to miss SAFF Cup 2008 due to sickness.

REFERENCES

Bisati, Afroz Ahmad, *Religio-Political Role of the Jama'at-i Islami in Jammu and Kashmir*, M. Phil. thesis, Srinagar: Shah-i Hamadan Institute of Islamic Studies, Kashmir University 1997.

Constitution of the Jama'at-i Islami Hind, Delhi: Markazi Maktaba-i Islami, 1995.

Dalit Muslim: Unki Abadi, Samasyaen Aur Arakshan Mai Bhedbhav, Patna: All-India Backward Muslim Morcha, n.d.

Khan, Muhammad Faruq, *Hindu Dharm: Ek Muta'ala*, Delhi: Markazi Maktaba-i Islami, 1992.

Khan, Mumtaz 'Ali, 'A Brief Summary of the Study on Mass Conversions of Meenakshipuram: A Sociological Enquiry', *Religion and Society*, xxvii, December 1981.

Khan, Wahiduddin, *Hal Yahan Hai*, New Delhi: Maktaba al-Risala, 1985.

Sadiq, Sayyed Kalbe, 'Maulana Sayyed Abul Hasan 'Ali Nadwi: Ek Nazar-i Aqidat', in *Rabita*, Delhi, 2000.

Samuel, K.J., *An Islamic Understanding of Inter-Religious Relations: An Assessment of Dr. Asghar 'Ali Engineer*, M. Th. thesis submitted to the Faculty of the Senate of Serampore College, 2001.

Schimmel, Annemarie, *Islam in the Indian Sub-Continent*, Leiden and Cologne: E.J. Brill, 1980.

Section: IX

WRITERS

1. AHMED SOFA

Ahmed Sofa was born on June 30, 1943, at Gachbaria in Chittagong district of Bangladesh. He was a well-known writer, critic and intellectual from Bangladesh. He wrote novels, poetry and non-fiction essays. He also translated the writings of others. Ahmed Sofa was renowned for his intellectual righteousness as well as his radical approach to the understanding of social dynamics and international politics. Ahmed Sofa was himself an institution who became larger than his works.

Sofa helped establish the anti-communalist Bangladesh Lekhak Shibir (Bangladesh writers' camp) in 1970 to "organise liberal writers in order to further the cause of the progressive movement". Sofa's career as a writer began in the 1960s. He never married. After receiving his secondary and higher secondary education in Chittagong, he studied at the University of Dhaka. Although he never paid much stress on formal education, he received his MA degree in political science and later did research work for a PhD; but he was not able to earn the degree. An autodidact and a confirmed bachelor, Sofa was an independent thinker.

Sofa was a very intelligent and original writer. He started writing creativity in the 1960's and left his mark through his stories, novels, poems, essays, critical works, translations, juvenile literature, and composition in other such areas. He had also edited many literary magazines. He is considered a successful writer of fiction and used his own personal experience as the basis of his stories and novels.

It is his uncommon personality traits that brought Ahmed Sofa into the limelight. He was bold in expressing the truth. He was outspoken. At the same time, he was very affectionate towards the younger generation who gathered around this all-knowing man who lived like a saint. He was never seen hankering after name and fame in a trivial sense. He hardly practised religion but his religious belief was unquestionable.

"Life is a compromise", Ahmed Sofa subscribed to this theory. Ahmed Sofa, much like a shining successor of his enlightened teachers, Prof. Abdur Razzak and Prof. Ahmed Shariff, was one among only a handful of intellectuals and thinkers who always put the nation's interests above everything else. While many of his brilliant associates and colleagues submitted themselves to the privileges and opportunities of the time, Ahmed Sofa felt content by remaining merely an isolated maverick. Yet it must be noted, his patriotism never took the turn of communalism or chauvinism. Indeed, Ahmed Sofa serves as a good example in that a person can have benevolence and a love for the mankind without betraying the allegiance and trust of his nation.

Ahmed Sofa was also not infallible. Many among us might find some of his views and stances "controversial" or/and "questionable" (for example, his "anti-Taslima Nasreen" views). Yet one thing would always remain true about Ahmed Sofa: he was honest with his beliefs; rather than any social-political or religious authority, Sofa listened to the call of conscience to live his life. The temptation of accolade or praise could not weaken his beliefs.

Sofa's fictions were often based on his personal experience. He protested social injustice and tried to portray the hopes and dreams of common people through his writing. One of the well-known essayists, critics and poets Sofa always handles his novels with a much meticulous thought and plan. In every novel he articulates innovation in both form and content. Without novelty in thought and characterization, in technique and narration, he never ventures for a novel. The trend of telling mere stories in novels never attracted him. Surya Tumi Sathi (The Sun the Companion) was the first with which Ahmad Sofa launched his novelist career. The book was written in 1964-65 and in the year 1967 it was published. The next one Onkar (The Om), very much appreciated nationwide and even in West Bengal, was written in 1972 and published in 1975.

In the year 1994, a different type of novel Alat Chakra (The Circle of Fire) came out of his pen, though the book was actually written ten years earlier. 1988 was the year in which Sofa wrote two novels, one was Aali Kenan, published in the same year, and the other Maran Bilash (Luxury in Death), printed in the following year. The novels, which came to the bookstores later on, are Gaavi Bittanto (Tale of a Cow, 1994), Ardhek Nari Ardhek Ishwari (Half Man Half Woman) and Pushpa Briksha Ebong Bihanga Puran (A Tale of Flowers, Plants and Birds), both published in 1996. Along with these eight novels Sofa is the author of hundreds of lyrics and poems, short stories and essays and columns. His Bangali Bushalmaner Mon is one of the most thought provoking and much hailed books in Bangladesh.

Any conscious reader would not fail to identify the two fairly long gaps in the period of his writing novels - the first was from 1973-1983 and the next was 1989-1994. Surya Tumi Sathi was composed in the first years of Sofa's 20s. The whole story of the novel centres around Hashim, a youth whose father was a convert to a Muslim from a Hindu. The religious conflict of our society has been vividly painted in the book. The grandmother of Hashim Poddar Ginni rises above all orthodox rituals and thoughts of the dark society by taking the responsibility of Hashem's newly born baby in Hashem's house.

Living in a society where a Hindu does not even take food from a Muslim neighbour, Poddar Ginni, an aged and ordinary minded pious woman does not hesitate to come to see the dead body of her grandson's wife and thus humanity takes the upper hand above all other things. It is true that the whole story has been narrated in a very conventional way and nothing new has been introduced in the narrative technique but despite that the book has been acclaimed as a remarkable one in the annals of Bangladeshi novels for its characterization and the sincerity of the novelist to the analysis of social values.

But in Onkar, Ahmad Sofa comes out of the traditional tendencies of a novel writer. In this second novel he achieved his own individual qualities as a novelist in the context of form and content. The 24-page novel gives a pen picture of assimilation of an extraordinary theme in a simple story. In the story, due to his father's unwise activities, the narrator is trapped to marry a mute girl. Having no other alternative to save his own family, he has to do it. The mischievous father-in-law arranges for him a job also. In his town house in Dhaka, his sister, who resides with him there, practises songs with a harmonium.

Once it is discovered that his speechless wife herself is trying to make sounds with that musical instrument. All these make the narrator-husband more sympathetic to his wife and it inspires the woman more and more to speak. One day after the death of Asad in 1969 while a procession passes by their house, in her natural tendency the housewife comes out to the veranda and assays to voice like the slogans, but alas, it is only blood that flows out of her throat and she dies. In the novel the socio-political condition of the then society as well as the socio-familial environment has been delineated very minutely and skilfully.

The next novel of Ahmad Sofa is Alat Chakra. Liberation-time helpless Bangladesh in Kolkata is the focal point of the story. The story of the speaker Daniel and his lover-friend Tayeba works as a thread of the loosely related episodes, though in the same scenario. Under the shade of Daniel-Tayeba, the novelist possibly intends to bring out all the political and pseudo-political aspects of people in the then Kolkata, driven off from Bangladesh.

Different opinions of different people about the liberation of Bangladesh, its possibility, its way to success have been moulded here. On December 3, 1971, when India declared war against Pakistan and the independence of Bangladesh became certain, the cancer patient Tayeba passes away in the blackout night. About the novel the other thing must be mentioned that the integrity that Onkar attained earlier seems a bit loosened here.

After only four years of Alat Chakra, Aali Kenan came into light. Ahmad Sofa created an existentialist character in the novel in a very true Bangladeshi context. The political scenes from Ayub Khan to Sheikh Mujib have also been portrayed vividly.

Death in Maran Bilash, as a comfort, is on at par with Aali Kenan. It is about the spontaneous talks of a minister at his deathbed. From 12:13 in the night to the dawn, the minister opens his mind to his attendant cum political follower Moula Box. In these episodes the whole life of the minister has been pictured - from his boyhood to his maturity. All the misdeeds of his life as the minister are revealed here one after another. In a society where immorality is the only ladder for a politician to climb the top gets an exposure in this novel. The hateful activities of the minister include such misdeed like poisoning his younger brother, having sexual relationship with a woman of his mother's age, burning the headmaster in his house with a communal attitude etc.

After his Onkar and Aali Kenan, Gaavi Bittanto is also a very significant novel that will get a permanent place in the history of Bangla novel. In a very satiric milieu Sofa has placed the supreme institution of our country - the Dhaka University. Making caricatures of the people of this highest education centre, Sofa has tried to ridicule the whole society in general. In Gaavi Bittanto the author actually attempted to expose the so-called intellectuals of our society.

Sofa's novels are generally small in size. Even the bigger ones like Alat Chakra, Gaavi Bittanto and Surya Tumi Sathi are of 129, 110 and 93 pages only. But surprisingly, Sofa is always successful in making his creations in such small volumes. All his novels draw the attention of the reader for their compactness. Almost never the plots of his novels are loosened.

Concerning his language and form, Sofa attained his best from the very beginning. In Surya Tumi Sathi, the story is narrated in a third person narrative, the technique which he pursued in his later novels like Aali Kenan, Maran Bilash and Gaavi Bittanto. In his other novels Onkar and Alat Chakra, he went for a first person narrative technique. But in novels excluding Alat Chakra, the aspect that rolls on with immense success is his objectivity.

It is, as if, from a distant place the author observes everything of his story - the characters and the incidents. Such honest and courageous observation is only possible for Ahmad Sofa, personally who is not a man of general track. Constant experimentation and novelty are the hallmark of all his works. When a new book of the author emerges, we find in it a new Ahmad Sofa coming alive and attractive as is seen in the context of his novel Pushpa Briksha Ebong Bihanga Puran.

His essays mostly revolved around Bengali Muslims. He wrote about their history, society, and politics.

His major works are:

Novels

- 1967: Surya Tumi Sathi (Sun, you are my companion)
- 1975: Uddhar (Rescue)
- 1989: Ekjan Ali Kenaner Utthan Patan (The rise and fall of one Ali Kenan)
- 1990:Alatachakra (A circle of fire)
- 1993: Onkar (The chest-note)
- 1994: Gabhibrttanta (Accounts of cows)
- 1996: Ardhek Nari Ardhek Ishvari (Half woman and half goddess)
- 1996: Puspabrksa O Bihangapurana (Flower tree and the accounts of birds)
- 1996: Dinga Binga Burgan (Alarms, Bells, and Whistles)

Short Stories

- 1969: Nihata Naksatra (Murdered Star)

Non-fiction

- 1973: Buddhibrttir Natun Binyas (New exercise of intellect)
- 1976: Bangali Musalmaner Man (The Mind of the Bengali Muslim)

- 1993: Ahamad Chaphar Prabandha (Essays of Ahmed Sofa)
- 2008: Ahmed Sofa-r Chithi (Letters of Ahmed Sofa), Khan Brothers and Co.

Ahmed Sofa died on July 28, 2001, in Dhaka, Bangladesh.

2. AKHTERUZZAMAN ELIAS

Akhteruzzaman Elias was born on February 16, 1943, in Gaibandha District, Bangladesh He is a renowned novelist and short story author. Although he wrote only two novels, critics place Elias in the pantheon of great Bengali novelists. In the context of the novels of Bangladesh, he is possibly the second person highest applauded after Syed Waliullah.

He was born at his maternal uncle's home in the village of Gotia in Gaibandha District. His paternal home was in Chelopara, close to Bogra town. His father, Badiuzzaman Muhammad Elias, was a member of the East Bengal Provincial Assembly (1947-1953) and Parliamentary Secretary of the Muslim League. He finished his Matriculation from Bogra Zilla School in 1958, Intermediate from Dhaka College in 1960, and BA (Hons) and MA from the University of Dhaka in 1964.

Although he has not scripted a lot of literary works he is believed to be one of the foremost fiction authors of Bangladesh.

He has scripted only two novels and twenty-two short stories.

Novels

- 1987: Chilekothar Sepai(The Soldier in an Attic) - details the psychological journey of an individual during the turbulent period just prior to Bangladeshi independence in 1971. This novel also contains what is arguably the most genuine description of life in Puran Dhaka, the old and distinctive part of Dhaka.
- 1996: Khoabnama (Tale of Dreams) - Khoabnama depicts the socio-political scene in rural pre-partition Bangladesh.

Short story collections

- 1985: Dudhbhate Utpat (No Peace in Milk and Rice)
- 1989: Dojokher Om (The Warmth of Hell)

Essay collections

- 1997: Shongskritir bhanga shetu (Broken Bridge of Culture)

Akhtaruzzaman Elias has got many awards, some of which are:

- 1977: Humayun Kabir Smrti Puraskar
- 1983: Bangla Academy Sahitya Puraskar
- 1987: Alaol Sahitya Puraskar
- 1996: Ananda Puraskar
- 1996: Saadat Ali Akhand Puraskar
- 1996: Kazi Mahbubullah Gold Medal
- 1999: Ekushey Padak (posthumous)

3. FAREED ZAKARIA

Fareed Zakaria was born on January 20, 1964, in Mumbai, Maharashtra, India. He is an India-born American journalist, writer, and television host specializing in international relations.

His father, Rafiq Zakaria, was a politician associated with the Indian National Congress and a Muslim scholar. His mother, Fatima Zakaria, was for a time the editor of the Sunday Times of India.

Zakaria attended Cathedral and John Connon School in Mumbai, Yale University and consequently got a Ph.D. in Government from Harvard University, where he studied under Samuel P. Huntington and Stanley Hoffmann.

Zakaria is generally looked upon as a political moderate or centrist. In foreign policy terms, he is a "realist" (i.e., someone who believes that American foreign policy should be led by a concept of its national interest). His first book, From Wealth to Power, argues that countries that grow affluent and powerful inevitably expand their sphere of interests abroad. He sees America as a reluctant great power in the late 19th century because it was a strange creature — a strong nation with a very weak central state.

Zakaria is an advocate of free markets, both at home and abroad. He believes that America should embrace globalization and free trade. He is an internationalist, writing consistently in favour of American engagement with the world, multilateralism, and efforts to help alleviate global poverty and disease. He has often argued that helping countries to modernize their economies and societies is a more secure path to growth and liberty than pushing for elections and democracy.

His second book, The Future of Freedom, develops this latter theme more fully. Zakaria argues that democracy works best in societies when it is preceded by "constitutional liberalism," which he defines as the rule of law, rights of property, agreement, and personal freedoms. He has scripted that historically liberty has preceded democracy, not the other way around. He has argued that countries that simply hold elections without broad-based modernization—along with economic liberalization and the rule of law—end up becoming "illiberal democracies". For this reason, he has been critical of the manner in which the Bush administration has pushed its democracy agenda forward, relying on elections in Iraq, the Palestinian Authority, and Lebanon as the solution to those countries' problems and minimizing the building of the institutions of law, governance, and liberty.

After the 9/11 attacks, Zakaria wrote an important cover-story essay for Newsweek named "The Politics of Rage: Why Do They Hate US?". In it, he argued that Muslim terrorism has its origins in the stagnation and dysfunctions of the Arab world. Decades of failure under tyrannical regimes, all claiming to be Western-style secular modernizers, has produced an opposition that is religious, violent, and increasingly globalized. Because the Mosque is the one place where people can gather in an Arab country, that is where the resistance to these regimes grew. Because Islam was the one language that could not be censored, it became the language of resistance. He argued for a generational effort to create more open and lively societies in the Arab world, thereby helping "Islam enter the modern world".

In a June 11, 2007 cover essay, Zakaria criticizes "fear-based" policies on terrorism, immigration, and trade, and argues that beyond George W. Bush the world needs an open and confident United States.

While Zakaria at first supported using military force against Iraq, he argued for a United Nations-sanctioned operation and occupation with a much larger force (approximately 400,000 troops, alike to what General Eric Shinseki had argued for). He also demanded a Bosnia- or Kosovo-style occupation that was international, rather than American, in nature. He wrote a Newsweek cover essay, the week the Iraq war began named "The Arrogant Empire," which detailed the failures of the Bush foreign policy in the run-up to the war.

He was an early and aggressive critic of the occupation, arguing against the disbanding of the Iraqi army and bureaucracy, which the administration accomplished under the guise of "de-Baathification." He predicted that accelerating the build-up of the Iraqi military would create a Shia and Kurdish army that would exacerbate the sectarian tensions in the country. Four months into the occupation, his columns bore such titles as "Iraq Policy Is Broken," and in September 2003, he wrote a cover story for Newsweek named "So What's Plan B?" In a February 2005 issue, the week before Iraq's elections, he wrote, "no matter how the voting turns out, the prospects for genuine democracy in Iraq are increasingly grim." In his March 5, 2007 Newsweek cover essay, Zakaria demanded a reduction in American troops in Iraq to 60,000 by the end of 2007.

In his 2006 book, State of Denial, Washington Post journalist Bob Woodward wrote that, on November 29, 2001, a meeting of Middle East experts and analysts was convened at the request of then Deputy Secretary of Defence Paul Wolfowitz. The outcome of the meeting was a report for President George W. Bush concerning American policy toward Afghanistan and the Middle East in the wake of the September 11, 2001 attacks, a report that supported the subsequent invasion of Iraq. Zakaria told The New York Times that he attended the meeting for a couple of hours but that he "thought it was a brainstorming session" and didn't recall being told that a report for the President would be produced.

Zakaria is a naturalized citizen of the United States. He presently resides in New York City with his wife, Paula Throckmorton Zakaria, son Omar, and daughters Lila and Sofia. Zakaria has weighed in on his Islamic background on only one occasion, telling the Village Voice, "I sometimes find myself reluctant to be pulled into a world that's not mine, in the sense that I'm not a religious guy."

After directing a research project on American foreign policy at Harvard, Zakaria became editor of the magazine Foreign Affairs, and, in 2000, an editor of Newsweek International. He writes a weekly foreign affairs column that appears in both the domestic and international editions of Newsweek. His book, The Future of Freedom: Illiberal Democracy at Home and Abroad, (Norton) was published in 2003.

He is the writer of From Wealth to Power: The Unusual Origins of America's World Role (1998) (Princeton University Press), The Future of Freedom (2003), The Post-American World (2008) and co-editor of The American Encounter: The United States and the Making of the Modern World (Basic Books).

Zakaria hosted the weekly TV news show, Foreign Exchange with Fareed Zakaria, for PBS, and, from 2002 to 2007 a news analyst with

ABC's This Week, with George Stephanopoulos. His new weekly show, Fareed Zakaria GPS, premiered on CNN in June 2008.

In 1999, he was named "one of the 21 most influential people of the 21st Century" by Esquire and in 2005, he won the World Affairs Councils of America's International Journalist Award. He serves on the boards of Yale University, the Trilateral Commission, the Council on Foreign Relations, New America Foundation and Columbia University's International House. Zakaria has appeared on The Daily Show with Jon Stewart, a record of eleven times.

4. HUMAYUN KABIR

Humayun Kabir was born on February 22, 1906, in Faridpur, present day Bangladesh. Humayun Zahiruddin Amir-i Kabir or Humayun Kabir was an Indian educationist, politician, author, philosopher.

His father, Khan Bahadur Kabiruddin Ahmed, was a Deputy Magistrate in Bengal and a forward looking man. His grandfather was earlier granted the title of Khan Bahadur by the British government. He came first, with star marks, in his matriculation examination in 1922. He was educated at Presidency College, Calcutta, finishing his Intermediate in Arts (I.A.) in English with first class third, and Calcutta at University, where he finished his B.A. (Honours) and M.A. in English with first class first. He won a scholarship to Exeter College, Oxford, where he finished his degree in 'Modern Greats', i.e. Philosophy, Political Science, and Economics with a first class in 1931.

In 1932, he was invited by Sarvapalli Radhakrishnan to join as a lecturer at the newly founded Andhra University. Later, he was a Joint Education Adviser, Education Secretary and then Chairman of the University Grants Commission in Delhi. He was the Minister of State for Civil Aviation, Education Minister of India twice, under the Prime Ministerships of Jawaharlal Nehru and Lal Bahadur Shastri. He was also Scientific Research and Cultural Affairs Minister. In 1965, Indira Gandhi offered him the Madras Governor's post, which he refused. In 1956, he was elected as a Member of the Rajya Sabha, and from 1957-1969 he was a Member of the Lok Sabha. He was instrumental in dislodging the Congress government in West Bengal and forming the United Front government in 1969. He was one of the co-drafter of the UNESCO 1950 statement named The Race Question.

His major works are:

- 1936: Imanuel Kant
- 1941: Poetry, Monads and Society
- 1942: Sharat Sahityer Multattva (The main theory of the literature of Sharat Chandra Chattopadhyay)
- 1943: Islamic Politics in Bengal
- 1945: Rabindranath Tagore
- 1945: Banglar Kavya (The poetry of Bengal)
- 1951: Marxbad (Marxism)
- 1961: Mirza Abu Talib Khan

He died of heart attack in Kolkata on August 18, 1969.

5. JAVED AKHTAR

Javed Akhtar was born on January 17, 1945, in Gwalior, Madhya Pradesh, India Javed Akhtar is an Urdu and Hindi (Hindustani) poet, lyricist and scriptwriter from India. Some of his most successful work was done in the late 1970s and 1980s with Salim Khan as half of the script-writing duo accredited as Salim-Javed. Akhtar continues to be outstanding in Bollywood and is a sought-after lyricist.

Javed Akhtar was born on January 17, 1945, in Gwalior State (now Gwalior, Madhya Pradesh) to Jan Nisar Akhtar, a Bollywood film songwriter and Urdu poet, and Singer Safia Akhtar, a teacher and author. His lineage can be traced back to seven generations of authors. The greatly respected Urdu poet Majaz was his maternal uncle and the works of his grandfather, Muzter Khairabadi, are looked upon as a milestone in Urdu poetry. Akhtar has one sibling; his younger brother is renowned psychoanalyst Salman Akhtar. After his birth, his parents moved to Lucknow, Uttar Pradesh, and later to Aligarh.

Young Javed Akhtar lost his mother at a tender age and his father often moved back and forth between Lucknow and Mumbai, so he and his brother spent most of their time with relatives. At the age of eight, he was admitted to the sixth class in a famous school of Lucknow, the Colvin Taluqdars' College. From Lucknow he moved to Aligarh to live with his maternal aunt. He took admission in a famous school of Aligarh, the Minto Circle. The school is part of renowned Aligarh Muslim University.

He finished his matriculation from Aligarh Muslim University. After finishing his matriculation, Akhtar got into and began attending Saifiya College in Bhopal where he earned a B.A.. He was a keen debater in college and won the Rotary Club Prize often. He arrived in Mumbai on October 4, 1964. In his early years living in Mumbai, he managed to write the dialogue for a minor film for Rs. 100. Sometimes, he used to work as an assistant.

Javed Akhtar is the father of the film director Farhan Akhtar, the father and son duo have recently worked together in movies such as Dil Chahta Hai, Lakhshya, Rock On!! etc. the latter script was scripted by Javed. Javed Akhtar has not worked with his old associate Salim Khan, the father of Salman, Arbaaz, and Sohail Khan since their split up.

Javed used to write his scripts in Urdu, which were then scripted out in Hindi by his assistant. Another assistant would type out a one line summary in English. His association with Salim lasted till 1980. After this, Javed wrote some scripts on his own but mainly moved into writing lyrics for films, in which he attained remarkable success.

Javed Akhtar's songs are rhythmic, reflective on life and very melodic and catchy. Javed has also attempted more serious Urdu poetry aside from writing lyrics for movies. A prominant set of his works were compiled in Tarkash, which was also rendered into audio in his voice. Singers such as Jagjit Singh and the late Nusrat Fateh Ali Khan have sung some of his non-movie poetry.

Presently, Javed Akhtar is also a judge together with Anu Malik, Kailash Kher & Sonali Bendre on India's renowned singer hunt, Indian Idol 4. He is also on the advisory board of Asian Academy Of Film And Television.

His father Jan Nisar Akhtar was also a renowned Urdu poet. Javed's original name was Jadoo, taken from a line in a poem scripted by his father - "Lamba, lamba kisi jadoo ka fasana hoga". He was given an official name of Javed since it was the closest to the word jadoo.

Javed Akhtar was married to Honey Irani, a script-writer for Hindi films, with whom he had two children Farhan Akhtar, a film director and Zoya Akhtar. He is also the uncle of director Kabir Akhtar. His marriage proposal to Honey Irani was made on his behalf by Salim to her mother Perin Irani. Salim gave an unflattering description of Javed to her and portrayed him as a drunkard who visited prostitutes. This event was later parodied in one of Salim-Javed's most renowned films, Sholay, with the character of Jai proposing to Basanti's aunt (mausi) on behalf of his friend Veeru (played by Amitabh Bachchan, Hema Malini and Dharmendra respectively). Another opinion is that this scene was motivated by an old poem by an Urdu poet from Hyderabad, India.

After Javed's divorce with Irani, he married actress Shabana Azmi, the daughter of another renowned Urdu poet, Kaifi Azmi.

Javed Akhtar has won 5 National Film Award for Best Lyrics and 7 Filmfare Best Lyricist Awards for his Hindi lyrics. In the year 2004–2005, all the nominated songs were scripted by him.

He was granted the Padma Shri by the Government of India in 1999 and received the Padma Bhushan in 2007. In 2007, he even received Filmfare Lifetime Achievement Award.

Famous movies scripted by him are:

- 1971: Haathi Mere Saathi
- 1971: Andaz
- 1972: Seeta Aur Geeta
- 1973: Zanjeer
- 1973: Yaadon Ki Baaraat
- 1974: Haath Ki Safai
- 1974: Majboor
- 1975: Deewaar
- 1975: Aakhri Daao
- 1975: Sholay
- 1977: Immaan Dharam
- 1977: Chacha Bhatija
- 1978: Don
- 1978: Trishul
- 1979: Kaala Patthar
- 1980: Shaan
- 1987: Prem
- 1998: Kabhi Na Kabhi
- 2004: Lakshya

6. KHURSHID AHMAD

Khurshid Ahmad was born on March 23, 1932, in Delhi, India. He is a scholar, economist, author, and Muslim activist. He holds Bachelors degrees in Law and Jurisprudence, Masters degrees in Economics and Islamic Studies, and an Honorary Doctor's degree (Ph.D.) in Education, and an Honorary Doctor's degree (Ph.D) in Islamic Economics conferred by the International Islamic University Malaysia IIUM.

Khurshid Ahmad is a productive author with many books, articles, seminar papers and translations to his name.

Khurshid Ahmad became a member of Islami Jamiat-e-Talaba (IJT) in 1949 and was elected as the Nazim-e-Ala (President) of the same organization in 1953. He officially became member of Jamaat-e-Islami Pakistan in 1956 and is at present Naib Ameer (Vice President) of the organization. In addition to many other duties, he is presently also the editor of the seminal Tarjuman al-Quran, a monthly publication started by Sayyid Mawdudi in May, 1933.

Prof. Ahmad has been editing a number of ideologically oriented magazines and periodicals. He has authored and edited about 70 books in English and Urdu combined and contributed to a large number of magazines. He has so far participated in over 100 international conferences and seminars in personal and also representative capacities.

His in-depth comparative study of the oriental and also occidental philosophies in religion, academics, economics, constitutional matters and commitment for Islam has led him to be entrusted with key positions in the national and also international organizations on these socio-economic and other multidimensional fields. During his life, he has held the following positions:

- Professor at the Karachi University (1955-68).
- Vice President, Standing Conference on Jews, Christians and Muslims in Europe, Berlin and London (1974-78).
- Member, Advisory Council, Centre for the Study of Islam and Christian-Islamic Relations, Selly Oak Colleges, Birmingham UK (1976-78).
- Federal Minister of Planning and Development and has been Deputy Chairman of the Planning Commission, Govt. of Pakistan (1978-79).

- Member, National Hijra Committee, Govt. of Pakistan (1978-83).
- Member, Supreme Advisory Council, International Centre for Research and Islamic Economics, King Abdul Aziz University, Jeddah (1979-83).
- Chairman, International Institute of Islamic Economics, International Islamic University, Islamabad (1983-87).
- President, International Association of Islamic Economics, Leicester, UK (1984-92).
- Member of Senate of Pakistan for two terms (1985-97)
- Member, Committee of Jurists to Evaluate Islamic Laws in Sudan (1986-87).
- Member, International Review Committee, Islamic Research and Training Institute, Islamic Development Bank, Jeddah (1988-89).
- Member of Senate of Pakistan (2003 to date).

In opinion of his pioneering work and contributions towards the growth of Islamic Economics as an academic field, he was granted the First Islamic Development Bank Award for Economics in 1988.

His contributions to the Muslim cause were also acknowledged in the form of King Faisal International Prize,1990, which is the equivalent of the Nobel Prize in the Islamic World.

In appreciation of his services in Islamic Economics & Finance, he was given 5th Annual Prize of American Finance House, LaRiba, USA in July 1998.

He has given lectures and speeches at many renowned universities around the world like Warwick (UK), Harvard (USA), Washington St. Louis (UK), UofT (Canada), and IIUM (Malaysia).

7. MUHAMMAD ZAFAR IQBAL

Muhammad Zafar Iqbal was born on December 23, 1952, in Sylhet, Bangladesh. He is a very popular Bangladeshi writer of children's books and science-fiction and also a well-known columnist. He is a professor of Computer Science at the Shahjalal University of Science and Technology, though originally educated as a physicist.

His father, Foyzur Rahman Ahmed was a police officer and because of his fathers occupation, he travelled various parts of the country as a child. Zafar Iqbal was inspired by his father for writing at an early life and wrote his first science fiction at the age of seven.

First publication of Zafar Iqbal's science fiction came at the famous weekly "Bichitra" as he wrote a short story titled "Kopotronik Bhalobasha" (Kopotronik Love). One of the readers claimed the story as a plagiarism to make Iqbal annoyed and he wrote a series of stories under the title as a result.

He passed SSC from Bogra Zilla School in 1968, and HSC in 1970 from Dhaka College. He joined in Dhaka University at the department of Physics in 1972. In 1976, Zafar Iqbal went to University of Washington in USA to obtain his Ph. D.. There he again met his Dhaka University classmate Yasmeen Haque, and a year later they were married. In 1992, Iqbal decided to come back to his country what according to him he had planned to do the day he had left the country. He and his wife have two children, son Nabil and daughter Yeshim, who translated the book "Amar Bondhu Rashed" (Rashed, my friend) written by her father. His elder brother Humayun Ahmed is a living legend, and considered one of the most popular writers of Bengali Language. Younger brother Ahsan Habib is the editor of satirical magazine, 'Unmad' (Mad) and a cartoonist as well as popular writer.

Iqbal studied Physics at the University of Dhaka and graduated in 1975. He obtained his PhD from the University of Washington in 1982. He completed his post-doctoral training at the California Institute of Technology from 1983 to 1988. He joined Bell Communications Research (Bellcore), which is now known as Telcordia Technologies in 1988 and worked there as a Research Scientist until 1994. Since 1994, he is a professor and the Head of the Department of the Computer Science and Engineering of Shahjalal University of Science and Technology.

Zafar Iqbal started writing since his college days and became very popular with his teen-adventure novels, a rarity in Bangla literature in the late 1970s. His writing career was interrupted when he came to study and work in the USA. While abroad, his first two science fiction books came out, meeting great critical and popular acclaim. He returned to Bangladesh in early 1990s, leaving his career in the US, and joined Shahjalal University of Science and Technology to teach Computer Science and also Physics. After his return, he took up the causes of promoting science to young children, building a first-rate science education program at the university, and promoting freedom of thought. His latter cause and his opposition to the religious fundamentalism put him in direct conflict with the religious fanatics.

Although he writes fiction and non-fiction for grown-ups, he is at his creative best with his novels for adolescents. The young people in his novels are everyday boys and girls, seeking and finding adventure in their otherwise unremarkable and modest lives. They go through tough times with a wonderful sense of optimism and wide-eyed curiosity. A couple of his novels have been made into motion pictures.

Iqbal writes a regular column in the popular Daily Prothom Alo called Sadha-Sidhe Kotha (Simple Talk). He has written numerous columns apart from this regular one as well.

Some of his famous works are:

- 1976: Kopotronik Sukh-Dukkho (Copotronic Joy and Sorrow)
- 1977: Mohakashe Mohatrash
- 1986: Dekha Alo, Na dekha Rup
- 1988: Crugo
- 1988: Triton Ekti Groher Nam (Triton, the Name of a Planet)
- 1992: Biggani Sofdor Alir Moha Moha Abiskar (The Great Inventions of Sofdor Ali, the Scientist)
- 1993: Jara Biobot (The Biological Robots)
- 1993: Tukunzil
- 1993: Omikronik Rupantor (Omicronic metamorphosis)
- 1995: Trinitry Rashimala (The Trinitry Sequence)
- 1996: Onuron Golok
- 1997: Pri
- 1999: Metsys
- 2000: Amra O Crab Nebula
- 2000: Jolojo (Born in Water)
- 2001: Project Nebula
- 2002: Trātuler Jagat (Tratul's World)
- 2004: Obonil (Infra-Blue)
- 2006: Ruhan Ruhan
- 2008: Andhokarer Groho

He was awarded Bangla Academy Award in 2004 and Best dramatist award in the Meril-Prothom Alo Awards in 2005.

Iqbal lives and work from Sylhet, Bangladesh.

8. SALMAN RUSHDIE

Sir Ahmed Salman Rushdie was born on June 19, 1947, in the city of Mumbai, India. He is an Indian-British novelist and essayist. He first attained fame with his second novel, Midnight's Children (1981), which won the Booker Prize in 1994. Much of his early fiction is set in any case partly on the Indian subcontinent. His style is often classified as magical realism, while a dominant theme of his work is the story of a lot of connections, disruptions and migrations between the Eastern and Western world.

His fourth novel, The Satanic Verses (1988), led to protests from Muslims in many countries, some of which were violent. Faced with death threats and a fatwa (religious edict) issued by Ayatollah Ruhollah Khomeini, then Supreme Leader of Iran, which demanded him to be killed, he spent almost a decade largely underground, appearing in public only sporadically. In June 2007, he was appointed a Knight Bachelor for "services to literature", which "thrilled and humbled" him.

He also holds, in France, the highest rank — Commandeur — in the Ordre des Arts et des Lettres. In 2007, he began a five-year term as Distinguished Writer in Residence at Emory University. In May 2008, he was elected to the American Academy of Arts and Letters. His most recent novel is The Enchantress of Florence, published in June 2008. In July 2008, Midnight's Children won a public vote to be named as the Best of the Booker, the best novel to win the Booker Prize in the award's 40-year history.

The only son of Anis Ahmed Rushdie, a Cambridge University-educated attorney turned businessman, and Negin Butt, a teacher; Rushdie was born in Mumbai, India. He was educated at Cathedral and John Connon School in Mumbai, Rugby School, and King's College, Cambridge, where he studied history. He worked for two advertising agencies (Ogilvy & Mather and Ayer Barker) before becoming a full-time author.

Rushdie has been wedded four times. His first wife was Clarissa Luard, to whom he was wedded from 1976 to 1987 and with whom he has a son, Zafar. His second wife was the American novelist Marianne Wiggins; they were wedded in 1988 and divorced in 1993. His third wife, from 1997 to 2004, was Elizabeth West; they have a son, Milan. In 2004, he wedded the Indian actress and model Padma Lakshmi, the host of the American reality-television show Top Chef and that marriage ended on July 2, 2007.

In 1999, Rushdie had an operation to correct a "tendon condition" that, as per him, was making it increasingly difficult for him to open his eyes. "If I hadn't had an operation, in a couple of years from now I wouldn't have been able to open my eyes at all," he said.

His first novel, Grimus (1975), a part-science fiction tale, was generally ignored by the public and literary critics. His next novel, Midnight's Children (1981), nevertheless, catapulted him to literary fame. It also substantially shaped the course that Indian writing in English would follow over the next decade. This work won the 1981 Booker Prize and, in 1993 and 2008, was granted the Best of the Bookers as the best novel to have received the prize during its first 25 and 40 years respectively. It still receives accolades for being Rushdie's best, most flowing and motivating work.

After the success of Midnight's Children, about the birth of the modern nation of India, Rushdie wrote Shame (1983), in which he depicts the political turmoil in Pakistan, basing his characters on Zulfikar Ali Bhutto and General Muhammad Zia-ul-Haq. Shame won France's Prix du Meilleur Livre Étranger (Best Foreign Book) and was a close runner-up for the Booker Prize. Both these works of postcolonial literature are characterised by a style of magic realism and the immigrant outlook of which Rushdie is very conscious, as a member of the Indian diaspora.

In his later works, Rushdie turned towards the Western world. In the 1980s, he visited Nicaragua, the scene of Sandinista political experiments, and this skill was the basis for his next book, The Jaguar Smile (1987). Ironically, in an interview at San Francisco University promoting The Jaguar Smile, he advocated that students should not write what they wanted to write, but what they couldn't help but writing. He referenced a work in development, that came out the following year...

In 1988, his most debatable work, The Satanic Verses was published. He followed this with The Moor's Last Sigh (1995), a family epic ranging over some 100 years of India's history. The Ground Beneath Her Feet (1999), presents an optional history of modern rock music. The song of the same named by U2 is a setting of lyrics in the book, hence Rushdie is accredited as the lyricist.

Several of Rushdie's post-1989 works have been critically acclaimed and commercially successful. His 2005 novel Shalimar the Clown received, in India, the esteemed Crossword Fiction Award, and was, in Britain, a finalist for the Whitbread Book Awards. It was shortlisted for the 2007 International IMPAC Dublin Literary Award.

In his 2002 nonfiction collection Step Across This Line, he professes his admiration for the Italian author Italo Calvino and the American author Thomas Pynchon, amongst others. His early influences included James Joyce, Günter Grass, Jorge Luis Borges, Mikhail Bulgakov, and Lewis Carroll. Rushdie was also a personal friend of Angela Carter and praised her greatly in the foreword for her collection, "Burning your Boats."

Rushdie has quietly teachered younger Indian (and ethnic-Indian) authors, inspired a whole generation of Indo-Anglian authors, and is an important author in postcolonial literature in general. He has received a lot of plaudits for his compositions, along with the European Union's Aristeion Prize for Literature, the Premio Grinzane Cavour (Italy), and the Writer of the Year Award in Germany. He is also a fellow of the Royal Society of Literature and Commandeur des Arts et des Lettres. Rushdie was the President of PEN American Centre from 2004 to 2006.

He opposes the British government's introduction of the Racial and Religious Hatred Act, something he writes about in his contribution to Free Expression Is No Offence, a collection of essays by many authors, published by Penguin in November 2005. Rushdie is a self-described atheist, and a distinguished follower of the British Humanist Association.

In 2006, Rushdie became member of the Emory University faculty as Distinguished Writer in Residence for one month a year for the next five years. Although he enjoys writing, Salman Rushdie says that he would have become an actor if his writing career had not been successful. Even from early childhood, he dreamed of appearing in Hollywood movies (which he would later realize in his frequent cameo appearances).

Rushdie also engages in more popular forms of public discourse. For instance, he had a cameo appearance in the film Bridget Jones's Diary based on the book of the same name, which is itself awash with literary in-jokes. On May 12, 2006, Rushdie was a guest host on The Charlie Rose Show, where he interviewed Indo-Canadian filmmaker Deepa Mehta, whose work has also faced violent protestations, about her 2005 film, Water. He also appears in the role of Helen Hunt's obstetrician-gynaecologist in the film adaptation (Hunt's directorial debut) of Elinor Lipman's novel, Then She Found Me. In addition, in September 2008, he appeared as a panelist on the HBO program, "Real Time With Bill Maher".

The publication of The Satanic Verses in September 1988 caused immediate dispute in the Muslim world because of what was perceived as an irreverent depiction of the prophet Muhammad. The title refers to a disputed Islamic custom that is related in the book.

On 14 February, 1989, a fatwa requiring Rushdie's execution was proclaimed on Radio Tehran by Ayatollah Ruhollah Khomeini, the spiritual leader of Iran at the time, calling the book "blasphemous against Islam". A reward was offered for Rushdie's death, and he was thus forced to live under police protection for years afterward. On 7 March, 1989, the United Kingdom and Iran broke diplomatic relations over the Rushdie dispute.

Rushdie came from a Sunni Islamic family but says that he was never really religious. In 1990, in the "hope that it would reduce the threat of Muslims acting on the fatwa to kill him," he issued a statement in which he claimed, "he had renewed his Islamic faith, had repudiated the attacks on Islam in his novel and was committed to functioning for better understanding of the religion across the world."

His books often focus on the role of religion in society and conflicts between faiths and between the religious and those of no faith.

Rushdie advocates the application of higher disapproval, pioneered during the late 19th century. Rushdie calls for a reform in Islam in a guest opinion piece printed in The Washington Post and The Times in mid-August 2005. Excerpts from his speech:

"What is required is a move beyond tradition, nothing less than a reform movement to bring the core notions of Islam into the modern age, an Islamic Reformation to combat not only the jihadist ideologues but also the dusty, stifling seminaries of the traditionalists, throwing open the windows to let in much-required fresh air. It is high time, for starters, that Muslims were able to study the revelation of their religion as an event inside history, not supernaturally above it. Broad-mindedness is related to tolerance; open-mindedness is the sibling of peace."

In 2006, Rushdie stated that he defended comments by the then-Leader of the House of Commons, Jack Straw, criticising the wearing of the niqab (a veil that covers all of the face except the eyes). Rushdie stated that his three sisters would never wear the veil. He said, "I think the battle against the veil has been a long and regular battle against the limitation of women, so in that sense I'm completely on Straw's side."

Rushdie continues to come under fire from much of the British academic establishment for his political opinions. The Marxist critic Terry Eagleton, an erstwhile admirer of Rushdie's work, attacked him for his positions, saying he "cheered on the Pentagon's criminal ventures in Iraq and Afghanistan". Nevertheless, he consequently apologized for having misrepresented Rushdie's opinions.

His works in chronological order are:

1975: Grimus

1981: Midnight's Children

1983: Shame

1987: The Jaguar Smile: A Nicaraguan Journey

1988: The Satanic Verses

1990: Haroun and the Sea of Stories

1992: Imaginary Homelands: Essays and Criticism

1992: Homeless by Choice

1994: East, West

1995: The Moor's Last Sigh

1997: The Firebird's Nest

1999: The Ground Beneath Her Feet

1999: The Screenplay of Midnight's Children

2001: Fury

2002: Step Across This Line: Collected Nonfiction

2005: Shalimar the Clown

2008: The Enchantress of Florence

2008: The Best American Short Stories

9. TASLIMA NASREEN

Taslima Nasreen was born on August 25, 1962, in Mymensingh, Bangladesh. She is a Bangladeshi ex-physician turned feminist writer who describes herself as a secular humanist. From a humble literary profile in the late 1980s, she attained a meteoric rise to global fame by the end of the twentieth century, for her disapproval of Islam and of religion in general.

As, come back to Bangladesh was not possible, Taslima settled in Calcutta, India after considerable stay in Paris and Stockholm. In 2007, in the teeth of social protest, the government of India kept her in confinement in an unrevealed location for many months under tight security cover. Suffocated, she decided to quit India and finally shifted to Sweden once again. However, she continued to urge upon the Indian government for come back to India. Finally, on August 8, 2008, she again landed in India. She is reported to be staying with an ex-Swedish diplomat in the suburbs of Delhi at an unrevealed location.

She studied medicine at the Mymen Singh Medical College and after graduating in 1986, she worked as a government physician till 1994.

She began writing poetry while she was still at high school and published a poetry leaflet named Snejuti from Mymen singh in early 1980s. She published her first anthology of poems named Shikore Bipul Khudha (tr. Hunger in the Roots) in 1986. It was an anthology of 38 poems compiled between 1980 and 1984. She specialized in writing short lyrics based on personal skill.

She succeeded in drawing attention of a wider readership when she started writing columns in the weekly magazine Khabarer Kagoj, encouraged by her second husband Naimul Islam Khan. She wedded him after divorcing poet Rudra Muhammad Shahidullah. Her alleged anti-Islam compositions caused dispute all over Bangladesh, and her feminist stance began to crystallize during the course of these articles. Her own skill of sexual abuse during adolescence and her work as a gynaecologist where she routinely examined young girls who had been raped, inspired her a great deal in writing about the treatment of women in Islam.

Her literary entry in the type of fiction began with the publication of a 76 page novella named Lajja. The Government banned the book and, allegedly a Muslim fundamentalist group declared a death sentence. In 1993, she was charged with blasphemy. An arrest warrant was issued and Taslima went into hiding. After two months she surrendered to the High Court and instantly left Bangladesh after receiving bail. Since 1994, she has dwelt in a lot of countries in exile including France, Sweden and India. In the meantime, she has published a number of fictional and autobiographical accounts, in addition to poetry. Her autobiographical compositions have also proved to be provoking and have faced governmental sanctions in India and also Bangladesh. Taslima was writing her sixth autobiographical book, Nei Kichu Nei (There is nothing), but the continued movement against her through 2007 and expulsion from Calcutta disrupted further writing.

The writer's other autobiographical works are Amar Meyebela (My Girlhood), Utal Hawa (Wild Wind), Dwikhandito (Split up into Two). Sei Sob Andhakar (Those Dark Days) and Ami Bhalo Nei, Tumi Bhalo Theko Desh (I am not well, stay well my homeland).

Ka, published in Bangladesh, is a self-censored variation of Dwikhondito published in India. Dwikhondito is said to contain critical comments on the prophet Muhammad. The latter was also banned in India by the Calcutta High Court in the state of West Bengal on November 18, 2004.

Apart from Lajja, Taslima's first four autobiographical volumes have been banned in Bangladesh. Police were told to confiscate all copies of Wild Wind. The Home Ministry in Bangladesh claimed that they "contain anti-Muslim sentiments and statements that could destroy the religious accord of Bangladesh." In November of 2003, the West Bengal government in India banned the sale, distribution and collection of Taslima's Dwikhandito, the third part of her autobiography. Nevertheless, the ban was lifted by the High Court in September 2005.

Till November 22, 2007, Taslima dwelt in the city of Kolkata, India, but was forced to leave the city in a rush, following security concerns raised by a violent agitation by many Islamic groups in the city that were calling for a stay on further extension of her Indian visa. Possibly urged on by the Bengal government, she flew to Rajasthan where she stayed in a hotel in Jaipur for one night. Due to threats by Muslim groups in Rajasthan, she was moved to New Delhi from where she was allegedly moved again to an unrevealed location.

India's External Affairs Minister Pranab Mukherjee assured Nasreen a "shelter" in India, but urged her to "refrain from activities and expressions" that may hurt the sentiments of Muslims in India and harm relations with friendly countries. Recognizing the mounting social pressure, Taslima apparently agreed to a compromise formula. On November 30, 2007, Taslima decided to remove three pages from her book Dwikhondito (Split up into Two). The book has been criticized by Muslims as "anti-Muslim". Taslima made a statement saying: It had not been her intention to "hurt anybody's religious sentiments...Now that some people in India have said they are upset with what I have said, I have decided to drop the debatable portions of the book and have told the publisher to take necessary action...After these portions are removed, I think there will be no more scope for dispute and all the tension so far caused should die down." Major authors of India welcomed the move.

Taslima's life in exile commenced when she left Bangladesh in 1994 to avoid arrest. As of 2008, Taslima has been living in exile for more than 14 years. Although she is still a citizen of Bangladesh, she has in the meantime been granted Swedish citizenship. She enjoyed living in developed countries like France and Sweden where she had the freedom of speech and could choose a life style that she preferred. But as time passed by, she became keen to come back home. But she could not come back to Bangladesh since she didn't have a valid Bangladeshi passport anymore. In 1993, when she appeared at the airport for travelling to India, her passport was confiscated by the Bangladeshi immigration department on a charge of attempting to hide her real profession.

Nevertheless, when after she left Bangladesh in 1994, Bangladesh Embassies abroad refused to renew her passport and at once stage the validity of her passport expired. In this condition, she decided to move to Calcutta, a city in India very close to Bangladesh. She enjoyed living in Calcutta where she could speak in her mother tongue. The government of India extended her visa to stay in India on a periodic basis. Taslima requested the Indian government to grant her Indian citizenship. After a big agitation in spread over October and November, she was forced to leave Calcutta and the government of India kept her in an unrevealed location close to New Delhi. In March 2008, Taslima decided to leave India and came back to Sweden. Incidents in India during 2007 motivated Taslima to begin writing a new book to be named Narir kono desh nei" (tr. A woman has no country).

The most recent blow came in September 2007, when a movement was initiated in West Bengal by Muslim extremists and communist sympathizers calling for expulsion of Taslima from India. As a consequence, she has been forced to leave Calcutta and seek refuge in New Delhi.

A protest, named by the militant Islamist "All India Minority Forum", against granting of Indian visa to Bangladeshi origin author Taslim Nasreen turned Kolkata into a scene of flaming vehicles and scampering school children on November 21, 2007, forcing the deployment of army in the city after almost 15 years. A call for a road-blockade went out of control as thousands of frenzied people from central Kolkata's Islamic-inhabited areas unleashed a free-for-all for hours. Taslima was first moved from Kolkata to Jaipur, a day after violent protests rocked Kolkata over her stay in India. She was then moved to New Delhi the following day. The Intelligence Bureau kept her in a 'safe house' inside a National Security Guards complex in Delhi.

The writer's defenders, along with some Islamic figures such as Dr. Mansoor, claim, she is being used by the West Bengal government as a way of diverting attention from the dispute between the state and Islamic farmers in the rural district of Nandigram. Fourteen people were killed and reports of further violence have continued to shock India. Taslima said: "I'm writing a lot, but not about Islam, It's not my subject now. This is about politics. In the last three months, I have been put under severe pressure to leave Bengal by the police.".

Since the last week of November 2007, Taslima was kept in 'safe custody' somewhere in New Delhi by the government of India. On January 9, 2008, she was selected for the Simone de Beauvoir feminist award in appreciation of her writing on women's rights. Nevertheless, she refused to go to Paris to get the award, fearing that she would not be permitted to re-enter India. She explained that 'I don't want to leave India at this stage and would rather fight for my freedom here.' She had to be hospitalized for three days with many objections. In a letter to London-based human rights organization Amnesty International, India's former foreign secretary Muchkund Dubey urged to exert pressure on government of India so that the Bangladeshi writer's current predicament gets over and she can come back to her home in Calcutta.

In December 2007, Taslima Nasreen wrote a piece that was circulated through internet groups. It was named The Vanishing. The post began; "Where am I? I am certain no one will believe me if I say I have no answer to this apparently straightforward question, but the truth is I just do not know". In this post, Taslima alleged safe custody in India was "a conspiracy to murder my essence, my being, once so courageous, so brave, so lively, so playful." With reference to her living in India she said, "I am a guest in this land, I must be careful of what I say. I must do nothing that violates the code of hospitality. I didn't come here to hurt anyone's sentiments or feelings." "...It is like a slow and lingering death, like sipping delicately from a cupful of slow acting poison that is gradually killing all my faculties." It remains unascertained who wrote or translated this piece on behalf of Taslima. On March 18, 2008, prior to leaving India, in a piece named Need to escape from death chamber published in a Calcutta daily, Taslima complained that, finding it pointless trying to destroy her mind, the Indian government attempted to destroy her physically. From Delhi she flew to London and while transiting through Heathrow Airport, she refused to disclose her destination. She told the press that since her face was now recognisable, she could easily become a target of fundamentalists. Disclosing the destination would affect her security. On March 20, 2008, she was reported to have landed in somewhere in Europe. Finally, Taslima, who holds a Swedish passport arrived in Sweden on March 19, 2008, Wednesday, and was admitted to a cardiac clinic in Uppsala. The Swedish media has been silent about her and it is alleged that they are not permitted to communicate with her.

Taslima has received a number of international awards in appreciation of her uncompromising demand for freedom of expression. Nevertheless, the Ananda Purashkar was granted in 1992 to her as a recognition of her literary achievement.

Her major works are:

Poetry

- 1986: Shikore Bipul Khudha (Hunger in the Roots)
- 1989: Nirbashito Bahire Ontore (Banished Without and Within)
- 1990: Amar Kichu Jay Ashe Ne (I Couldn't Care Less)
- 1991: Atole Ontorin (Captive In the Abyss)
- 1992: Balikar Gollachut (Game of the Girls)
- 1993: Behula Eka Bhashiyechilo Bhela (Behula Floated the Raft Alone)
- 1994: Ay Kosto Jhepe, Jibon Debo Mepe (Pain Come Roaring Down, I'll Measure Out My Life for You)
- 1995: The Game in Reverse: Poems and Essays by Taslima Nasreen
- 1996: Nirbashito Narir Kobita (Poems From Exile)
- 2000: Jolopodyo (Waterlilies)
- 2004: Khali Khali Lage (Feeling Empty)
- 2005: Kicchukhan Thako (Stay For A While)
- 2007: Bhalobaso? Cchai baso (It's your love! or a heap of trash!)
- 2008: Bondini (Prisoner)

Essay collections

- 1990: Nirbachito column (Selected Columns)
- 1991: Jabo na Keno jabo (I will not go; why should I?)
- 1992: Noshto meyer noshto goddo (Corrupt prose of a corrupt girl)

- 1994: ChoTo choTo dukkho kotha (Tale of trivial sorrows)
- 2007: Narir Kono Desh Nei (Women have no country)

Novels

- 1992: Oporpokkho (The Opponent)
- 1992: Shodh (Revenge)
- 1993: Nimontron (Invitation)
- 1993: Phera (Return)
- 1993: Lajja (Shame)
- 1994: Bhromor Koio Gia (Tell Him The Secret)
- 2002: Forashi Premik (French Lover)

Autobiography

- 1999: Meyebela (My Girlhood)
- 2002: Utal Hawa (Wild Wind)
- 2002: Meyebela, My Bengali Girlhood - A Memoir of Growing Up Female in a Muslim World
- 2003: Ka (Speak Up)
- 2003: Dwikhondito (Split-up in Two)
- 2004: Sei Sob Andhokar (All those darkness)
- 2006: Ami Bhalo Nei, Tumi Bhalo Theko Priyo Desh (I am not okay, but you stay well my beloved homeland)

REFERENCES

Dawat-i Islami Ka Nishana: Fard Ya Ijtima?-Muraslat Maba'in Sayyed 'Abdul Qadir Aur Wahiduddin Khan Ki Raushni Mai, Idara-i Nashr ul-Huda, Hyderabad, 1990.

Deendar Anjuman-Ajmali Ta'aruf, Hyderabad: Deendar Anjuman, n.d.

Engineer, Asghar 'Ali, *Muhammad as a Liberator*, Mumbai: Institute of Islamic Studies, 1988.

Masud, Khalid (ed.), *Travellers in Faith: Studies of the Tablighi Jama'at as a Trans-National Movement for Faith Renewal*, Leiden: E.J. Brill, 2000.

Mathew, George, 'Politicisation of Religion: Conversion to Islam in Tamil Nadu', *Economic and Political Weekly*, 19-26 June 1982.

Menon, V.P., *The Story of the Integration of the Indian States*, Mumbai: Orient Longman, 1956.

Shadid, Wasif and van Koningsveld, Sjoerd, 'Loyalty to a Non-Muslim Government: An Analysis of Islamic Normative Discussions of the Views of Some Contemporary Islamicists', in W.A.R. Shadid and P.S. van Koningsveld (eds), *Political Participation and Identities of Muslims in Non-Muslim States,* Kampen: Kok Pharos, 1996.

Siddiqui, Naim, *Hindustan Main Fasadat Aur Unka 'Ilaj*, Delhi: Markazi Maktaba-i Islami, 1989.

Bibliograhpy

Ahmrad, S. Maqbul, 'Madrasa System of Education and Indian Muslim Society', in S.T. Lokhandwala (ed.), *India and Contemporary Islam*, Simla: Indian Institute of Advanced Study, 1971.

Ahmed, Imtiaz (ed.), *Caste and Social Stratification Among Muslims in India*, Manohar: Delhi, 1978.

Akhtar, Shabbir, *A Faith For All Seasons: Islam and the Challenge of the Modern World*, Chicago: Ivan R. Dee, 1991.

Alam, Javeed, 'Communalism Among Muslims: The Majlis-e Ittehad ul-Muslimeen in Hyderabad', in T.V Sathyamurthy (ed.), *Region, Religion, Caste, Gender and Culture in Contemporary India*, New Delhi: Oxford University Press, 2000.

al-Hamidi, Khalil Ahmad, *Tehrik-i Islami ke 'Alami Asrat*, Delhi: Markazi Maktaba-i Islami, 1994.

Ali, Abdullah Yusuf 'Ali, *An English Interpretation of the Holy Qur'an*, Bombay: Bilal Books, 1996.

Ali, *Ejzz, Jihad*, Patna: All-India Backward Muslim Morcha, n.d..

Ali, Sayyed Hamid 'Ali, *Hindustan Mai Firqavarana Fasadat Ka Masla*, Delhi: Markazi Maktaba-i Islami, 1992.

All-India Backward Muslim Morcha, Patna: All-India Backward Muslim Morcha, n.d.

Ally, Muhammad Mashuq ibn, 'Theology of Islamic Liberation', in Dan CohnSherbok (ed.), *World Religions and Human Liberation*, Maryknoll: Orbis Books, 1992.

Ansari, Abdul Haq, *Qaumi Yekjuhati Aur Islam*, Delhi: Markazi Maktaba-i Islami, 1996.

Ansari, Muhammad Hasan, *Hazrat Maulana Sayyed Abul Hasan 'Ali Nadwi: Hayat Aur Karnamey Aur Unke Malfuzat-Ek Ajma'ali Khaka*, Lucknow: Maktaba-i Jami'at ulMu'minat, 1999.

Azmi, Sheesh Muhammad Ismail, *Ahd-i Saltanat ke Fuqaha, Sufia Aur Danishwaron Ki Nazar Mai Hindu Ki Haisiyat*, New Delhi: Islamic Book Foundation, 1998.

Baghpati, Matin Tariq, *Da'wat-i Haq Aur Ghayr Muslim*, Delhi: Markazi Maktaba-i Islami, 1994.

Bahadur, Kalim, *The Jama'at-i Islami of Pakistan: Political Thought and Political Action*, New Delhi: Chetana Publications, 1997.

Bari, Sayyed 'Abdul Bari, *Azad Hindustan Mai Muslim Tanzimey*, New Delhi: Institute of Objective Studies, 2001.

Bedar, 'Abid Reza, 'Post-Independence Indian Islam', in S.T. Lokhandwala (ed.), *India and Contemporary Islam*, Simla: Indian Institute of Advanced Study 1971.

Bisati, Afroz Ahmad, *Religio-Political Role of the Jama'at-i Islami in Jammu and Kashmir*, M. Phil. thesis, Srinagar: Shah-i Hamadan Institute of Islamic Studies, Kashmir University 1997.

Constitution of the Jama'at-i Islami Hind, Delhi: Markazi Maktaba-i Islami, 1995.

Dalit Muslim: Unki Abadi, Samasyaen Aur Arakshan Mai Bhedbhav, Patna: All-India Backward Muslim Morcha, n.d.

Dawat-i Islami Ka Nishana: Fard Ya Ijtima?-Muraslat Maba'in Sayyed 'Abdul Qadir Aur Wahiduddin Khan Ki Raushni Mai, Idara-i Nashr ul-Huda, Hyderabad, 1990.

Deendar Anjuman-Ajmali Ta'aruf, Hyderabad: Deendar Anjuman, n.d.

Engineer, Asghar 'Ali, *Muhammad as a Liberator*, Mumbai: Institute of Islamic Studies, 1988.

Faridi, Fazlur Rahman, *Tahaffuz-i Shari'at Aur Millat-i Islamiya-i Hind*, Delhi: Markazi Maktaba-i Islami, 1996.

Faruqi, Mumtaz Ahmad, *Muhammad 'Ali: The Great Missionary of Islam*, Lahore: Ahmadiyya Anjuman-i Isha'at-i Islam, 1966.

Ganagalu, Pandit Sayyed Qasim Ganagalu, *Hindu-Muslim Unity in the Person of His Holiness Maulana Siddique Deendar Channabasaveswara*, Hyderabad: Deendar Anjuman, 1990.

Gellner, Ernest, *Post-Modernism, Reason and Religion*, London and New York: Routledge, 1992.

Gilani, Sayyed 'Ali Shah, *Rudad-i Qafas*, vol. 1, Srinagar: Al-Huda Publishing House, 1993.

Hamid, Sayyed, 'Maulana 'Ali Miyan', in *Rabita*, Delhi, 2000.

Hasan, Muhammad Nafis, *Meri Tamam Sarguzasht: Sayyed Abul Hasan 'Ali Nadwi*, New Delhi: published by the author, 2000.

Hasan, Mushirul, *Legacy of a Divided Nation: India's Muslims Since Independence*, London: Hurst & Company, 1997.

Hindu-Muslim Ekta Ko Todne Wali Samvidhan Ki Dhara 341 Mai Sanshodhan Ke Liye Jihad, Patna: All-India Backward Muslim Morcha, n.d.

Hussain, Siddiq, *Hidayat Namah Banam Ghayr Muslim Salatin*, Hyderabad: Deendar Anjuman, 1398 1977/78.

Islahi, Muhammad Yusuf, *Izzat Ki Zindagi Aur Muslamanan-i Hind*, Delhi: Maktaba-i Zikra, 1999.

Islahi, Sadruddin, *Tehrik-i Islami-i Hind*, Delhi: Markazi Maktaba-i Islami, 1994.

Islahi, Sultan Ahmad, *Maulana Abul Lais Islahi Nadwi: Shaksiyat Ke Chand Numaya Pahlu*, Aligarh: Idara-i Ilm-o-Adab, 1996.

'Islam, Liberalism and Democracy', *Progressive Perspective*, vol. 4, no. 11, November 1995.

'Islamic Mission and Inter-Religious Dialogue in a Minority Context: The Jama'at-i Islami of India', *Islam and Christian Muslim Relations*, vol. 13, no. 1, 2002.

Jama'at-i Islami Hind: Policy and Programme (April 1999-March 2003) (henceforth *Policy and Programme*), Delhi: Jama'at-i Islami Hind, 1999.

Jones, Kenneth W, 'The Arya Samaj in British India', in Robert D. Baird (ed.), *Religion in Modern India*, New Delhi: Manohar, 1995.

Kashmiri, Ashiq, *Tarikh-i Tehrik-i Islami Jammu Aur Kashmir: 1947 Se 1970 Tak*, Srinagar: Jama'at-i Islami of Jammu and Kashmir, 1984.

Khan, M.A. Saleem, *Early Muslim Perception of India and Hinduism*, New Delhi: South Asian Publishers, 1997.

Khan, Muhammad Faruq, *Hindu Dharm: Ek Muta'ala*, Delhi: Markazi Maktaba-i Islami, 1992.

Khan, Mumtaz 'Ali, 'A Brief Summary of the Study on Mass Conversions of Meenakshipuram: A Sociological Enquiry', *Religion and Society*, xxvii, December 1981.

Khan, Wahiduddin, *Hal Yahan Hai*, New Delhi: Maktaba al-Risala, 1985.

Masud, Khalid (ed.), *Travellers in Faith: Studies of the Tablighi Jama'at as a Trans-National Movement for Faith Renewal*, Leiden: E.J. Brill, 2000.

Mathew, George, 'Politicisation of Religion: Conversion to Islam in Tamil Nadu', *Economic and Political Weekly*, 19-26 June 1982.

Menon, V.P., *The Story of the Integration of the Indian States*, Bombay: Orient Longman, 1956.

Miller, R.E., 'Modern Indian Muslim Responses', in Harold G. Coward (ed.), *Modern Indian Responses to Religious Pluralism*, Albany, NY: State University of New York Press, 1987.

Moazzam, Anwar, 'The Indian Muslim: A Dilemma of a Dual Personality', in S.T. Lokhandwala (ed.), *India and Contemporary Islam*, Shimla: Indian Institute of Advanced Study, 1971.

Moghni, Abdul Moghni, *Hindustan Ke Liye Mustaqbil Ka Naqsha-i 'Amal*, Delhi: Markazi Maktaba-i Islami, 1994.

Mujahid, Abdul Malik, *Conversion to Islam: Untouchables' Strategy for Protest in India*, Chambersburg: Anima Books, 1989.

Nadwi, Abdullah Abbas, *Mir-i Karavan*, New Delhi: Majlis-i 'Ilmi, 1999.

Nadwi, Abul Lais Islahi, *Jama'at-i Islami Ka Maqsad Aur Tariq-i Kar*, Delhi: Markazi Maktaba-i-Islami, 1989.

Nadwi, Khalid Beg Nadwi, *Fitna-i Channabasaveswara*, Tumkur, 2001.

Nadwi, Muhammad Ayub, 'Sayyed Abul Hasan 'Ali Nadwi Aur Tehrik-i Payam-i Insaniyat', in *Rabita*, Delhi, 2000.

Nadwi, Rizwan Ahmad, 'Sayyed 'Abul Hasan 'Ali Nadwi: Shaksiyat-o-Kirdar', in *Rabita*, Delhi, 2000.

Nadwi, S.M. Rabey Hasan, 'The Philosopher of Islam: A Close-Up', in Shariq 'Alavi (ed.), *The Fragrance of the East*, January-June 2000.

Nadwi, Sayyed Abul Hasan, *'Asr-i Hazir Mai Din Ki Tahfim-o-Tashrih*, Lucknow: Dar ul-'Arafat, 1980.

Nasr, Seyyed Vali Reza, *The Vanguavd of the Islamic Revolution: The Jama'at-i Islami of Pakistan*, London and New York: I.B. Tauris, 1994.

Nath, Ram, *Dalit-Muslim Unity: Why? And How?,* Bangalore: Dalit Sahitya Akademy, 1995.

Nazirullah, Abul Sami Muhammad, *Deendar Anjuman Kya Hai*?, Hyderabad: Deendar Anjuman, n.d.

Noor, Farish A., *New Voices of Islam*, Leiden: International Institute for the Study of Islam in the Modern World, 2002.

Omar, Irfan A., 'Islam and the Other: The Ideal Vision of Mawlana Wahiduddin Khan', *in Journal of Ecumenical Studies*, vol. 36, nos. 3-4, summer-fall 1999.

Parekh, Abdul Karim (ed.), *Murshid-i Ruhani Musleh-i Ummat Hazrat Maulana Sayyed Abul Hasan 'Ali Nadwi Urf 'Ali Miyan Sahib Ke Khutut Mufassir-i Quran Hazrat Maulana 'Abdul Karim Parekh Sahib Ke Nam*, Delhi: Farid Book Depot, 1999.

Qadri, Sayyed Ahmad 'Uruj, *Fasdat Ka Ilaj*, Delhi: Markazi Maktaba-i Islami, 1989.

Quraishi, Muhammad 'Abdur Rahim, 'Muslim Personal Law Tehrik Hazrat Maulana 'Ali Miyan Ke Daur-i Sadarat Mai', in *Rabita*, Delhi, 2000.

Rahmatullah, 'Curse of Allah on Muslim Religious Leaders For Flouting Koran', in V.T. Rajshekar (ed.), *Curse of Allah*, Bangalore: Dalit Sahitya Akademy 1997.

Sadiq, Sayyed Kalbe, 'Maulana Sayyed Abul Hasan 'Ali Nadwi: Ek Nazar-i Aqidat', in *Rabita*, Delhi, 2000.

Samuel, K.J., *An Islamic Understanding of Inter-Religious Relations: An Assessment of Dr. Asghar 'Ali Engineer*, M. Th. thesis submitted to the Faculty of the Senate of Serampore College, 2001.

Schimmel, Annemarie, *Islam in the Indian Sub-Continent*, Leiden and Cologne: E.J. Brill, 1980.

Shadid, Wasif and van Koningsveld, Sjoerd, 'Loyalty to a Non-Muslim Government: An Analysis of Islamic Normative Discussions of the Views of Some Contemporary Islamicists', in W.A.R. Shadid and P.S. van Koningsveld (eds), *Political Participation and Identities of Muslims in Non-Muslim States,* Kampen: Kok Pharos, 1996.

Siddiqui, Naim, *Hindustan Main Fasadat Aur Unka 'Ilaj*, Delhi: Markazi Maktaba-i Islami, 1989.

Sikand, Yoginder, 'The *Fitna* of *Irtidad:* Muslim Missionary Responses to the *Shuddhi* Movement of the Arya Samaj in Early Twentieth Century India', *Journal of Muslim Minority Affairs*, vol. 17, no. 1, 1997.

Smith, Wilfred Cantwell, *Islam in Modern History*, Princeton: Princeton University Press, 1957.

Umm Zubayr, *Tabligh Kaise Ki Jai*, Delhi: Markazi Maktaba-i Islami, 1997.

Umri, Sayyed Jalaluddin, *Dharmik Logon Se Nivedan*, New Delhi: Madhur Sandesh Sangam, 1994.

Upadhyaya, Ved Prakash, *Kalki Avatar Hazrat Muhammad*, Hyderabad: Deendar Anjuman, 1991.

Vajpeyi, Dhirendra K., 'The Politics of Paradise: Islam, Identity and Politics in India', in Arvind Sharma (ed.), *Hinduism and Secularism: After Ayodhya*, Basingstoke and New York: Palgrave, 2001.

Wright Jr, Theodore P, 'Hindu-Muslim Stereotypes in South Asia', *Journal of Asian and African Affairs*, vol. 3, July 1991.

Index

I

J

K

L

M